D0912159

JOHN
CALVIN

A PILGRIM'S LIFE

HERMAN J. SELDERHUIS

Translated by Albert Gootjes

IVP Academic
An imprint of InterVarsity Press
Downers Grove, Illinois

Inter-Varsity Press
Nottingham, England

InterVarsity Press, USA
P.O. Box 1400, Downers Grove, IL 60515-1426, USA
World Wide Web: www.ivpress.com
Email: email@ivpress.com

Inter-Varsity Press, England
Norton Street, Nottingham NG7 3HR, England
Website: www.ivpbooks.com
Email: ivp@ivpbooks.com

InterVarsity Press®, USA, is the book-publishing division of InterVarsity Christian Fellowship/USA®, a movement of students and faculty active on campus at hundreds of universities, colleges and schools of nursing in the United States of America, and a member movement of the International Fellowship of Evangelical Students. For information about local and regional activities, write Public Relations Dept., InterVarsity Christian Fellowship/USA, 6400 Schroeder Rd., P.O. Box 7895, Madison, WI 53707-7895, or visit the IVCF website at <www.intervarsity.org>.

Inter-Varsity Press, England, is closely linked with the Universities and Colleges Christian Fellowship, a student movement connecting Christian Unions in universities and colleges throughout Great Britain, and a member movement of the International Fellowship of Evangelical Students. Website: www.uccf.org.uk.

Design: Cindy Kiple

Images: John Calvin: Eric Lessing/Art Resource, NY
   cross pattern: Klaus Rademaker/iStockphoto

USA ISBN 978-0-8308-2921-7
UK ISBN 978-1-84474-375-9

Printed in the United States of America ∞

Library of Congress Cataloging-in-Publication Data

Selderhuis, H. J., 1961-
 John Calvin: a pilgrim's life / Herman J. Selderhuis.
  p. cm.
 Includes bibliographical references (p.) and index.
 ISBN 978-0-8308-2921-7 (pbk.: alk. paper)
 1. Calvin, Jean, 1509-1564. I. Title.
 BX9418.S35 2009
 284'.2092—dc22
 [B]

                      2008046021

British Library Cataloguing in Publication Data
A catalogue record for this book is available from the British Library.

P	19	18	17	16	15	14	13	12	11	10	9	8	7	6	5	4	3	2	1
Y	25	24	23	22	21	20	19	18	17	16	15	14	13	12	11	10	09			

CONTENTS

INTRODUCTION

Life is a steeplechase: there are dangers everywhere, and God himself, who has put most of the obstacles in our way, watches to see whether we make it over them. Such is John Calvin's view of life—and of God. Calvin never spoke of life as something fun, and his own wasn't. Many of his followers concluded that there shouldn't be any fun in life, and here they misunderstand him.

Calvin runs the race of this life, falling all the while, picking himself up again and again, and looking forward to the finish, which he calls "the reflection of the life to come." The race wears him out, often seeming to pointlessly bring him back to the place he started, and yet there remains something to look forward to. Calvin stays on the course in faith that the God who makes the race so difficult also secures the runner's finish. At times, Calvin understands nothing of his God, but still hews closely to him and calls others to do the same. Without that God, life is nothing.

Calvin wanted things to be otherwise, but he had no choice. This is his greatest problem: there is so much he wants to do, but cannot. He wants to be free, but God always stands in the way. As so many others then and now have also seen, Calvin seems to be aware that even his own character is often only another obstacle in his way. Calvin pleads for freedom, but prays for providence. Doesn't he see that these two just do not go together? Or is this precisely what gives life its edge—a battle between the human race that wants to run free, and the God who wants to keep a tight rein on things?

Does this make Calvin more exciting as a person than his dull appearance suggests?

In this book, Calvin is approached as neither friend nor enemy; I just do not categorize him in that sense. I feel nothing for Calvin either way, but I am fascinated by him as a person. Without intending to, he created a world-wide community of believers, arousing as much scorn as admiration and accomplishing so much in spite of his many limitations. I have tried to tell the story of his life to discover what he was like as a person. Since Calvin himself claimed that we learn most about people from their letters, the most important source for this book is his correspondence. Because I hope it will get us closer to Calvin himself, there are few references to secondary literature.

Much more can be said about Calvin than what is in this book, but I hope the story told here will reveal a very interesting person hidden behind per-ceptions of him as a somber academic. At first glance, he is no more than a bookish man with a long goatee who spent his entire life chopping away at dry doctrine with an occasional pause to burn some odd heretic in his spare time. In the coming of Jesus Christ, the Bible tells us, God clothes himself in the skin of another to transform each human being into another person. Maybe, just maybe, we will see another transformation if we ourselves crawl into Calvin.

It is well worth trying to get under his skin, and—if you get that far—I will let you out again at the end. I promise.

ORPHAN

(1509-1533)

FATHER

The family into which John Calvin—actually Jean Cauvin—was born on July 10, 1509, was a little different. They lived in Noyon, a small town in Picardy in northern France, where in 1551 the inhabitants held a big celebration when a rumor that Calvin had died reached their ears. The celebrations were a little premature, since a year later Calvin wrote that he had outlived Noyon after hearing that the town had been sacked by Habsburg troops, and that his parents' house was the only building still standing. Calvin—no wonder—saw this as a miracle!

Calvin's father and brother both came into conflict with the church—or rather, the cathedral—of Noyon, though both were also employed by it. His father, Gérard, had come from a family of dock workers and coopers in the fishing town of Ponte-l'Evêque, but left for Noyon, some three miles away, to start a new career. In this town with its beautiful cathedral, he became a successful lawyer and also looked after the financial affairs of the church. Some disgruntlement arose when the clergy accused him of underhanded dealings in connection with the estate of two priests, and as a result

Gérard was excommunicated on November 13, 1528. At the time, this was by far the worst thing that could ever happen to anyone, both temporally and eternally. Gérard died while still outside of the fellowship of the church on May 31, 1531, but his oldest son Charles managed to obtain absolution for him, so that he received a Christian funeral and was buried in consecrated ground. Charles was a priest, but in that capacity showed two character traits that, considering that his younger brother John showed them as well, must have run in the family: belligerence and stubbornness. Charles too was excommunicated, for first insulting one colleague from the Noyon cathedral and then hitting another—not exactly the kind of behavior one expects from a priest. On his deathbed in October 1537, he was offered absolution and last rites, but refused both and so was buried far away from his father, outside of the churchyard in unconsecrated ground under the gallows. Later, when John Calvin came into conflict with Rome and ended up outside of this church, he was, in a sense, simply continuing a family tradition. The one difference was that his theology did away with the distinction between consecrated and unconsecrated ground, and so it was no problem for him when he was buried neither in a churchyard nor under a gallows, but in an unmarked grave in a quiet cemetery in Geneva.

MOTHER

Let us leave Calvin's death and burial for a later chapter and return to his family. From the information that has come down to us, it appears that Calvin's parents had seven children, two of whom were girls. Of these, one was called Marie. Two of the family's sons, Antoine and François, died at an early age. Very little is known of the family's children, however, aside from the facts that Charles was the oldest, John the second, and that another son also named Antoine would follow Calvin around for some twenty-eight years. Very little is also known of Calvin's mother, Jeanne Lefranc, but the little we do know of her allows us to understand much about him. She was apparently both beautiful and pious, and her deep religious devotion seems to contrast with what appears as mere outward appearance in her husband. Calvin thus grew up in an environment of piety, with a mother said to have devoted herself to her children. He remembered her as a devout woman who took him on pilgrimages as a child. It was with her that a young Calvin once ended up in Ourscamp, close to Noyon, kissing a relic of Saint Anne. Neither the kiss itself, nor the fact that it was bestowed on a relic, fit with many of the current common images of Calvin, but closer to his own day it was to this same Anne that Martin Luther had promised to become a monk when he was caught in a terrible thunderstorm. So Calvin's first kiss was a corpse, at a time when he was unaware that such things and others would only get better.

Of greater significance, however, was Jeanne's death in 1515, which left Calvin motherless at the age of six. His father, who would die when Calvin was twenty-one, remarried and his new wife, herself a widow, bore Gérard two daughters. As a child, though, Calvin no longer had a mother. Instead, the church increasingly became his mother, informing Calvin's later affirmation of the traditional Christian dictum that no one can have God as Father who does not have the church as mother. Calvin's relationship to the church at that time was somewhat peculiar, since in spite of everything, Gérard had been able to arrange a position for his son as chaplain at La Gésine chapel in the cathedral of Lyon. In terms of ecclesiastical responsibilities, this was little more than a farce; at the time one could hold such a post and receive its income while paying another (at a lower wage, of course) to do the actual work. At the church of St. Martin de Marteville in 1527, Calvin took on an additional position in the same way, and in 1529 he took yet another as pastor of Pont-l'Évêque through the mediation of his friend Claude de Hangest. Mother church thus provided the means for young Calvin to devote himself to his studies and, ironically, so begin to distance himself from her.

TEACHERS

The scarce details we have strongly suggest that Calvin grew up in middle-class circumstances. His family could not have been poor at any rate, since his father had to pay school fees whereas many other children received a bursary. Whether the family's home would have provided visible evidence of their affluence can no longer be known. In 1918, German forces struck Noyon (again!) and bombing destroyed Calvin's home. It was later replaced with a small Calvin museum. After a short time at Noyon's Collège de Capettes (named after the caps that were part of the school uniform), Calvin left his hometown for Paris in August 1523—the same month in which Jean Vallière was burned as the first Lutheran martyr in France. Calvin was accompanied by three sons of the house of de Montmorts, a branch of the de Hangest family, whom he had befriended through his father's professional network. The contact Calvin had with these nobles was already a sort of schooling in itself, one that would remain useful to Calvin. Throughout his entire life, he smoothly established and carefully maintained relationships with people of high standing. He remained aware of class differences, however, acknowledging his middle class background to Claude de Hangest in 1532. Calvin represented himself as an ordinary son of ordinary parents, and of average intelligence, someone who associated with people from the upper crust but did not belong there himself. As a fourteen-year-old boy he boarded with his uncle Richard, a locksmith, who lived close to the great gothic church of Saint-German L'Auxerrois, next to the Louvre, which in those days was still a palace. Here Calvin first studied under a tutor, whom he referred to as a "dumb man" *(homo stolidus)*. Yet, within a month of his arrival, he matriculated at the university of Paris through his admission to the Collège de la Marche as *martinet* or oppidan. That Calvin was only fourteen years old at the time says nothing one way or the other about his intellectual abilities. It was not unusual to enter the university at fourteen, and Calvin, in fact, may even be said to have begun a little on the late side. He was by this time also old enough to latinize his name from Jean Cauvin to Ioannis Calvinus. That's how we ended up with "John Calvin."

De la Marche would be very significant for Calvin's ability in Latin. The renowned Latinist Mathurin Cordier, who must rank among the founders of modern pedagogy, worked there. He was greatly concerned for the spiritual well-being of children, and saw learning to read and write well as expedients for learning to live well. Calvin worked intensively with this man for three months, and as thanks for what this contributed to his knowledge of Latin, his commentary on 1 Thessalonians was dedicated to Cordier in 1550. Since Cordier also instructed his students in the love of Christ, Calvin had great respect for his teacher as a Christian as well. In fact, the two became such close friends that they stayed in contact, and toward the end of his life Cordier rejoined Calvin in Geneva after previously working there with him from 1536 to 1538. Significantly, Calvin's relationship with his teacher also reveals a deep respect for those who were in authority above him. Cordier was not only his teacher but also a father figure, and as will become evident below, such people remained important to Calvin throughout his entire life.

ASSAULT

Aside from Cordier, there was not much to recommend the Collège de la Marche, above all because its environment was too liberal for anyone desiring to become a priest. This was actually what Calvin's father intended for him, and within a few months he was transferred to the Collège de Montaigu in the Quartier Latin, where he became a boarding student. Intellectually, the move was certainly an improvement, but this institution was known for launching nothing less than an assault on the physical condition of its students. Hygiene at de Montaigu was so appalling that Erasmus, whose own stay at the college left him with bad health and an abundance of lice and fleas, wrote that he knew many others who had still not overcome the illnesses they had contracted there. Writing thirty years after his studies at the Collège de Montaigu, Erasmus recalled the hard beds, sleepless nights and spoiled food as if he had spent the previous night in his old school. We find no such complaints about the college from Ignatius of Loyola, founder of the Jesuits, whose four years there overlapped with one of Calvin's, but François Rabelais referred to it as the "college of lice" and likewise wrote that, if he were king of Paris, he would set fire to the entire building, including the teaching staff.

The accommodations were lacking, but the education was solid, ethically moral and theologically conservative. In this place for the training of future priests, Calvin received a good education in the subjects that belonged to the so-called faculty of arts. These were the preparatory subjects required of all students before they made choices for further studies in theology, law or medicine. The focus was on rhetoric and logic, knowledge of culture, languages, and nature, and throughout it all the skill of engaging in learned disputation received considerable emphasis. In his extracurricular activities, Calvin secretly read the forbidden books of that time, which were considered provocative and even dangerous by some. To avoid any misunderstanding, it should be noted that these were the writings of Luther and Melancthon, with the latter's generally considered to be the more dangerous insofar as they were more persuasive and captivating than those of Luther.

Calvin lodged with the Nation de Picardy, as in that day students were grouped by country of origin. At the Collège de Montaigu, Calvin also acquired the nickname *accusativus*, which was not meant as a compliment. The name appears to have had nothing to do with grammar, but with a perception that Calvin felt a moral obligation to tell on others to the administration. This allegation was not completely just, and a look at the later Calvin will reveal that he—just like Erasmus and Ignatius—would receive more from the Collège de Montaigu than only a weakened constitution.

FATHERS

In short, Calvin's intellectual life was progressing well, and he stood out for his diligence, intelligence and impressive memory. However, when he had almost finished with the preparatory curriculum of the general arts subjects so as to be able to devote himself entirely to theology, his father ordered him to drop his theological studies and begin an education in law. The reason for this was that by that time the elder Calvin (who, as related above, had been excommunicated for refusing to give an account of the proceedings for the testaments of two members of the clergy) had had enough of theology and anything ecclesiastical. John, always obedient, as he would continue to be throughout his life, did exactly as his father wished. In this Calvin displayed a trait that would show again very often in his relationships with others, and which explains much about the things he did or refused to do. Just as he wanted to do all that God asked of him, so also he wanted to be obedient to all who, as he saw it, were appointed by God over him. Gérard's will was to be obeyed as law even though it had changed because he had come into conflict with the church. Additionally, though, Gérard's decision was also based on the realization that career opportunities and thus chances of financial success were much greater for Calvin in law than in theology. Many years later Calvin wrote that he obeyed his father as was naturally appropriate, but that in the end God in his providence turned the course of his life—and from his words it is more than clear that he was very happy with that turn. Even Calvin's father would have to cede to the law of the fatherly will of God. Or, as Calvin would put it—more than twenty years later!—in a letter to Melchior Wolmar: "my father sent me to study law, and the death of my father once again turned me aside from that road."

STUDENT

During the time when Calvin still had to deal with his earthly father, toward the end of 1527 or the beginning of 1528 (the exact date cannot be determined), he went from Paris, where only ecclesiastical or canon law was studied, to the university of Orléans, a renowned center for legal studies where a program in civil law was also available. Calvin's father wanted his son to become a lawyer or judge but above all to stay out of ecclesiastical law. In Orléans Calvin received instruction from a man equally as renowned as the university: Pierre de l'Estoile. But after little more than a year— most likely in May 1529—he left for Bourges with his friends François Daniel and Nicolas du Chemin. Since 1517 Bourges had been under the protection of Marguerite d'Angoulême, sister of King Francis I of France, and had served as a sort of center for reform-minded critics. Here Calvin attended the lectures of Andrea Alciati, as renowned as de l'Estoile, who had arrived only a month earlier. Like many others who had taken leave of conservative Orléans, Calvin was attracted to Alciati's fresh, humanistic method of teaching Roman law from the Latin source texts. Calvin's earliest biographers report that he worked extremely hard, and that he was in the habit of skipping meals and working until midnight only to wake up early the next morning to go over the previous day's material once more before attacking the new subject matter. Calvin's routine resulted in exceptional knowledge as well as exceedingly bad health—building on his experience in Paris on both counts. Soon Calvin was tired of Alciati's tendency—actually rather common among professors—to criticize his colleague de l'Estoile continually. Along with his fellow students, Calvin was also rather critical of Alciati's spoken Latin, as we see in his first extant publication, the preface to a work by his fellow student Nicolas du Chemin (*Antapologia*, 1531). According to Calvin, Alciati could write very beautiful Latin in his books, but he spoke it like a country bumpkin. Alciati had introduced him to the world of Italian humanism, but aside from this Calvin was very disappointed.

AMBITION

In October 1530, Calvin returned to Orléans—on foot, as many people in his time did—and in February 1531 he obtained his bachelor's degree in law *(licentié ès loix)*. From there he went to Paris with the specific goal of finding a printer for his first book, a commentary on *De clementia,* by the classical thinker Seneca, but he made a detour via Noyon in order to visit his father and make an appearance in the church to which he was, in fact, appointed as chaplain. During his stay, Calvin's father became so sick that his death was expected, and when it did indeed occur on May 26, 1531, Calvin was forced to stay in Noyon for sixteen days. What a remarkable scene that must have been—a chaplain in the place where he was not really the chaplain, a brother with the family to which he did not really belong, and a motherless son with his dying father to whom he was not really that close to begin with—for sixteen days, as a person who did not have the gift of patience! His father's death meant complete freedom to break off his studies in law, and so Calvin returned to Paris. He had, of course, been diligent in his legal studies as was expected of him, but his heart was set upon the arts, and at the Collège Royal he could study them to his heart's content. This institution had been formed by the initiative of King Francis I and remained under his protection. The king had appointed five humanist teachers who were in, but not of, the university. This was a clear royal signal to the reigning theological tendency at the university. The Collège—independent and academic—could guarantee the reforming trend, something made particularly evident in its focus on the three languages of humanist learning: Hebrew, Greek and Latin. Not that long ago (1523) at the Sorbonne it had been decided that all translations from Hebrew and Greek sources were of no value for the church and were in fact dangerous. Within France, a virtual crusade was launched against French translations and against works that supported such translations. The Collège was thus an interesting and cunningly progressive institution. Calvin was surrounded there by scholars who wanted to work, learn, and teach from original sources, including the Bible, which was exactly in line with his own interests. He received instruction in Hebrew, although it is not known from whom. Calvin had an interest in this language but would never become an expert in it, even if his knowledge did suffice to allow him to read from the Old Testament. In this he surpassed Erasmus, who did not know Hebrew and who was in fact afraid that learning the language could lead to a fall back into Judaism. Calvin, on the other hand, was convinced that one could learn from Judaism, and this conviction provided him a foundational and positive appreciation for the Old Testament.

Calvin had two goals in Paris, to study and to publish, but because he was so busy with the latter he did not attend many lectures. Nevertheless, while there he became so absorbed in the Bible that his biographer Colladon reports that he began to preach from it in the areas surrounding Orléans and Bourges during an extended stay there in 1532 and 1533. As an aside, we note that we have no idea whatsoever as to the reason for this stay. The period from May 1532 to October 1533 is in all events a bit of a mystery, but in the wall of the Augustinian monastery of Bourges there is a veranda that is referred to as "the chair of Calvin," and nearby in the Marché aux Poissons one can see a rock from which Calvin is said to have preached. As an official clergyman he had the right to preach, of course, but it is strange that this chaplain, who had never previously made much of his ecclesiastical work and instead had intended to become a jurist, had now become an evangelist. What had happened to Calvin? According to his own words, one Father had won the battle against the other. "Although I did everything to do the will of my father, God in his providence yet made me turn to another way."

CONVERSION

Just as the death of Calvin's mother was directly related to his new bond to the church as mother, so the death of his father directly affected his bond to God as Father. On the basis of the evidence it is somewhat easier to trace Calvin's relationship to the church than his relationship to God, and so questions as to the moment at which and the path by which Calvin came to faith always come up. Though these questions have been of no concern to Calvin's biographers, many others have nevertheless attempted to settle them. Conversion, however, is a matter between God and a human being. As a result, biographers have found hardly any material, and certainly have not been able to give an exact date to anything. Despite all of this, however, Calvin's conversion has too often been modeled after those of Paul, Augustine and Luther, and an alternate category has been ignored. Calvin's conversion could very well have been like that of Timothy, who the Bible notes was already a believer as a child with his mother and grandmother. Calvin referred to his conversion as *subita*. If this word is translated as "suddenly," Calvin's conversion would indeed belong in the same category as Paul's. *Subita,* however, should actually be translated as "unexpected," indicating that Calvin had not expected to be converted. Even more significant is the fact that in speaking of his conversion he probably did not even mean a conversion from unbelief to belief, but rather a change in terms of church, by moving to a "purer doctrine" *(purior doctrina).* Calvin himself tells us that he held on stubbornly to papal superstitions and that he was too old to be pulled out of that swamp. (Writing at the age of forty-eight, and referring to the time when he was barely twenty, perhaps Calvin considered himself already old at that time.) Another of his arguments cuts even deeper, namely that out of obedience to the church *(ecclesiae reverentia)* he did not dare to make the step until he truly saw things differently. This raises the issue as to the time or moment at which Calvin no longer saw any good in the Catholic church and began to consider the reform-minded side of the Christian religion. This question too is easier to ask than to answer. Much evidence suggests that Calvin's conversion began toward the end of his twenties, but even that was really nothing more than a beginning: Calvin himself writes that at first he had little appreciation for the Reformed teaching.

That Calvin was not quickly won over is evident from a conversation he had in Paris in June 1531 with the sister of his friend François Daniel. Daniel's sister had entered a convent and, to the chagrin of her brother, was on the point of making her vows of poverty, chastity and obedience. Daniel thus sent Calvin and another friend, Nicholas Cop, to see her. Calvin wrote that he had made no attempt to dissuade Daniel's sister because that was not why he had made the visit. Instead, he had gone no further than to tell her that she should not do anything in her own power, and that she should also reflect carefully before doing anything. Evidently Calvin was not directly opposed to her decision and only wanted to tell her that she should make her vows relying on God's direction and power. Later, when Calvin gained an appreciation for the new doctrine, he expressed himself more radically on this subject, but he would continue to promote piety, chastity and obedience.

A DIFFERENT GOD

It is perhaps better to leave the mystery of Calvin's conversion for what it is, and to draw a parallel between it and his view on the presence of Christ in the Lord's Supper. In both cases it is not about the *how* but rather about the *that,* and especially about the fruit of the *that*. More important than the preceding questions is the core of the issue, and for Calvin the core was that he was once again in a right relationship with God, which meant that God in his mercy had called him when he was lost *(quand il m'a appellé du temps que i'estoye perdu)*. Calvin had already known God, but he had known him more as Judge than as Father because of the way the church had wrongly portrayed him. The unexpected transition to another theology also unexpectedly confronted him with a different God, the real God as Calvin now understood him.

> I was his archenemy, and in me there was not even a semblance of obedience toward him at all, but I was rather full of pride, full of maliciousness, arrogance and a diabolic obstinance to resist God and to plunge myself into eternal death. And this would indeed have happened, had not God in pity received me and unlocked for me the endless treasures of his mercy.

For Calvin this was the heart of the matter, as well as a matter of the heart. With this the questions as to the *when* and the *how* fall away, and furthermore, one understands why Calvin devoted himself so fiercely to God's cause: thankfulness for being saved from ruin.

Calvin was thus already a believer before he had a conversion in terms of church, and he wanted that belief to be characterized by what the Bible calls a life in the fear of the Lord. Such fear is to be understood as respect, akin to that which children have for their parents, and that Calvin had especially for his father. In Calvin, however, this fear also has an element of anxiety, though not in the neurotic sense described by twentieth-century psychologists and subsequently read back into figures like Luther and Calvin. Instead it is the anxiety of a person who is keenly aware of guilt before God. Calvin said he knew the feeling of the author of Psalm 130, who cried out to God from the depths of his guilt. One's conscience is tormented by an awareness of being a sinner and having to appear before a righteous and wrathful God, and one's conscience finds heavenly rest when it knows forgiveness and renewal. For Calvin the conscience is not a second God, but God himself speaking to human beings, and it is virtually impossible to count the number of times he writes about the conscience and its need to be at rest. Calvin's problem was that he had experienced Catholic preaching as a burden on the conscience without the comfort of forgiveness that is to follow. "There were always those torments of conscience which made you feel as if you were in hell. . . . I experienced it myself that way." Over against this strain on the conscience is the freedom of the Christian. This was why Calvin also had issues with the food- and fasting-prescriptions of Rome. God permits us to eat with a clear conscience all the things he has given us, and for that reason when Rome forbids certain kinds of meat on certain days, our freedom is curtailed and we are caused to doubt with each and every bite. For Calvin, conversion meant freedom, a liberation from the torments of the conscience, from the feeling that whatever he did was sinful and wrong. Calvin experienced freedom from all of this and found peace in his conscience. According to him, "there is no greater good one can inherit on this earth."

Calvin's decision to end his legal studies had little to do with his conversion. He had had little use for this study to begin with, not only in terms of its content but also because at that time he was still rather shy—certainly no advantage for one who intends to become a lawyer. Moreover, Calvin wanted his choice to make it perfectly clear that he had no desire to follow in his father's footsteps, especially in view of what he had made of his career in law.

Life

As a youth, Calvin experienced many things; nothing truly exceptional for young people of that time, but these experiences were rendered more acute through his conversion. Here we should think especially of his constant experience of being a stranger, of being on the road, of continually having to let go. Even if there is a sense that life here on earth is nothing more than a passage we run through in all haste, there is no contempt for this world. While on the road, we are to live as Christians, and Calvin's description of that life is clear and concise. We are renewed by the Spirit of God, renewed to be children of God, and a sign of this is that our physical desires no longer master us, "but that the Spirit of God reigns in us, that we give evidence of our adoption, that we walk in the fear of God, holding to him as our Father and giving God the honor that is due him. That is the essence of what it means to be a Christian." This is transparent and clear language, and it was appealing at a time when many craved religious clarity and simplicity. Calvin himself was among those who thirsted for such clarity, and once he came to know God, he also wanted to know everything about him. This fostered a frantic aversion to anything that even smelled faintly of idolatry, which he opined could be found aplenty in Rome.

WATCHDOG

With Calvin's conversion, the rest of his life can actually be summed up as well. Calvin had found God—he would probably say that God found him, but the result is the same: Calvin became God's advocate. He would devote every minute of the rest of his life to the defense of God and of his cause. Calvin's is the story of that one God and that one man. He wanted nothing more than to defend God against any attack that deprived him of his due, that made him appear small, or portrayed him as a tyrant or conversely as some kind of Santa Claus. The virtually impossible task he took upon himself was to keep God beyond humanity's reach, and yet at the same time make him the full concern of humanity. One could call Calvin a theological jurist or a juridical theologian, but he was in fact simply a shepherd's watchdog who wanted to protect the sheep, keep the flock with the shepherd and in so doing take the shepherd under his protection. Calvin made himself God's advocate.

Calvin did ask himself, however, who that God really was. Calvin warned against unrestrained theological speculation and wanted to keep closely to the Bible. God accommodates himself to us when he speaks, and babbles with us like a mother with her child. The Bible must be seen in that way as well. It is not a book in which all things are described in an exact, scientific way, but a book where an account of the facts—which are indeed facts and not merely stories or myths—is given such that both young and old can grasp them. It is in this way that God speaks about himself. For this same reason there is also an unknown and unknowable side to God. If God accommodates himself when he speaks, who is he really? Suspense is always present when Calvin talks about God, and at times he himself does not understand God at all. Throughout his entire life Calvin busied himself with the question of who God really is, continuing his search for the Father he had found.

JOB SEARCH

Those who have such high spiritual goals must also see to it that there is bread to eat. In Calvin's time, one applied for a post in the academic world by presenting a substantial publication. Calvin did this in 1532 with the publication of his commentary on *De clementia*. As its title suggests, Calvin's work dealt with the harmonious life recommended by Stoicism, that ancient philosophy that longed for a state of being unaffected by emotions. As nice as this title may sound, Calvin's intent was not to surreptitiously reach the French king who mercilessly battled the Protestants under the guise of a philosopher beyond suspicion such as Seneca. The work cannot even be seen to relate closely to Calvin's faith. His commentary on *De clementia* says nothing of his religious convictions and was only intended to satisfy the common academic norms. As regards Stoicism and the apparent similarities between Stoic philosophy and Calvin's thought, one is still a long way from proving that the latter finds its roots in the former. Still, this suggestion is often made, and Calvin is said to have attempted to pass through all the circumstances of his life and of this world as emotionlessly as possible. This in turn is supposed to have been behind all those tough characters in the Reformed world who burn with fanaticism but stay ice-cold in the face of need, sickness and death. Calvin himself wrote that the Stoic ideal was in many ways similar to the virtuous Christian life, but added that the Stoic concern was a matter of one's own conscience, whereas Christianity was about service to God. In short the only message Calvin meant to communicate with his first book was that he wanted a place among the academic elite. An earlier edition of Seneca's *De clementia* had been published by Erasmus, who had suggested that subsequent improvements by another scholar would be good. Calvin's youthful overconfidence was such that he thought he was the one who could indeed do it better, and for that reason he did not hesitate to point out errors Erasmus had made here and there. In the preface Calvin wrote of himself—in conformity with the humanistic norm of modesty bordering on false piety—as such a simple young man that there was no reason to imagine that he would one day become well known. And yet Calvin is actually trying to gain a reputation for himself with this very book! This reveals another of Calvin's traits, and one could say that in this way he was like his *Institutes* which changed externally, but internally remained the same over the course of time. Calvin described himself as a shy person who was not at ease in company. That may well have been the case, but once he had begun to write, all shyness fell away. It appears as if the brakes came off when he no longer saw people, but only pen and paper. His shyness was therefore only part-time, as is already apparent here at the beginning of his career.

In the commentary on *De clementia*, Calvin wished to display the extent of his knowledge and cited no less than sixty Latin and twenty Greek classics, including several church fathers. Clearly, he had a sharp mind. He knew by heart the classics such as Cicero, Virgil and Tacitus, and was very familiar with the corpora of Plato and Seneca. For these reasons, Calvin also had high expectations for his book. "The dice have been cast," he wrote to his friend François Daniel. An expression from the world of gambling in Calvin?! He had gambled that he would make it but should have known that gambling brings no luck. The book was a flop—all the more pitiful since he had paid for the cost of printing himself, as well as for the purchase and delivery of one hundred copies to be distributed for free in Orléans. He also attempted to persuade the professors in Paris to adopt his book to be used as course material, but this brought him nothing but debt and frustration. The whole affair leaves us with a rather heartbreaking image of a young man who tried so hard to belong, to climb higher, to make the jump from one social class to another, and in the process ended up between the two. On the other hand, if a twenty-one-year-old makes his own rather bold claims to competency, then gives further evidence of immodesty by criticizing other senior scholars in suggesting it is high time for a good commentary on Seneca's *De clementia* to finally appear, he should not be surprised if those same scholars look down on and ignore him. The results, at any rate, were a failed job search, a book that flopped and a lonely junior scholar with few prospects.

A CHOICE

Another unstable factor in Calvin's life was the situation in France. King Francis I had some leanings toward reform, even if only to irritate his two rivals, the emperor Charles V and the pope. In that European struggle between the French kingdom, the German empire and the Roman Church, Luther was used by each of these powers to strengthen their own position.

Within France, there was considerable receptivity to Luther's message, though there was no direct connection to Luther. He was, after all, just a German. The reform movement in France was called *évangélisme*, and in most cases had more to do with inner convictions than with outward choices. Calvin himself did not separate quickly from Rome, even after he had already been of evangelical conviction for several years. What helped was the fact that he associated with the "wrong" people: his cousin Robert d'Olivetan, with whom Calvin was very close, belonged to the confirmed Lutherans, as did his beloved teacher Melchior Wolmar. People are variously influenced by those around them. Thus we see that while Calvin was in Noyon in August of 1533 to fulfill some aspect of his chaplaincy he joined in a prayer gathering against the plague with his colleagues in the chapter of the Catholic cathedral.

On the other hand, however, his reforming side is also clearly visible when at the end of October of that year he reported negatively about a play in which students criticized the reforming principles of Marguerite d'Angoulême, the sister of King Francis I. On the basis of this, Nicolas Cop, Calvin's friend and the new rector of the Parisian university, delivered a rectoral speech inspired largely by Calvin on November 1 (All Saints' Day), which brought him into conflict with the theologians of the Sorbonne. Calvin said that these events motivated him to speak out precisely because Marguerite was a believer who was devoted to true teaching. Marguerite was a very interesting woman for many reasons, certainly in terms of Calvin's ideals and norms: she could read Hebrew, Greek and Latin, and speak Italian, Spanish, English and German. She had gathered around her a circle composed of culturally sophisticated and church reform-minded progressives. This circle was led by Guillaume Briconnet who, as bishop of Meaux, attempted to realize the ideal of Faber Stapulensis, the real leader of the French reform movement: to make the Bible accessible to all the people so that Christ could work salvation in their hearts by his Word. Calvin was also a participant in this little circle, but once again his problem was that he did not easily fit the profile of either of the circle's two main constituencies. He did not really belong wholly either to the openly reformed party or to the

reform-minded elite, and yet there were ways in which he actually belonged
to both. Here is a tension that can be seen in all of Calvin's life and thought:
the tension within himself as an educated elitist who actually wants to serve
the common people; the tension between a scholarly humanist and a popular
reformer. Calvin himself is the man in whom Erasmus and Luther must come
together: in terms of style he wants to stay with Erasmus; in terms of content
he must opt for Luther. As a result, Calvin wrestled his whole life long with
the question of the proper relationship between culture and religion. Beyond
this, little is known about this period in Paris other than that he lectured on
Seneca and that a surviving report from one hearer tells that the audience
was greatly impressed by the learning of "this Calvin."

ESCALATION

Late in 1533, Calvin had the opportunity to become an ecclesiastical jurist
near Orléans, but the prospect held little interest for him. Was he to occupy
himself with useless things? This question speaks volumes since Calvin
needed money, had in his mind already dismissed the church, and wanted to
become an academic but found that there must be more useful things for
him to do even if he did not know what these were.

In the courts and in the theological faculty, however, people began to
take sides, spurred on by Cop's speech, who, as noted before, chose All
Saints' Day (November 1) to propagate as rector the ideas of Erasmus and
Luther, adding an appeal to use not swords, but words, to fight for the
truth. The Parisian theologians warned the king against these Lutherans,
and he responded with a series of arrests that began within the month. The
king, however, did not want to act too directly against the reformers since
he needed the help of the German Protestant princes in face of the threat
posed to France by the emperor and the pope. Just when the situation appeared to settle down somewhat, things got out of hand with the *affaire des
placards*. Cop had urged a war of words, and on the night of October 17,
1534, pamphlets promptly appeared which described the Mass as an intoler-
able abuse. They were not just posted here and there, however. One pamphlet made its way to the door of the king's own bedroom in his castle at

d'Aboise. As one would expect, he had quite a shock the next morning when he realized that someone had been able to get within a few meters of him without being noticed. Weren't these people linked to the fanatics in Münster who only a short time ago had intended to bring about a new heaven on earth and had instead caused all hell to break loose? The king immediately saw these things as a spiritual battle, and on the next day organized a procession and public prayers that God might bring these shameful people to repentance. Apparently unconvinced, however, that prayer and processions alone would solve the problem, he followed up with persecution and bloodshed. Even with the support of the German princes hanging in the balance, the king claimed he was left with no choice. This was no longer an exclusively theological matter; it had become political, just as had happened in the battle against the Anabaptists, whose radicalism and rejection of infant baptism had turned society upside down. The attack on the Mass as an institutional means of grace was seen in the French context as an attack on the king himself. Church and monarchy were so closely related that any who raised their hands against the church raised them against the king himself, and in so doing brought all of France into danger.

The situation escalated to the point that Cop fled to Basel. Since it was known that Calvin had contributed significantly to Cop's speech, Calvin considered it wise that he should leave as well and thus arrived in Angoulême in March 1534. It appears that the preceding events were the proverbial last straw for Calvin, and on May 4 he renounced the income from his chaplaincy. This step was further necessitated by the requirements of canon law, according to which he would have to decide at age twenty-five whether he wanted to continue in the church and be ordained as a priest, or to give up his ecclesiastical career altogether. Calvin chose to end his ministerial service—and yet he did not: the chaplain did not become a priest but he did become a pastor.

IMAGE

Before moving on to the next stage in Calvin's life, we need to consider how Calvin was viewed by others and how he viewed himself. Exactly what he looked like at that time is not known, but surviving portraits leave the impression that in those days Calvin still looked young and fresh—not quite so pale and skinny as he appears in later pictures. The prevailing image of Calvin rests on those later pictures, however, and it must be noted that such representations of his physiognomy certainly have been of little advantage to him. The image is of a rather unsociable person who can barely find anything to enjoy in life. It is the image, as suggested in a well-known survey work, of one who seemed to have taught the law rigorously with little respect for the gospel revealed in Christ. This is the dominant image of Calvin. It may remain to be seen whether this image represents Calvin as he really was later in life, but we can already see that it does not match up with Calvin in his early years. Instead, as we have seen in this chapter, he was a person who was forced to be independent early on, who followed his father's way and yet sought his own while doing so. He was one of those students and young academics open to new ideas, new challenges, new forms of church and scholarship. He brought a fresh approach, he was progressive, interested in renewal and driven by the new experience of life promoted by the renaissance and humanism. This is the image of Calvin as he was in those early years, and as he would in fact remain. Needless to say, this is quite different from the typical image of Calvin portrayed as a boring churchman with a pointed beard who gazes darkly out into the world.

Calvin wanted to be free and independent, ideals that can also be seen in his view of the church. His 1532 letter to du Chemin in which he asked for a little bit of money since he was broke provides a typical example of this desire. The note ends with the promise that du Chemin will receive his money back within a few days and be able to cross Calvin's name off his list of debtors. Calvin wanted to be indebted to no one—he wanted to be free and independent—and he wanted the same for others with respect to himself. We see this in the announcement of the publication of his Seneca commentary to François Daniel, in which Calvin suggested that it would be great if Daniel were to buy a hundred copies, but added that his friend was not to feel obligated in any way by the complimentary copy he included.

Calvin did not want to dictate to Daniel but rather wanted to allow him to make a completely independent decision.

SEAL

Calvin designed his own seal, and simply in so doing betrayed a certain kind of self-consciousness. More revealing than the production of the seal, however, were its images and words, which said so much about his drive. The seal depicted a hand, and within that hand a heart. Everything was summed up in this. Calvin wanted to give his whole heart to God *prompte et sincere*— "willingly and honestly"—as was written around the image. These two characteristics were in clear evidence throughout Calvin's life: the *prompte* in his incessant, persistent and sometimes apparently thoughtless diligence, and the *sincere* likewise. Many things could be said about Calvin, but he was at any rate open and honest; others always knew what they were up against in him. Yet the seal also said more, since the hand with the heart was bookended by the letters *I* and *C,* which could stand for *Ioannes Calvinus* but also for *Iesus Christus.* This may seem confusing, but actually made things crystal clear: it was Calvin's desire that all that concerned him and all that concerned Christ should be perfectly aligned but should also actually come together as one. He was neither the first person with such a vision, nor the last, and he was certainly not the only one. But in Calvin the importance of this vision certainly stands out. Identifying one's own cause with that of God, one can accomplish a great many things, but one can also become vulnerable and potentially incapable of distinguishing between work and home any longer.

Calvin did not like to talk about himself—at least that is what he said. His commentaries and sermons, however, reveal quite a lot about him just as the novels, plays and poetry of other authors do of their authors. He can be found, if only one looks for him in his work, and this will indeed be done in what follows. Calvin spoke more directly about himself in his correspondence, and from this emerges the image of a person who is confident (and assertive) in his call to be a prophet, but also a person who is much less confident in himself.

SELF-IMAGE

"Who I am, you know, or at any rate you ought to know. I am a man for whom the righteousness of our heavenly Father is so important, that I allow no one to move me from a most strict devotion to this righteousness." With these words to Ami Perrin, Calvin declares himself and describes his manner of life from the time of his conversion to his death.

His claim in a letter to Sadoleto that he did not like to speak about himself *(De me non libenter loquor)* has been interpreted widely as evidence that Calvin would not talk about himself at all. A careful reading of his letters and commentaries proves this false, however, and reveals much about Calvin as a person. The fact that in his writings and sermons he often uses "we" when he means "I" provides an additional key to a better understanding of Calvin.

As noted previously, Calvin did not have a great self-image. In his letters he frequently mentioned a number of his own negative characteristics of which he was conscious but which he also found difficult to hide. He admitted that it was difficult for him to maintain peace with moderation and tolerance, although he did his best "against his nature." He said that in writing he often became more fiery than he actually intended, even though "it is not my nature to fight it out with such coarse rudeness." This character trait also amazed the Catholic theologian Bartholomeus Camerarius, who had several discussions with Calvin in Geneva about the freedom of the will. Camerarius did not understand how Calvin could be so sharp in his writings and so easygoing and friendly face-to-face.

Calvin's vehemence also explains why he could defend Luther when the latter had once again lashed out harshly. When Calvin wrote to Farel that he preferred to live in isolation, part of the reason for this was his realization that his presence could work people up. He wrote the same to Melanchthon. It would be better for himself as well as for others if he withdrew a little, but God continually put him back on stage. God had given him his role in the play *(theatrum)* that is this world. He wanted to do something about this shortcoming, writing to Heinrich Bullinger that he tried to write in such a way that others would not become angry. Along the same lines, a colleague from Basel, Simon Grynaeus, admonished Calvin for being too sharp in his reaction to Peter Kuntz, a preacher at Bern, reminding him that Kuntz came from a family of simple farmers, whereas Calvin had a more educated and cultured background.

In the course of his dispute with the fanatical Lutheran theologian Joachim Westphal, Calvin noted in his second response that he had perhaps been too harsh. He had been shocked by his own violence, and wrote to Bullinger: "I see that I was more heavy-handed that I had intended to be." He wrote that he did not understand very well how this could have escaped him in his dictation, and later admitted that he had had difficulty restraining himself when responding to Westphal.

In contrast to all of this, Calvin wrote in the preface to his commentary on the Psalms: "I have to admit that by nature I am timid, soft and of little courage," referring to his *pusillanimitas* or smallness of heart *(Ainsi, combien que ie me recognoy estre timide, mol et pusillanime de ma nature)*. Elsewhere he openly wrote: "timid as I am and have always been, as I confess" *(timide comme ie suis, et comme ie l'ay tousiours esté, ie le confesse)*.

HONEST KID

Though aware of his own faults, Calvin did think he lived as he had taught others to live, a claim the truth of which is more and more corroborated by research. The criticism of his lifestyle and the various accusations of immorality that were already in circulation during his lifetime appear to have been unfounded. It was impossible for him not to speak the truth and in fact would have gone against his very nature. He loved being straightforward and open, but in that openness he often went too far. As a young theologian, he criticized the experienced Reformer Martin Bucer, claiming that he could act no differently: "I prefer to make my complaint against you openly rather than to suppress my annoyance and so cause it to grow." He found it more honest "to give offense in my boorish simplicity than in hypocrisy to praise someone." Anyone who thought Calvin was a sycophantic slimeball knew nothing of him at all, and he considered nothing better than that others should speak as openly with him as he did with them.

When Bullinger let it be known that he had problems with Calvin's criticism of his book on the Lord's Supper, Calvin gave an elaborate defense of the way he had written: "I have always loved simplicity, and never cared much for cleverness." Even opponents praised him for his clarity, and Calvin wanted at all costs to avoid the impression that he was cleverly hiding things. "My way of teaching is too simple to be considered suspect, and at the same time too detailed for it to be called unclear." Thus he said nothing different in Zürich than in Geneva. He claimed that it was his principle to be frank and consequent in speech and that in his experience this had been the way in which even the strictest hardliners could be brought around to moderation. He wanted to avoid long-windedness, which he claimed to see in Augustine among others. He also admitted, however, that his terseness could cause offense. He just was not sure, and claimed that it was a result of his lack of self-confidence: "I have so little self-confidence that I prefer to follow my own nature than to admonish others." Shame is another feeling Calvin often felt. He asserted that he took no pleasure in exposing the evil of Rome, but rather was ashamed by it. When ill, he was ashamed of being able to do so little. Calvin was transparent, open and straightforward, and this made him both vulnerable and sensitive to criticism.

He did indeed see himself as God's watchdog: "A dog barks when it sees that its master is being attacked. I would be a real coward if I saw God's truth being attacked and remained quiet without making a sound."

In a letter to Bucer, Calvin anticipated what Bucer might say about him: "You will probably say that I have a habit of hurling lightning bolts in letters, and being mild in personal contact." Calvin thought differently about this: "I like to be clear, and whether in a letter or face to face, I cannot restrain myself when I want to express my meaning clearly in words. Openness is of more use than craftiness, and so I prefer simply to say what I mean."

Writing in 1538, Calvin claimed that his openness was a strategy intended to separate the person from the issue, and he was proud to have achieved this. He debated Albert Pighius, a Catholic theologian from Kampen, only when the latter was alive and only on the basis of his doctrine. He reacted vehemently against Sadoleto because he felt attacked not in his person but in his office. Calvin claimed that the fierce treatment he received from Michael Servetus—whose life, as will be seen further on, was brought to an end at the stake in Geneva with Calvin's help—never bothered him. Servetus' defamations of Calvin were like "the barking of a dog at a pile of manure," and just two hours before Servetus was burned, Calvin maintained he had not battled him for personal reasons. "I do not hate you, I do not despise you and I did not want to be hard in pursuit of you."

HUMAN BEING

Nevertheless, Calvin's entire life and work clearly show that he was not an emotionless stone. A glimpse of this is caught in his reaction to the news that Luther had been content with Calvin's work. "If we are not appeased by such moderation, we must be completely of stone. I am really appeased. I wrote something that satisfied him." Neither was fear foreign to him. As late as 1562 Calvin could speak of his fears under persecution thirty years earlier. In a sermon on 2 Samuel, he looked back on his time before his flight from France and related that he had been scared to death: "I was so afraid that I wanted to die to be rid of those fears."

Calvin was simply a human being, and we will follow him on his remarkable journey.

PILGRIM

(1533-1536)

ON THE ROAD

"We are always on the road." With these words Calvin not only expressed his view of life in general but unconsciously summed up the story of his own life as well. The same is true of his spiritual offspring, since *on the road* can be understood both literally and spiritually. Over the centuries, Reformed Christians have often lived as sojourners, refugees and emigrants, but they have also seen themselves as being "on the road" spiritually since heaven has become their new homeland—the journey will finally end only when they have arrived there. Believers are "just sojourners on this earth, so that with hope and patience they strive toward a better life." If heaven is one's homeland, one can, at one and the same time, feel at home both anywhere and nowhere.

The road to heaven is not an easy one. It is a narrow road, as depicted in a painting of two clearly separate roads that could and can be seen in many Christian homes. On the one side is that terrifying yet seductively easy broad road that leads to destruction. On the other is the very promising but difficult narrow road that leads to eternal life. The painting brings to mind two concepts that were fundamental to Calvin's speech and thought: labyrinth and abyss. For Calvin, these are the two forms of the ultimate experience of misery.

Calvin took the word *labyrinth* from the humanistic tradition, where it was used pejoratively against scholasticism. For him, it represented a way of thinking that entangled a person and caused him or her to lose the way to God and self. In this life, humans find themselves in the labyrinth by nature. Only by holding onto the Scriptures as onto Ariadne's thread—or, to use a Christian expression, as a guide for the journey to eternity—can one escape from the labyrinth unscathed. As to the "abyss," people end up in it when they fall from God's ways, when they overturn his order and disregard his peace. Calvin himself had come to the very edge of the abyss when his eyes were suddenly opened to his guilt before God. To think of him in that situation as entirely hopeless and in extreme despair, however, fits neither with the prevailing image of Calvin discussed in the previous chapter, nor with the real Calvin. He himself described the experience as having been knocked down by God's wrath. God brought him to the abyss, to the very edge of ruin but at the last moment saved him. This experience in which guilt and grace, election and providence, came together would determine Calvin's view of humanity, the church and the world.

WORLD

The world is in constant change; there is no stability in it. Calvin spoke of the uncertainty of this existence and of the chaos in this world numerous times just in his commentary on the Psalms. Heaven may offer stability and rest, but the world is characterized by upheaval and instability. The whole world has been turned on its head. Calvin refers to the abhorrent disorder that overshadows the order of God's providence. God himself, however, is hard at work in the midst of the disorder, "since God everywhere lays traps for us, digs pits, throws all kinds of obstacles in our way, and finally encloses us in the abyss." It is as if God is toying with us, and our lives are little more than playthings. God puts us on a track and gives us a small obstacle-course to run. It is a short race; he soon takes us back to himself again. Life is short and means very little. Wherever we look there is despair. We are spoiled even within, and we are but mirrors of death. Are not all the events of this life nothing but a prelude to the final destruction *(praeludium interitus)?* "As humans we are like dry grass, we can wither away at any moment, we are never far from death, indeed it is as if we are already living in the grave." Our life "hangs as if from a silk thread," and we are "surrounded by a thousand deaths." This experience begins from the moment of birth: "leaving the womb is the entrance to a thousand deaths." Life simply flies by, and it is as if we have only just been born before we die again. There are dangers everywhere.

> If only you look up, how many dangers threaten us from there? But if you look down at the ground, how many poisons do you find there? How many wild beasts that can tear you to pieces? How many snakes? How many swords, pits, stumbling blocks, ravines, caved-in buildings, stones and flying spears? In short, we cannot take a single step without encountering ten deaths.

In the city, many accidents are just waiting to happen, but if one goes out into a forest without knowing the way, one soon runs the risk of becoming prey to lions or wolves. According to Calvin, even our own bodies are already full of all kinds of maladies, let alone all those threats to us from outside!

> If you step onto a ship, you are only one step away from death. If you climb onto a horse, your foot only needs to slip and your life is in danger. Just walk through the city streets one time, and there are as many dangers as there are roof tiles on the houses. If you or your friend are carrying a weapon, injury lies in wait.

Thus Calvin could come up with a virtually endless list of dangers to show that human life is in constant threat and amounts to very little.

Nothing is certain, everything is in danger, and "it appears as if the heavens are crashing down, the earth is being moved, and the mountains rooted up." Calvin calls life "a churning river" and finds the human condition "as desperate as that of someone in the grave or of those who met their end in a labyrinth." Life takes place "in an ominous labyrinth," and one escapes only by trusting to God's providence. Those who do not are in hell already, hell being for Calvin the agony of fear and uncertainty, "since there is no more terrifying agony than to tremble from fear and uncertainty." Given his vision of human existence, it is no wonder Calvin sought refuge in providence and predestination.

PREDESTINATION

Now that predestination has been mentioned it seems best to treat this complicated issue right away. A stumbling block for both friends and foes, it must be dealt with at some point since many consider this doctrine distinctive of Calvin. As the mother of the doctrine of election, the doctrine of providence belongs to this discussion as well. Predestination is but a small part of the whole discussion of providence but nevertheless has been the specific focus of attention. The image of an arbitrary, merciless God as tyrannical as Calvin himself, of a theological system that filled psychiatric wards and led people to commit suicide, cannot be left unmentioned in this book. Unfortunately, many who came after Calvin did indeed make a real mess of things. Opponents deliberately misrepresented his views; many of his own followers foolishly brought their church members to a state of mental despair through their preaching and pastoral work.

Needless to say, Calvin's own views were very different. Through the fall into sin, humanity broke with God, is now excluded from life and is under judgment. All are fallen. God, however, came with a plan of salvation, and this means that whoever believes in Christ is freed from judgment and receives eternal life. "But," asked Calvin, "how is it that one person believes and another does not?" The difference must depend on God's choice, for if the choice were made by humans, God would be dependent on what they do. This would leave us with a weak God and—what may be worse—with believers who lack certainty. If, on the other hand, the choice depends entirely on God, he receives the greatest degree of glory and the believer receives the greatest degree of certainty—this is the doctrine of election! That God decided not to lead all people to faith means that there were people he did not choose, people he left under judgment and thus actually condemned. This is exactly why Calvin spoke of a *decretum horribile*. The term has nothing to do with horror, but everything to do with the shivers. It is not a "horrible decree," but a decision that causes us to tremble and shiver all the same. This decision also humbles us. Calvin often spoke of a *humilitas*, expecting this as the basic attitude of humanity before God.

Calvin found that the notion of an electing or decision-making God left people not only humble but also at peace. This was true of the idea that God was at work in all things, that nothing happened by chance, and that everything comes from his Fatherly hand. If, however, this is the way things are, one must also be willing to learn something from that hand of God. If, for example, terrible things happen to one in this life, one can learn that this world is passing away, that one must seek true rest elsewhere, that with God even setbacks aim at the good, that one must be humble, that one needs forgiveness of sins, and the list goes on. If God does nothing randomly, there must always be something to learn. God works with a goal, and so all Calvinists seek so to do as well. As Calvin sees it, something of lasting value must always come from everything that happens.

PRESIDENT

Those who do not connect and relate "predestination" and "providence" with the concept of being "on the road," however, will never understand any of these ideas. For Calvin, providence and election are not merely doctrines to teach, but realities to experience, and those who abstract these teachings out of life can only handle them in a way that further extinguishes life. In 1534, Calvin fled from Paris and found refuge with the du Tillet family in Angoulême. As a pilgrim he did not know what would happen next, but he did know that God would take care of him. Calvin described God's inimitable ways as he himself had experienced them. "When I thought things would settle down, all of a sudden I was confronted with all kinds of things I had not expected. When I thought I no longer had a place, unexpectedly a little nest was prepared for me. And all that by the hand of God who will himself take care of us if we commit ourselves to him." As an orphan, Calvin had already been somewhat lost in the world, and this only increased when he had to flee France. Only his faith in God's sovereign choice and in his almighty care brought him back to his feet, moved him along and kept him on the road. This would also be true later for members of his church in Geneva and Strasbourg, for Protestant galley-slaves, for persecuted Huguenots, and for the Pilgrims, but it was most significantly true first and foremost for Calvin himself. In short, Calvin's view of predestination and providence can only be understood if one keeps one eye on Calvin as he walks the road of his life and the other on the campaign Calvin ran with the motto "God for president" (*Ego me in uno Dei praesidio contineo*). God stands preeminent in every way—at the beginning, at the end and at every moment in between. Calvin would not have been able to take even a step if he did not know that his president was awake when humans were asleep, when they were losing their ways in the labyrinth or standing at the edge of the abyss. God is in control, and this is true in his choice for me as a believer, and in his care for me as a human being.

Calvin also still saw the guiding hand of God the Father behind all those father figures he encountered throughout his life—many of whom so often used threats to force him forward on the road he actually did not want to take. Often he did not understand God's intentions but saw in retrospect that it was good to trust his guiding hand. Calvin said he had experienced God's providence in his life and understood himself as keeping company among those biblical figures with whom he so closely identified. "Why," Calvin asked, "would that which was true for them and for me not be true for every other person?" Calvin had already described this experience in the first edition of the *Institutes*, that is to say, when he was a refugee in Basel without any idea as to where he would end up. In the 149 sermons Calvin preached from 1554 to 1555, he dealt with the same topic even more extensively, reflecting on the question of Job, which was in fact also the question of Calvin and of his compatriots: the question of God's incomprehensible ways. For Calvin nothing could be worse than to depart from God's way, even though he would so often and so readily have preferred to take another road. "I would most like to withdraw" is a thought expressed in varying forms in virtually every phase of his life. Calvin was, as it were, harnessed to God's cart with blinders on to prevent him from turning aside from the road to which God had led him. In that state one can only go forward, trusting in God's direction. Predestination means that one cannot lose faith, providence that one cannot lose the way.

ANGOULÊME

Until May 4, 1534, Calvin was still an official member of the Roman Catholic clergy, and so during his stay in Angoulême, he was called several times to preach in Latin for the chapter. The rest of the time he laid low, and in terms of church led what he would come to loathe as the life of a "Nicodemite," that is, a life resembling Nicodemus (Jn 3) who dared not come out openly for his faith. In January 1534, Calvin really began to immerse himself in the Bible and in patristics. He found the materials he needed in the library of the du Tillet family in the castle at Angoulême. "I am advancing very well in my studies," Calvin wrote to his friend François Daniel in 1534, "although I am actually doing a whole lot of nothing." Calvin did not want to make too many changes, however, since God could always do the opposite of what one might expect or plan. He had not at all expected to find himself a "quiet nest." The castle at Angoulême became Calvin's little nest and at the same time his fortress, his Wartburg. It was, perhaps, less grand than the castle of Eisenach where Luther had stayed, but for Calvin it was just as significant. Here he felt safe, in God's hand. Calvin's words sound pious, but they probably had as much to do with the contentment he experienced in the solitude of delving into his books in peace and quiet. This bookish contentment distinguishes both Calvin and those who followed after him. Reformed Christians removed all else from their churches in order to direct attention only to the Word, and they cleared all else from their shelves to make room for books. Calvin insisted that faith consists not only in experience but also in knowledge, and this has fortified the reading culture of Reformed Christianity in which one who does not study cannot be converted either. Calvin is almost always portrayed with a book in hand and several others around him. This was how he passed his time in Angoulême and also in Ferrara. He wrote books, he bought books, and in his letters he described his pain in times of having to sell books. Later, his academy in Geneva would have an impressive library, and this became a distinguishing mark of all Reformed institutions. It is thus no wonder that studies of primary schools in the seventeenth century have shown that Reformed children scored higher than their Lutheran or Roman Catholic contemporaries. When a Reformed child sits in church, there is nothing to do but listen or read because there is nothing to look at, and at home it is barely any different.

In order to promote listening, Calvin wrote six sermons reform-minded believers in the area could read aloud. On November 1, for example, preaching about the saints might be replaced by preaching about sanctification. On the feast of the Virgin Mary, preaching about her would give way to preaching about her Son. He also wrote a book, first of all for himself, which dealt with a question that had always interested him: what happens to the soul when the body dies? The book is called *Psychopannychia,* which literally means "the soul awake," though the book itself is actually about the sleep of the soul. In it Calvin opposes the idea that at death the soul enters a state of sleep, and he defends the position, later found in the Heidelberg Catechism, that the soul goes "immediately" to be with Christ and lives there awake. For Calvin, this was a better alternative to the doctrine of purgatory than the soul sleep taught by certain Anabaptists. He had wanted to publish the book in 1534 but allowed himself to be persuaded otherwise by yet another older man in the role of a father figure, as would become the pattern of his life. Wolfgang Capito, a colleague of Bucer at Strasbourg, advised Calvin against publication, fearing that it would arouse too much controversy among the Reformed in France. Thus Calvin did not publish the book, at least not then: it did find its way into the market in 1545.

PARIS

The city along the Seine was the actual starting point for Calvin's pilgrimage. Prior to his departure from Paris, Calvin's travels had, somewhat unusually for students of his time, been limited to France itself. In the sixteenth century, students often made a grand tour of Europe, exploring universities—and professors—particularly outside of their home countries so as to gain experience and international contacts and to see something of the world. When Calvin had to leave France, it was quite a change for him, not only because it was his first time going abroad but especially because he *had* to leave—a different matter altogether from a choice to go somewhere else for a while. Taking Abraham as his great example, Calvin left his home country without knowing where he would end up, resolute in the conviction that God had called him to this—a conviction that at the time he felt less than he would later have others and himself believe. This was the beginning of Calvin's life as pilgrim, and it developed into a theme that, as noted previously, would play a major role in his theology and spirituality. Calvin learned from experience the painful reality of that passage from the letter to the Hebrews where we are told we have no enduring city here on earth. The same experience, however, later allowed him to preach in a most meaningful way to people who had become pilgrims themselves, who had left their cities and countries for their faith, and who believed that God had called them on this journey, helped them on the way, and would continue to help them just as he had done with all those pilgrims in the Bible.

The pilgrim theme also stood behind Calvin's repeated call to leave France. He did not claim a specific divine revelation for it but maintained that those who wanted to worship God with body and soul in good conscience could not merely listen to the words, "Leave your country" (Gen 12:1). On the other hand, those who chose to continue living under the papacy were not to act as religious fanatics. According to Calvin, there was no need to ascend a pulpit or start a procession. One simply had to live in one's situation as a Christian: avoid popish idolatry, speak and act in faith, but do not knock relics from a Catholic's hand and throw them into the dirt. One should be an example, but if God cannot be worshiped openly, he must be worshiped within the heart instead. This is another side of Calvin. He knew of the critique of those who said "that you can only be a Christian if you have first been in Geneva and have had your ears filled with preaching there." For Calvin it did not matter where you were a Christian, as long as you were sure to be on the outside what you were on the inside.

It was just this, however, that Calvin thought no longer possible in his home country. To put it another way, one could no longer live for God in France because God simply no longer dwelled there. Once Calvin had identified the king of France as Pharaoh, believers could do nothing except organize an exodus. Calvin remained consistent in his view of France: in 1561, when he had been living outside of it for twenty-six years, he wrote that though it was a country with a pleasant climate that attracted many foreigners, he never regretted no longer living there, nor did he want to return. How could one live in a country from which God's truth, true religion and eternal salvation had departed? In Calvin's view, if eternal salvation had departed from France, continuing to live there meant running a constant risk of losing sight of the truth. His departure was necessary, Calvin claimed, because the truth of the gospel, true religion and pure worship of God had also left France. Where these three aspects of genuine faith could not be found, Calvin did not want to be found. The reverse was true as well: wherever he was, those three aspects of genuine faith had to be as well, or they at least had to be in the process of arriving. If this was not possible in France, then Calvin would journey elsewhere, wherever that might be.

With these words the pilgrim-Reformer was born. Calvin was the mother of the refugee churches and the father of the Pilgrims. God no longer dwelled in France, but later he did live in Emden, and in the liberated Netherlands where he resided with the house of Orange, and thereafter in America, in South Africa and in Tasmania. Erasmus had said that the world was a monastery, meaning that one should live in the world as if one were in a monastery. Calvin held a similar view but with a small twist. The world was not a monastery but the Promised Land—that is to say, the Promised Land can be found wherever the Word is preached. As such, the Promised Land is mobile, moving because God does not sit idle *(non otiosus)* but is constantly in action. God cannot do nothing and may even travel; in earlier days he used a pillar of cloud and now a moveable pulpit. Where the Word of God is preached, heard and practiced, there is the Promised Land. There, in fact, is heaven on earth.

Basel

The city of Basel had broken with Rome in 1529, and by the time Calvin arrived there with Louis du Tillet in 1535, it had become a center for people who were not inclined to consider Rome the only true church. For Calvin, Basel held a number of advantages, such as the presence of Nicolas Cop, a concentration of printers, and the fact that it was still close enough to France that he could follow developments there. He was also able to further his training in languages. He studied closely with Simon Grynaeus, an expert in Greek, and according to Beza he attended the Hebrew lectures of Sebastian Muenster. In Basel, Calvin developed contacts with many other Reformers, such as Heinrich Bullinger, Leo Jud and Pierre Viret, with whom Calvin would work throughout the rest of his life. Erasmus also established himself in this city in July 1535, but whether Calvin ever met him is not known. Just to be on the safe side, Calvin took on a pseudonym and became known as Martinus Lucianus, the surname being an anagram for "Calvinus."

Calvin wanted quiet, to live the life of a scholar, and at that time his attitude was more like that of Erasmus than that of Luther. He had problems with the church but wanted to avoid conflict and thought he could accomplish this simply by avoiding the things that disturbed him. This proved impossible, however, and so already in Basel the preaching and teaching that would become Calvin's lifelong tasks came together. In terms of the first, Calvin wrote a foreword to a French Bible translation produced by his relative—most likely, his cousin—Olivetan, as well as an introduction to the New Testament. The whole work was published in July of 1535 and was a notable event because at that time Rome still held that translations into the vernacular would only cause confusion. Calvin directly opposed this and wrote that God had placed his pupils in all ranks and positions, yet this did not necessarily mean all order in the church was turned on its head. Calvin assured spiritual and political leaders that lay access to the Bible posed no danger for the church or for society at large. Calvin would surely have done his best to make the language of this translation as elegant and readable as possible—by this contributing to, as well as criticizing, his cousin's work.

He later wrote in the foreword to the so-called Geneva Bible that Olivetan's translation was still a little awkward here and there and departed from currently conventional French. Calvin thus went over the text very carefully, not only because when it comes to God's Word not even the best is good enough but because aside from this theological motive, he simply wanted clarity as a humanist. And as a Frenchman, Calvin finally wanted to avoid anything that might make people think that French was a barbaric tongue.

Calvin's introduction to Olivetan's New Testament was special, serving as a systematic theology in miniature. In a couple of sentences he laid out the meaning of Christ and the necessity of faith. Of course, there is nothing remarkable in itself about Calvin producing what might resemble a small systematic theology: he had already done something similar in a little book he finished in 1535 and published in 1536.

A Little Book

This little book was the rather simple prototype of what by 1559 would grow into a balanced, mature edition of the *Institutes*. Just as with children, the book kept its name and main characteristics, but in growing up it gained experience, size and weight. Given that it matched his professional aspirations in no way, it is a little strange that Calvin succeeded in the market with this particular book. Such a publication would gain him no respect in the academic world. In fact, his explicit choice in favor of persecuted Reformed believers in France put him at risk of being left altogether outside of the circle of the academic elite. Even if there were scholars who had leanings toward Luther and his thought at that time, they were as yet unwilling to make them public and to put them in print. Perhaps the total failure of the commentary on Seneca had made Calvin reflect on and repent of his earlier ambitions. At any rate, in 1535, this new book was intended to provide an overview of biblical doctrine for the French Reformed believers who, in Calvin's own words, "hungered and thirsted after Christ," but knew little of the Scriptures. It was also Calvin's response to the persecutions in France; he thought it would be an unjustifiable betrayal on his part if he were to keep silent and not stand up to the attacks they were suffering. Re-

ferring to the *Institutes,* a preacher from Basel announced the appearance of
"a catechism from a certain Frenchman, addressed to the king of France."
As a religious textbook, it was like many others published at the time. Calvin's catechism had many similarities to that of Luther: both treated law,
faith and prayer as their most important themes, consisting of explanations
of the Ten Commandments, the Apostles' Creed and the Lord's Prayer.

Calvin became especially well known through this book. Between 1536
and 1559, he cut out, added and moved great amounts of text, and despite
several intermediate versions was really satisfied only with the final edition.
By the time of the 1559 edition, however, the work had grown tenfold in
size. The result was that, though highly praised, it was seldom read. For
centuries, Calvin's thought has been analyzed almost exclusively on the basis of the *Institutes,* as if it were the only book he wrote or as if the rest of his
writings have nothing significant to add. To some, this left Calvin appearing
overly dogmatic, and so scholars began to turn to his commentaries, letters
and other smaller works. Here they indeed encountered more aspects of the
man and his thought. This discovery was actually late in coming: ironically,
Calvin himself had already said that his commentaries "contain more than I
would be allowed to say without being immodest." All the same, the Calvin
unveiled by these newer studies was not all that different, and those who
already find the *Institutes* too dogmatic will find little they like in the rest of
his writings. His teaching on election and reprobation gain color and some
added context, but they remain the same. In the end, it is no wonder that
Calvin claimed the *Institutes* was his most important work.

SECOND GENERATION

The success of Calvin's book was also related to the late date of his birth. He
belonged to the second generation of Reformers, and therefore knew the
writings of the early Reformers—at least he knew those that had been written in or translated into Latin or French, since he did not know German. As
a result, Calvin could survey and use their treatments of a number of essential
theological themes and developments. One can think, for example, of the
battle between Luther and Zwingli over the Eucharist, the polemics between

Luther and Erasmus on free will, disputes with the Anabaptists on baptism, covenant, the value of the Old Testament and the relationship between church and state. Calvin was able to pluck the fruit of these discussions and thereby avoid many paths that had turned out to be dead ends. Another distinguishing feature of his work, made clear specifically by the *Institutes,* was the fact that Calvin had never received any formal theological training. To a degree, this freed him from the material and formal baggage imposed by the study of scholastic handbooks and carried by the average theologian. The freedom of his work was further developed by Calvin's humanism, which drove him to work from original sources with the aim of producing formulations that were as clear as possible. Among his sources one finds such Reformers as Luther, Bucer, Zwingli and Oecolampadius; the church fathers, especially Augustine; early church history, including the ecumenical councils; and the most important source, the Bible. If one compares different editions of the *Institutes,* the fruit of Calvin's exegetical work in the Holy Scriptures becomes more and more visible, and it can rightly be said that the *Institutes* grew from the expansion of Calvin's knowledge of the Scriptures.

The most remarkable part of the book, however, was not the actual content, but the one part that remained the same throughout the many editions. It was a letter, an open letter to "the almighty and most exalted monarch, Francis, the most-Christian king of France," in which Calvin tried to make perfectly clear that the Reformed were not revolutionaries, but rather harmless, and above all, fully biblical Christian subjects. Thus, argued Calvin, it was only reasonable that Reformed doctrine should be given a place in France, and in fact this would prove a great boon to the nation.

This letter reveals the characteristics of a student trained in law who was also a chaplain. Here the orator, lawyer, scholar and preacher all come together in a piece considered a masterpiece of French literature by friend and foe alike. How regrettable that the king did nothing with it.

NICODEMITES

With the *Institutes,* Calvin had made a clear choice, but the question remained whether everyone should do as he had done. In Basel, or later in

Geneva, it was not so difficult to speak and to act "Reformed," but what about in Reims or in Lyon where there was no Reformed church nearby? Calvin thought about this question many times. Can a Reformed believer still attend the Mass? What happens if one no longer participates? The importance of this question for someone living in the sixteenth century is difficult for someone living in the twenty-first to grasp. At that time, it was not only impressed from childhood that one had to attend Mass at least once a year, the eternal consequences of failing to do so were also clearly elaborated. Consequences for one's temporal existence were even more radical and also more immediate. When an internal choice for the Reformation became external as well, it meant a break with community, neighbors, family and even clients.

Nicodemus was a person who had earlier struggled with such questions. In the Scriptures he was noted among the disciples of Christ, but for fear of his colleagues he did not dare make that association public. Nothing negative is said about this in the Bible, and in fact it is noted there that Nicodemus, along with Joseph of Arimathea, who was in a similar situation (Jn 19:38-42), ensured Jesus' burial. Nevertheless, the name "Nicodemite" had negative connotations. Even Calvin thought that Nicodemus had been dealt an injustice, and pointed out that he had later come out openly for his beliefs. Calvin, however, still used the name "Nicodemites" for those who continued to attend the Mass but had already distanced themselves from it in their hearts. When his old friend Nicolas du Chemin confronted him on the issue, Calvin argued that one ought to leave the apostasies of Babylon as soon as possible. The Bible clearly taught that Christians ought not be ashamed of the gospel, and this was to be the guiding principle, not feelings of fear or shame. Calvin knew that his position would draw criticism, so he added that his view had not originated in quiet meditation, but came from those martyrs who had endured cross, fire and oppression. One might view this as Calvin's variety of radicalism or fanaticism, but it would better reflect the sixteenth-century situation to consider it simply as Calvin's consistency when it came to making definite choices—choices he himself also made, even when others did not do what he thought was right.

ROUSSEL

Within the circle of renewal-minded critics in Paris, Calvin became good friends with Gérard Roussel. When Calvin chose to break with Rome, however, Roussel did not, and Calvin thought they ought to part ways. When Roussel was offered a position as bishop, he was faced with an uncomfortable dilemma: from such a position he hoped to bring about reform in the church, but he also knew that he would have to do work that he could not support. Calvin thought he could help his friend by showing him the way out of the Catholic Church. According to Calvin, it was impossible to be a Christian and yet remain financially dependent on an institution in which ungodly practices and views were accepted. "Among the great variety of obligations that are part of your office, there is nevertheless always that one of holding a Mass for departed souls as satisfaction for their sins." Calvin saw this as a debasement of the complete and once-for-all work of Christ and could not understand how his friend could participate in demeaning Christ's work and glory. Roussel ought to stop immediately, and seek not even a penny as recompense.

Indeed, every Catholic penny was stained with blood, since the priests were paid for performing services that belittled the shedding of Christ's blood. Any excuses Roussel might proffer did not matter: for Calvin it was as simple as a choice between Christ and Satan. Calvin attacked his friend fiercely and made it amply clear to him that he had to make a definitive choice. "You are fooling yourself if you think that you belong to the people of God when you are in fact a soldier in the army of the anti-Christ." Calvin accused Roussel of wanting to become a bishop for the power it offered, the privileges, the honor. In short he accused his friend of seeking a bishopric for his own interests. Above all, Calvin believed that as a French bishop, Roussel would be waging war against his home country and against the Reformed believers but would be forgetting one thing: "You are dealing here with God!" If as a bishop Roussel allowed the laity to be involved in idolatry, he would be handing them, as well as the priests under him, over to destruction.

In all of this, Calvin's tone is that of a person who has become very sharp in his anxiety; the content of what he has to say is that of one who sees no in-between, no *via media*. For him these were matters of black and white, and when Roussel chose to remain Catholic, Calvin believed they could no longer remain friends. Calvin's criticism of the Mass could also be found throughout the late Middle Ages. On this point, Calvin contributed nothing new. What was new, however, were the consequences Calvin drew from this critique. As he saw it, Roussel was a traitor, a deserter, one who sold Christ and crucified him. A choice must be made for one or the other, said Calvin. Either one stayed with Pharaoh or one followed Moses. Calvin's kind of consistency has typified Calvinism as well, and also explains its drive. Reformed people give their all. When they do something, they do it well, and others who do not follow in certain choices are unfortunately kept at a distance and declared outsiders. This is a search for power in isolation, but it runs the risk of excluding those who actually do belong.

Roussel became a bishop, and he reaped the rewards, but also paid the price of his dilemma. He worked fruitfully and gave inspired direction to the church for many years, but in 1550 he was stabbed to death by a Catholic of noble birth during a sermon in which he criticized the many saints' days.

Detour

As his homeland, France, continued to draw Calvin throughout his life—he referred to his country as *nostra Gallia* in his commentary on *De clementia*—and until the end of his life he did all he could to promote the reformation of the church there. Before the first edition of the *Institutes* was on the market in 1536, Calvin was already on his way with du Tillet to Renée (Renata) de France, daughter of Louis XII, duchess of Ferrara and known sympathizer with the reform movement. By that time it had become necessary for Calvin to take on a false identity, and he traveled to a village near Noyon as Charles d'Espeville. The name was worthy of a visitor to the duchess, and it would also have matched Calvin's appearance. If one considers the well-known painting made by Hanau in that time, Calvin was dressed as a noble, appearing as a real lord with a gold ring on his finger—a raised finger, no less! Calvin and du Tillet could stay at the court for no more than several weeks:

when a certain anonymous man left the worship service at the adoration of the cross openly and with loud protests, immediate and rather unexpected measures were brought against all there who were reform-minded and who were not wise enough to make a hasty exit.

Although Calvin did not spend a long time in Ferrara, he was still able to make contact with several prominent figures who could help the reform in and of France. Calvin maintained contact with Renée throughout his life, and when she returned to France in 1560, her palace became a place of refuge for Protestants. Calvin greatly admired her and even wrote to her from his deathbed. After returning to Basel, du Tillet and Calvin parted ways. Du Tillet went to Geneva, but Calvin traveled to Paris to settle some matters the nature of which we do not know, but he soon left Paris again with his brother and sister in order to make his way to Basel or Strasbourg, both centers of humanism and reform close to the French border. Either of them would make an ideal base of operations. Calvin may not have had a Pauline conversion, but he did have Petrine experiences throughout his life, often being taken where he did not want to go. The road to Basel and Strasbourg was blocked by troop movements in Lorraine as war dragged on between Francis I and Charles V. The dangers this posed to travelers forced Calvin to take a detour to the south in order to continue on to his destination. A southern detour meant going through Geneva—a place Calvin did not want to be.

THE NEXT FATHER

Free from the upheavals in France and in search of peace in Strasbourg, Calvin was to discover again that God was not going to make his life easy. He had once so desired to become famous, and now he would pay for that conceit since it was no longer possible for him to spend even a single night in Geneva *inconnu*. Louis du Tillet, one will remember, had traveled to Geneva and was at that time still Calvin's friend, and he was so enthusiastic about the arrival of the famous Calvin that he immediately told Farel. Du Tillet should not have done this, since Guillaume Farel, born in Gap in the Dauphiné and one of the most powerful and fanatical pioneers of the Swiss Reformation, had a plan for Geneva in which he saw a perfect role for Calvin.

Prior to Calvin's arrival, Geneva had already liberated itself from the political rule of the Duke of Savoy and the spiritual rule of its bishop. A disputation had been held between representatives of Rome and the Reformation, and afterward, in May of 1536, it had been decided to live "according to the Gospel," a decision which in fact set a course for creating a Reformed city. The decision was made by both the citizens and the council, and this wide support assured the departure of the bishop. The Genevans, however, still needed a capable person to realize their desire, and it was thus seen as nothing less than a gift from heaven when a man like Calvin came like an orphan to the city. In Geneva, Calvin had an experience very similar to that of his French king: waking up one morning, the whole world suddenly looked different. He did not merely find a pamphlet on the door to his bedroom, but rather a person in the bedroom itself with a threatening message. Farel had discovered where Calvin was, sought him out in his room, and informed him that it was clear that God had brought him to Geneva and that he wanted to keep him there as well. This was exactly what Calvin did not want to hear, since he rightly foresaw—and in this he was indeed a prophet—that the peace he had found would come to an end if he stayed in Geneva. Nevertheless, when Farel added that Calvin would find no eternal peace if he did not stay, he made his choice promptly, knowing eternal peace to be of greater worth than temporal peace.

> I had always and everywhere kept quiet about the fact that I was the writer of the *Institutes,* and I intended to keep it that way, until I was held back in Geneva, not by deliberation or persuasion, but rather by a terrible imprecation from Guillaume Farel, as if God straight from heaven violently laid his hand on me.

Calvin the orphan thus found another earthly father in Geneva in the sense that there was once again an older man who chose his road for him. Calvin had had absolutely no intention of staying in Geneva. He had come there by accident and wanted to move on as quickly as possible. According to Farel, however, his arrival was not an accident, and he would be going against God's will and way if he did not stay. When Farel added the threat that Calvin's lot would be like that of Jonah if he left this Nineveh behind him, this new father figure essentially became the wrathful heavenly Father, so that Calvin could do nothing but stay where he was. There were no great fish to save him in Lake Geneva, and so for Calvin the reference to Jonah made it clear enough that should he refuse, God's judgment would be called down upon his already fragile life.

This decisive event was a microcosm of God's providence about which Calvin spoke and wrote so much. From experience he knew that things did not occur by chance, and he consistently confronted his readers and hearers with this, though he also knew from his own experience that it was not always easy, and at times even less than pleasant, to accept God's providential dealings with patience and good cheer.

The confrontation with Farel was the beginning of a long, trusting but also complicated relationship. The father-son dynamic became one of mutual collaboration, and then a relationship where Calvin took the dominant role, thereby gaining a position from which he could teach Farel a lesson or two when necessary. For twenty years their correspondence averaged at least one letter per month, in addition to any personal meetings. Calvin first managed to get Farel's permission to go and finish some business in Basel. Along the way, several congregations asked him to stay with them, and this fact makes clear not only that Calvin had become well known but also that he no longer had the option to pursue his own plans.

Any hope for peace in the academic climate of the Collège had thus failed. Until the day he died, Calvin would find no rest, even though he had always dreamed of living that ideal life of the scholar, burying himself in his studies far away from all the worries of daily life. Instead of finding rest, Calvin ended up in one upheaval after another. The insecurity of his life was perhaps best demonstrated when Farel went to the city council to request a small salary for Calvin. The secretary made a record of it but evidently could no longer remember Calvin's name, identifying him as "that Frenchman" *(ille gallus)*. He was a foreigner in Geneva and would remain as such until only four years before his death, when he received citizenship. Until that time Calvin was officially a refugee with only a temporary residence permit.

PROBLEM

Another problem worsened the instability of Calvin's situation—the turmoil in which Geneva found itself at the time. In order to follow Calvin's story as it unfolded, it is necessary to take a look at the political circumstances of the Swiss territories. At that time, Geneva was not yet one of them, being a so-called free city, and its people were intent on keeping that freedom. They also wanted to keep their city "pure," a desire that had moved them to ban the Jewish colony in 1490 and burn a first witch in 1495, to be followed by another twelve by 1531. The big cities of Basel, Bern and Zürich had already aligned themselves with the Reformation a year earlier. In those cities, one concrete result was government control of the church, leaving pastors to preach and otherwise concern themselves no further with ongoing affairs. In this way, a sort of state church was created in Bern in 1532. That city wanted to expand its influence, and to that end the industrious Farel was sent out as a sort of missionary who, in spite of a first defeat, still managed to gain a foothold in Geneva. In 1533 the Catholic bishop left after a revolution that was more political than religious, and in the next two years the Reformation gained more and more ground. Images were removed from the churches, the Mass was forbidden by the city council, and the city took over the right of minting coins from the bishop, marking its coins with the telling words *Post tenebras lux* ("Light after the darkness"). Previously, during its episcopal period, Geneva's motto had expressed the hope that people would see light after the darkness: *Post tenebras spero lucem* ("I hope for light after the darkness"). The new motto indicated that this wish had been fulfilled. The darkness was gone, and on May 21, 1536, the citizens voted in the new light, swearing their desire to live with God's help and according to his Word. This had sounded great when facing a common enemy, but when the time came to give concrete expression to exactly what it meant to live according to God's law, it became clear that there were many different opinions. Was God's law to concern only the ecclesiastical domain or also the civil? To what extent was this to be worked out? Some inhabitants saw the Reformation as a liberation, so that they could live according to their own wills, while others considered it an opportunity to require each and every citizen to finally conform to God's law. At any rate, they had all had enough of the clergy—who had themselves noticed this as well. Before 1536, the city of 10,000 inhabitants had some 400 members of the clergy, a number which soon decreased by 97.5 percent, when only ten preachers remained. In the background was also a sort of anticlericalism with which Calvin would soon be confronted as well. Many things changed in this city through the revolution of the reformation, including a change from Latin to French for official documents.

Consistory

A more significant change, however, was the arrival of a new institution: the consistory. It was Calvin who invented the Reformed consistory, an institution that would be exported throughout the world from Geneva. The consistory was meant to be an independent ecclesiastical institution, but Calvin failed to have this realized for several reasons. First and principal among these was the constant collision between Calvin and the so-called Children of Geneva—the old families of Geneva, particularly the Berthelliers and the Favres—led by Ami Perrin, commissioner of the republic. They were not content to have a foreigner prescribe their laws to them, not now that they were finally free of the bishop, and especially not when they became aware that Calvin wanted to make changes to their lifestyle. There was also the influence of Bern, the city whose protection was needed by Geneva to keep the bishop and Savoy at a distance, the city that had helped Geneva to realize its reformation, but also the city that sought to bring Geneva under its control. All of this put restraints on Calvin and his consistory.

The *consistoire* met every Thursday for three or four hours, and the sinners—people who had done something against the Genevan norms of a biblical life—were made to appear before it at this time. The council

had the right to keep a sinner from the Lord's Supper one time, which was
to be a sign that this person had become distanced from God and thus also
from the church. In that society, this had considerable consequences, especially if it became clear that temporary or even permanent excommunication could follow. The latter meant exclusion from the Christian community, that is, from the city itself. For Bern, all of this was simply too
much. Not only were the Bernese not so keen on the whole concept of
excommunication, they also felt that ecclesiastical functionaries ought not
to have so much power.

The situation was thus rather simple: those who wanted freedom were in
favor of keeping good relations with Bern, while those who wanted to adhere
strictly to the Bible cared little for what Bern had to say. The Children of Geneva were among the former; the children of Calvin among the latter.

ORGANIZATION

In order to follow Calvin's story, it is also necessary to understand the structure of the Genevan government after the departure of the bishop. In essence, Geneva had become an independent city with an autonomous government that comprised several levels. The lowest level was the General
Council, in which all citizens and bourgeois had a place. "Citizens" were all
those born in Geneva, while the "bourgeois" were not subject to this re-
quirement but instead had to be at least twenty years old, possess land or a
building, or have an honorable vocation. One could only become a part of
this circle upon payment of a considerable sum or by showing oneself of
service to the city in a special way. The General Council met every February to vote for a number of other councils and commissions. Only on very
special occasions was an extra meeting held, such as the one for the vote in
favor of the Reformation in 1536. Above this General Council was the
Council of Two Hundred, and above that the Council of Sixty. The Council
of Two Hundred concerned itself with, among other things, appeals against
the highest institution of the city, the Small Council, composed of twenty-
five members who formed the daily government of the city. The Small
Council included four chairmen known as "syndics," who were elected

every year from the Small Council and acted as mayors. The Council of Sixty busied itself particularly with affairs involving other cities or territories. All of these councils were elected yearly, usually in reelections of the incumbent members. Two other institutions fell under the responsibility of the Small Council: the General Hospital—later designated by Calvin as the deaconry—and the Consistory. Although Calvin had intended it as a church council, it became in fact a semigovernmental institution, chaired by one of the syndics. In the consistory room, there were two benches. One of these was for the preachers of the city and of the several towns under city control. At the head of this bench Calvin sat as the *primus inter pares,* that is, as the chairman of the company of pastors. The other bench was filled with so-called elders, who were nevertheless appointed by the city council and were thus in fact civil servants. They too were elected yearly, and here also the majority held office simply through repeated reelection. As a rule, there would be twelve elders, two from the Small Council, four from the Council of Sixty and six from the Council of Two Hundred. If at all possible, they came from different parts of the city. The Consistory had two assistants appointed to it, one of whom was a secretary, who made detailed reports of every meeting. Although small in size in the beginning, the consistory eventually grew to a body of some twenty to twenty-five people, depending on the number of pastors.

BATTLE

Lying on his deathbed, Calvin reflected on the situation he had found in Geneva when he first arrived: "When I first came to this church, it was as good as nothing. They preached, and that was about all. They did indeed go out looking for images and burning them, but in no way was there a reformation. Everything was in a state of confusion." There was no way Calvin could put up with confusion. God had proceeded in an orderly manner with creation— everything had happened properly, and only through the fall into sin was it all thrown into disarray. Chaos and sin thus go together, as do order and Christian living. For others, however, Christianity meant freedom, so they had no problem with the fact that there was preaching and nothing further. Trouble was thus waiting in the wings, and things did indeed go wrong.

But there was also something else. The city had a problem of internal division that was more political than ecclesiastical. There were two groups, the *Guillermins* and the *Articulants*. The first group was named after Guillaume Farel, the second after the articles of the alliance, which repeatedly referred to the bonds between Geneva and Bern. It was Bern that had freed Geneva from the episcopal yoke, and as often happens with liberators, Bern thought it had the right to decide how things were to be done in Geneva. The pressure exercised by Bern was unwanted by some, but for others it was exactly the kind of help the city needed against the threatening powers of France in King Francis I's war with Charles V. Opinions were divided within the city. What were they to do? Were they to remain independent, or were they to fortify themselves by siding with Bern? Geographically speaking, Geneva was important for all parties, and this fact increased the pressure all the more. Geneva, as a Protestant city, was like the tip of a spear that prodded the side of Catholic southern Europe. Geneva was desired by all. In addition, the influx of refugees who slowly but steadily came into the city grew Geneva to 12,000 inhabitants in the 1540s, and 20,000 in the 1560s. This meant ethnic problems, as well as pressure on the housing, job and food markets. In short, Geneva was going through an exciting, but tense, time. When Calvin wrote several years later that the city suffered internal discord, he hit the nail on the head. This had already been a problem before the Reformation, when one group gladly recognized the authority of the bishop, while others wanted to be rid of it. Even then Geneva had had factions that fought and chased each other from the city. It was in the middle of these disputes that Calvin had arrived—and as a Frenchman no less. Within Geneva's own city walls, as well as between Geneva and Bern, there were more than enough things that had to be discussed, and as we will see, they would not be left alone for all that long.

STRANGER

(1536-1538)

ANOTHER MAN

For Calvin it was not fate but God who decided the course of his life. The man who had taken a detour and intended to pass through to Basel or Strasbourg was once again transformed, and another man went to work in Geneva, one who sought nothing but the justice of his heavenly Father, and who in seeking it would not be shamed by anyone or anything and would not be moved by anyone or anything, either. Calvin did not care if he were made a laughingstock, as long as God and the angels approved. In and behind this drive was the fear of the Lord, which had entered his heart at his conversion and would remain there until his death. His personality also offered all that was needed to persist: stubbornness, a readiness for self-sacrifice and a refusal to compromise. Furthermore, his teaching had all that was needed to succeed: a biblical foundation, simplicity and a clarity that made it accessible to all. He was consistent as well. What he wrote in a letter to the duke of Somerset in 1548 had in fact already been his teaching in 1536 and would continue to be his teaching until 1564:

Namely, that we see God as the only lord of our soul, and his Law as the only rule and spiritual instruction for our conscience, so that we do not serve him according to all kinds of foolish human regulations. Further that he wants to be served by us in spirit and with a clean heart. On the other hand, we admit that in us there is nothing but unrighteousness, that we are corrupt in all we think and do, so that our heart is an abyss of evil. We therefore doubt ourselves, deny any claim to our own wisdom, worthiness or aptitude for the good, turn to the fountain of all good which is Jesus Christ, and receive what he gives us, the reward of his suffering and death, so that we may be reconciled to God through it. Washed clean in his blood, we are now no longer afraid that our sins will prevent us from finding grace at his heavenly throne. Assured that our sins have been freely forgiven on the basis of his sacrifice, we find our rest and assurance of salvation. We are sanctified through his Spirit to devote ourselves to obeying the justice of God. Strengthened by his grace, we will be victorious over the devil, the world and the flesh. Finally, as members of his body, we do not doubt that God counts us among his children, and that we may with full confidence address him as our Father. It is clear to us that all that is said and done in the church goes back to the main point, that we, withdrawn from the world, are raised up to heaven with our Head and Savior.

To be sure, Calvin filled thousands of pages working this out more expansively, but it all comes down to nothing more than this one paragraph. Supporting his endeavor was an optimism that bordered on idealism.

Calvin was rather optimistic when it came to the church and the world and thought that quite a lot could be done. This is a remarkable characteristic that is rarely found among Calvinists in Europe anymore, but on the other side of the Atlantic it still remains. Calvin had this optimism at a time during which he himself noted that "all of Christianity is on the point of falling in ruins," and that Europe was a disaster (*afflicta est Europa*). Calvin, nevertheless, was too driven to be able to simply sit and wait for its complete destruction or for the return of Christ, and thinking that a good dose of *ora et labora* would rebuild the church and restore Europe, he went hard to work.

ANOTHER GOD

If it was nothing less than another man who went to work in Geneva, he brought with him nothing less than another theology—one might even say another God. Rome had frightened the people with "long sermons about the fear of God" without showing the way to grace. It kept "those wretched souls and their doubts trapped" and made them "flee from him and terribly afraid before his face." This was Calvin's view, typically brief and direct, of the image of God produced by the papacy. Calvin's God, however, was different. He was a wholly other God. Where Rome worked people into fear, Calvin wanted to put them at ease, though throughout the following centuries many have wondered how successful he actually was. There have been, after all, many in the Reformed tradition who have become spiritual victims of a God portrayed in sermons that were—as Calvin would have put it— more Catholic than biblical. We leave the matter with this remark, however, to return to Calvin himself.

With its view of God, argued Calvin, Rome undermined sin and gave the impression that you could once a year, such as at Easter, drop off all your sins at church as if you were leaving a neat little package at the post office. In reality, however, there was an "abyss of sins" whose depth could not be fathomed, and thus could not be numbered or confessed, either. With Rome, sins were finite in the sense that they could be counted. With Calvin, however, sin could not be fathomed, counted or measured, and was thus infinite. God's grace, however, was equally as infinite, so that the latter perfectly covered the former.

That Calvin continually spoke of God as Father did not mean he did not believe that God could punish in his wrath, and there were times Calvin drew awfully direct lines between sin and punishment. When imperial troops made life difficult for Protestants, Calvin wrote to Brenz that nothing could be done but to humbly beg God for mercy, "because he gives the godless free rein since we have offended God with our sins." Our calamities should not call up outrage in us, but should rather lead us to humble ourselves. One does not benefit from hardships suffered if they are not explicitly connected to one's own sins on the one hand and to God's punishing hand on the other. Calvin notes, however, that there is "barely one person in a hundred who pays attention to the hand that strikes," since people prefer to think about "why" they are suffering rather than seeking the blame and cause in themselves. Calvin constantly tried to turn people to God rather than encourage them to turn in upon themselves. His view of sin and punishment came down to this: those who look for God as Judge will find him as Father.

CLEAN-UP

That Calvin came with another God should not be surprising. He was, after all, fond of change, and by the end of his life so many things had changed that on his deathbed he advised that things should finally be left as they were. Before then, however, he was different, and labored to bring about a big clean-up: personally, ecclesiastically and socially. Calvin had little use for touch-up jobs, did only minimal renovation work, but extensive demolition and rebuilding. He made use of some of the older materials and styles, but the result was still something new. In the process, he tore down the entire humanist ivory tower. The ideal world into which he had once so badly wanted to retreat would have to be realized among the common people instead. God could not be given his due only in some part of human experience; even personal and social life must aim at the honor of God.

The clean-up process had to begin in any case with faith, but Calvin was dissatisfied with the way faith had been discussed. The most important theologians of the Middle Ages had argued that no one could be sure of eternal salvation if God had not given some special revelation. Anyone who had not had an experience like Paul's on the road to Damascus could do little more than hope that things would turn out for the best, while living what had been determined to be a Christian lifestyle. There was no more hope than this, and most believers would still need to spend an indeterminate time in purgatory anyway. With Calvin, however, there was no such thing as "hope" when it came to eternal life. It was a matter of certainty. And what is more, there was no need for purgatory to exist.

Faith might doubt, but it need and ought not. One may experience trials, and from time to time be very afraid in God's presence, but these things happen within the safety offered by the gates of assurance and are guaranteed by predestination. Calvin knew God as a judge and avenger of sin and evil, but faith turns to God's mercy, and because God is merciful, there is no reason for us to doubt.

As it happens, this does not produce smug, self-assured people, but humble believers who are painfully aware of their sin and guilt. Faith means placing one's confidence in God on the basis of one's knowledge of him. It is not merely intellectual or rational knowledge, but, once again using the image of a father, it is the knowledge a father has of his child, and a child has of his father.

ANOTHER CHURCH

Another man, another God and so another church also. Calvin set up a church in which a Christocracy, as it were, was joined with a democracy. There could only be *one* master, and that was Christ, so clearly present in the church through his Spirit that he needed no representation in the form of a pope. People were used by Christ, especially pastors, elders and deacons. Pastors, however, were to say nothing but what they heard from God. Elders stood at the gates of the kingdom of heaven only to open and close them. Deacons were nothing but financial couriers. They came from God, but from among the people, all of whom had an equal right to speak. With these democratic principles, Calvin also unleashed a fury of quarrels and schisms, but these cannot really be charged to his account. If everyone has the right to speak, if everyone can read the Bible, and if the Bible belongs to no one and everyone at the same time, there will always be the danger that quarrels will break out over who is right.

All the same, Calvin constantly sought a balance between being bound and being free, especially when it came to the church and matters of church order. "We know that each church is free to set up its own church order as it sees fitting and useful, because the Lord has not given us any specific directions in this regard." The strength of Calvin and Calvinism's view of the church was that each member had the same rights and duties. Each member, whether male or female, had a calling and a task, and was to be ready and responsible for service. Women were therefore included, although on the basis of Scripture Calvin saw no ground for admitting them to the offices of pastor or elder. According to him, the divine and natural orders required that a woman should teach her family at home privately but should not teach publicly in the church. Calvin's struggles with the texts that pertain to the place of women in the church are remarkable, since he wrestled with them more than many of his predecessors and contemporaries did.

At any rate a new kind of church was set up, a church with a simpler structure than that of Rome, but with more offices than that of Luther. It was in this church that Calvin was for the time the *primus inter pares*.

PASTOR

Calvin became the pastor of the beautiful St. Pierre cathedral in the old city, where not long before a bishop had been seated. It has been remarked that this was really no progress at all, since one bishop was simply replaced by another. Of course, Calvin was not officially a bishop, but he was the master, if not the dictator, of Geneva, wasn't he? One might easily draw the conclusion that Calvin was the tyrant of Geneva, but only if one pays no attention to dates. The city, for instance, had already decided to purify itself and adopt imperial law—including the death-penalty for heretics—as its norm when Calvin was still many miles away, and in fact still a student. The old image of Calvin the tyrant is not at all in line with the facts. He was indeed later portrayed together with some of his Reformer colleagues in massive, unmoving statues making up part of a wall on which the entire city appears to rest, but in reality he never had much say in Geneva—except possibly toward the end of his life. In Geneva, as throughout the rest of Europe, many politicians did not waste the opportunity to rejoice in the Reformation and the pious motive it offered them to take power over the church. The affairs of this city of 10,000 inhabitants were governed by the Small Council, consisting of twenty-five citizens, who chose four mayors each January. This council took care of the city's daily affairs, meeting three times per week. Twice per year all the citizens were assembled for the opportunity to express their opinions on important matters. The pastors had no business there. They could open their mouths to preach, but only at church, and in other matters they did well to keep quiet. This, however, was something Calvin never was good at.

PROFESSOR

Before becoming the pastor, however, this Frenchman had been appointed "lecturer in Holy Scripture," or as he referred to himself in a letter, "professor in Holy Scripture at Geneva." Toward the end of August 1536, before his official appointment, he began lecturing on the exegesis of the Pauline epistles. These lectures were apparently a success, because Oporinus, a printer and publisher at Basel, asked Calvin if he could publish them. In October, however, just when Calvin was settling into his work, he was sent to take part in a dispute at Lausanne organized by the local preacher Pierre Viret. The goal of this debate was to impress on the Catholics the unbiblical nature of what they were doing. Obedient to authority as always, Calvin went, but at first he stayed out of the discussion. This may have been on account of modesty or even unease, but he may also have thought: the more I keep out of it, the sooner we will be home. When someone falsely cited a church father, however, Calvin could no longer keep quiet and astonished those present with numerous patristic quotations from memory. Later that month Calvin also had to go to a synod in Bern for a discussion on the so-called Wittenberg Concord, a joint statement on the Lord's Supper by Luther, Bucer and others, with the hope that the Swiss would also go along with it. Nothing came of the Swiss participation in this synod, however. Later, on December 1, 1536, Calvin was invited by the Strasbourg Reformers Bucer and Capito to discuss the state of the church in Basel, Bern and Geneva. After that crazy month, Calvin would have realized that his life's work would concern the church more than the academy, and he would become more Reformed and less humanistic. He could find no rest, and it was as if he had embarked on the wrong boat, but out of obedience to and fear of the Captain he did not dare to jump overboard, deciding instead to take this journey to its unknown destination.

CALL

Calvin had never really wanted to become a pastor, and this had never been one of his reasons for coming to Geneva. But what did his will have to do with it? Here too things turned out differently from the way Calvin had envisioned them, and a year after his appointment as professor he was chosen as pastor. Now he was an official pastor, though he had no degree in theology from an academic institution and had not submitted to an ecclesiastical examination, both of which were elements he considered extremely important and that his followers would soon neatly regulate in all respects. Calvin's situation, however, posed no problem given that the Reformation was seen by its followers as nothing but a continuation of the existing church. Already existing church offices, including the office of chaplain, remained valid. Thus, even though Calvin had formerly renounced the income of his chaplaincy, he was nevertheless in the eyes of others an experienced and viable holder of church office. For Calvin, however, the most important aspect informing the holding of church office was a divine calling. How ought his own to be understood? In different respects, Calvin compared himself to David. Weren't they both poet, refugee and shepherd at the same time? He saw many similarities in the routes their lives had taken, even if something like the Bathsheba incident was in Calvin's case completely unthinkable— though he will have laid his eyes on more than just nice books. Calvin extended his comparison with David to calling as well, since he too was called to a higher office unexpectedly *(subita!)*. The Geneva archives clearly show he was no king, but Calvin was a prophet, and always kept the air of an Old Testament prophet about him. He would, in fact, hold their examples before his eyes throughout his life to help him—as he claimed—do battle against the dishonest priests and false prophets of his own time.

The matter of a divine calling was so fundamental for Calvin that one who really wanted to hurt him did best to attack him on this point. Louis du Tillet, a friend of Calvin who became estranged when he returned to Rome, apparently knew this as well. "I wonder whether you have actually been called by God, for you have only been called by men." He repeated the same in December: "I can only conclude that you have not received a call to the ecclesiastical office from God." Should this be true, Calvin would be completely in the wrong and there would no longer be any basis for his work. Calvin himself, though, had no doubts about his calling, and this helped him act with confidence and without fear, and to speak words of admonition as well as comfort. Calvin thought that he had both the right and the duty to speak freely as a prophet, and this was accorded to him. In this context, Calvin's words to Bullinger about his relationship with Luther are of great significance. He claimed not to flatter Luther, as many others did, often out of fear. Calvin added that he did not fear Luther but had maintained his freedom from him. For him the presence of freedom was more important than the absence of fear. It was this freedom that gave Calvin the room to let his heavenly Father take over from his earthly one, for in the end theology had been victorious over law, although both disciplines were concerned with the power of the word.

THE WORD

Calvin certainly had a gift with words, and it was evident not only in his biting sarcasm but also in his pastoral speaking and writing. He had the gift of explaining difficult theological concepts very simply, but he could also participate in abstract theological disputes on simple biblical themes that had been made complex. He could speak to common people but also with those of high standing. He was a sort of verbal decathlete modeled after the Old Testament prophet. His confidence can be explained from his sense of calling, his way of acting from his consciousness of himself as one of the prophets, or as the Bible calls them, in Calvin's words,

> watchmen . . . who always have to be on guard to be able to warn against evil and take a stand against it. Whenever they see that God is insulted, they are to become trumpets that wake those who sleep. Look, that is also why the Holy Scriptures give that name to the prophets whose task it is to watch over others, just as today to the ministers of the Word who as watchmen must keep a close watch on what is happening in order to rise up into action against evil, and to announce to those who stay fast asleep in their sins that they really cannot continue to mock God in this way.

Calvin saw his task as that of a watchman on the walls of Zion, and his actions can really only be understood in this way. He had a mission that he did not for a minute doubt. In a letter to Renée de Ferrara, he wrote that the Lord had revealed to him in the Scriptures that God had called him to office and had also given him the program that went along with that office. This was how Calvin could work as he did. As professor, pastor and bishop he constantly buried himself in the Bible in a most remarkable way. He read the Bible as his own biography—not an autobiography, for then it would no longer be God's Word. It was not he, nor any other human being, who had written it. According to Calvin, God used men who served as secretaries or amanuenses to write down his messages. These writers did leave their marks in the nature and style of what they wrote, but the contents of the messages were entirely from God, and as a result the Word is both trust-worthy and sure. Calvin clung to the Bible closely, not only because he so often encountered himself in it but also because he saw it as the one tangible but unmovable thing on earth. If for Rome the point of contact between heaven and earth was the altar, for Calvin it was the Bible—but both were in the church. Calvin held tightly to the fact that God has recorded his Words in the Scriptures. As humans, we tend to forget about God, to drift further and further away in each and every direction, to try to come up with one new religion after another, and for all these reasons the divine teaching simply had to be recorded. God ensured that this was done, from which we have the Scriptures.

EGYPT

The divine teaching of the Scriptures also makes clear that a Christian can-not participate in the Mass. Once he had parted ways with Rome, Calvin developed a strong aversion to the Mass, images and Nicodemites, all of which can be explained from his convictions.

> If someone were to ask what the essence of our faith really is, and what the truth consists in, you would end up at the following two points which not only occupy the most important place, but also envelop all other points and so form the entire substance of the Christian religion: knowledge of how

God can properly be worshiped, and secondly, knowledge of where salvation should be sought. If these two are cast aside, we can still boast of being a Christian in name, but our confession will be idle and in vain.

This conviction fits in no way with what happens in the Mass or with what an image represents. Calvin noted, however, that it was very difficult to impress upon people who are used to these images that they are on the wrong track.

> Just as one who cleans toilets makes fun of the people who pinch their noses when he happens to be near them, because he has himself been in that filth so long that he does not notice that awful stench anymore; so those who worship images and have by this habit become so hardened to that filth think that they are among the roses, and make fun of those who are bothered by the stench they themselves no longer notice.

Having been a refugee, Calvin's life was certainly no bed of roses, but his fellow believers in France suffered much greater hardships and were now confronted with the question of how to be Reformed in completely Catholic surroundings. Calvin gave his answer in the so-called Two Letters *(Epistolae duae)* of 1537, which twenty years later he would still call "extraordinary writings." The term *Two Letters* has a threatening ring to it, and this was indeed the case. In them Calvin dismissed the reform movement within Catholicism once and for all, as Luther had dismissed Erasmus. As far as Calvin was concerned, it was high time for some clarity in the situation, and he summed it up in one word: Egypt. Calvin referred to France as Egypt, and this could only mean one thing: flee, flee first of all from the Mass! For Calvin it was absolutely unthinkable that someone who sought reform would still participate in the Mass. Wasn't this the absolute pinnacle of idolatry? Didn't it encompass all that was wrong? Wasn't Christ's one sacrifice robbed of its merit when it was said not to be good enough, and needed to be repeated every single day? Think also of the idolatry with that little piece of bread! "For the God that the priest waves in the air when he makes all kinds of busy movements around the altar was not produced from heaven, but is rather produced of the same thing as the bread that one takes out of an oven." Clearly no one should take part in such sacrilege. This was to remain Calvin's view throughout the rest of his life, and when the religious discussions between Rome and the Reformation broke down in the 1540s, Calvin reiterated his view in a *Short Treatise Setting Forth What the Faithful Man Must Do When He Is Among Papists and He Knows the Truth of the Gospel*. There was nothing to do but to flee, just as Abraham did when God gave him that short but clear message, "Leave your country." This part of the Abraham narrative appears repeatedly in Calvin's writings, as does 1 Kings 18:21, where the Israelites were told they were wavering between two opinions if they did not come out clearly either for God or for Baal. It was as simple as that. A radical choice had to be made. For Calvin, a faithful believer could no longer stay in France. One ought to flee not out of fear for sword or fire, but so as to be able to serve God elsewhere with a clear conscience. The real problem faced by Reformed Christians in France was not that they might suffer and die for the faith, but that they might bring down the guilt of idolatry upon themselves. To avoid this, one simply had to flee.

CRITICISM

There was considerable criticism of this view, but Calvin brushed it off in his booklet *The Excuse of John Calvin Against the Complaints of Messieurs the Nicodemites of His Too Great Severity*. This work really offered no excuse, since Calvin wrote that his view had nothing to do with severity, but everything to do with the Bible. He would repeat the same to others, such as the unknown Frenchman who apparently approached him with a similar question in 1548. For Calvin, the Lord's Supper as instituted by Christ had about as much in common with the papal Mass as fire did with water. The Mass was an invention of Satan to destroy the real Lord's Supper. Not only was it idolatrous, it also reversed God's gift to the congregation and turned it into an offering from the congregation to God, and this was diabolic in the sense that it threw everything on its head. A return to Rome was absolutely unthinkable, and would in fact be "a crime that is incompatible with the Christian faith."

BISHOP

The other issue treated in the Two Letters was whether one could still occupy a position as bishop in a church with which you had already parted internally. This too was an existential question, particularly for the addressee of the second letter, Gérard Roussel, a member of the reform-minded party who was appointed bishop on February 2, 1536. At first there appears to be no problem whatsoever, as Calvin elaborately lays out the biblical foundations for the office of bishop, and from there proceeds to stress the scope, importance and essence of this office. With respect to its essence, Calvin notes that it is to be a shepherd to the priests and, through them, to the believers. Gérard, says Calvin, desires the power, privileges and honor of this office. But what about the task itself? Calvin emphasizes to Roussel that he is here dealing with God himself, so that if his priests are allowed to engage in idolatry at the Mass, Roussel is handing them over to destruction. Calvin slowly brings his argument to a climax, and then turns it into a confrontation. Roussel is a deserter and worse, since as bishop he would wage war against his home country and support idolatry as well. "And then I am not saying much when I call you a murderer and traitor of those who are your own." Roussel is selling Christ and crucifying him! According to Calvin, it is self-interest, pure laziness and fear that prevents the bishops from acting out against superstition. Roussel has to choose either to do something about it, or else to lay down his office. Things are as clear as they had been in Egypt: one either stayed with Pharaoh, or one followed Moses. For Calvin there is no such thing as middle ground, and if there were, it would be the Red Sea in which one would no doubt drown. The only question remaining is whether Roussel is still a brother, and with that question Calvin's break from Rome became a fact that has now lasted for centuries:

> For as long as you suck the blood from the poor by robbing and plundering
> them, and then pour it out and spill it; as long as you lay claim to a post as
> shepherd, and therein bring the sheep down in most vile treachery; as long
> as you are found among that herd of people whom Christ calls robbers and

bloodthirsty plunderers of his church; so long you can think of yourself as you wish, but for me you will be neither a good man, nor a Christian. Greetings.

Things between Calvin and Rome would never heal.

PROMISED LAND

If France was Egypt, Geneva must be the Promised Land. At least, that was how Calvin spoke and preached about the city, even though he was well aware that the Promised Land on Lake Léman came close to the new Jerusalem in no way. He actually opposed those who compared Geneva to Jerusalem. Geneva was still a long way from that, and it was even questionable whether it would ever come close. If one can believe Calvin, people in Geneva had done what Israel had done long ago. God gave deliverance, but they spoiled this gift. It was precisely against this that Calvin had to spring into action, just as the Old Testament prophets had done. This was how Calvin saw himself and his office as pastor, and from that conviction he both preached and exercised his office. Whether during the trying years in Geneva, or later when politics had shifted to his side, Calvin continued to preach both comfort and admonition.

To be clear, we should emphasize that it was not as if Calvin only went after the papists hammer and tongs; his sermons focused especially on his own people. Do we really understand God's mercy and our privilege, he once asked in a sermon, when we see how God has showered us with his gospel, while he has passed over so many other, much greater and richer cities? In Geneva, just as in Israel of old, men and women might be tempted to think that election meant rest and relaxation, but it was really about responsibility. Election was not a goal but a means to an end, a means to honoring God, and this is, and has always been, the problem: people do not want to submit to the yoke of Christ.

Just as God again and again took pity on Israel, Calvin thought he did on Geneva as well. He did this in 1536, but again in 1555 when things finally took a turn for the worse for Calvin's enemies. "Was the city not headed for ruin and destruction? But God stretched out his hand such that an unbeliev-able change can be seen. He planted the gospel here, founded his royal seat, chose for himself a dwelling-place and sanctuary." For Calvin it was clear that God really did care for Geneva.

LAW

According to the biblical narrative, God repeated the contents of the law when Israel arrived in the Promised Land, and this law prescribed that the people must love God before all else and love their neighbors as themselves. For Calvin, law simply returned after the gospel, but now as a guide for Christian living. The law was "an eternal rule for a pious and holy life." It was a permanent rule as found in a cloister, and so Calvin wrote the *regula* for an "Order of the Reformed." *Permanent* meant that the law was there to stay. And why not? Christ had not come with a new law, but brought the old law into our very hearts. This connection between law and gospel, justifica-tion and sanctification, brought about that terribly complex yet ever so ex-citing tension between freedom from, and bondage to, the law. God has freed us from slavery, but to avoid falling back into it we must almost slav-ishly bind ourselves to his law. Among the Calvinists this tension is perhaps most clearly evident on Sundays. One is free of one's daily work, but re-quired not to do it. One does not have to go to church, but one has the privi-lege. Great trouble awaits if one does not go, and rich feeling when one does! This is the feel of Calvinist freedom and bondage.

At any rate, all of this meant that Calvin had a hard time with anything and anyone that took God's law less seriously than he thought was biblically warranted. All such people, whatever the differences between them, he simply called *Libertines*. As far as he was concerned, they were right up there with the lawless, even if they sometimes lived very decent lives and only took the Bible less normatively than the Catholics and the Reformed did. Calvin encountered many such people inside and outside of Geneva, includ-ing in the Netherlands, where a certain Dieryck Volckertsz Coornhert pro-moted Libertine doctrine in his writings. Coornhert argued that there was no need to put one's life at risk for the sake of a few church ceremonies and that Jesus really did not ask his followers to become martyrs. His argument in favor of the Nicodemites was further accompanied by problems he had accepting the doctrine of original sin. For Calvin, this was enough to prompt him to write his *Response to a Certain Dutchman*. Libertinism had no boundaries and had to be opposed.

ANABAPTISTS

There was also that rather varied group known as the "Anabaptists." This group was behind the 1533 attempt to establish the new Jerusalem in Münster, whose few bright rays soon turned blood red, whose goal had been heaven but whose efforts ended in a hell. Despite this, many Anabaptists wanted nothing to do with violence and polygamy and were simply opposed to infant baptism, oath-taking and any form of war. Calvin did not differ from his fellow Reformers in his *stance* toward them, but he did in his *approach,* for he thought that these Anabaptists had a point when they stressed sanctification of life, imitation, dedication and devotion. They clearly saw the danger of infant baptism, which could be accompanied by the idea that, once baptized, one had made it. They understood that the Spirit not only brought people into communion with Christ but also changed them after his image. There was definitely something to be learned from them, and Calvin was more than ready to do so. He understood why they were bothered by the Reformed. "They are right to take offense, and we give opportunity for it and cannot excuse our damned slowness, which the Lord will not leave unpunished." Calvin's appeal for church discipline also matched well with the Anabaptist insistence on a Christian walk of life and on baptism as a beginning, not an end. He was very engaged with the Anabaptists, and even married an Anabaptist widow, providing a symbol of the way he dealt with them theologically. One had to win them over and bring them into one's own house. In terms of the church, one might even marry them by taking into one's own theological house the good that they bring with them. Calvin managed this masterfully. If today it can be said that Reformed Christians can learn from their evangelical brothers and sisters, Calvin made the same claim five hundred years earlier, though he would have insisted that the good that can be found in the evangelical camp should simply be reflected in Reformed life and thought. If one were to combine Martin Luther with Menno Simons, one would get John Calvin—a theologian of the Holy Spirit with a great knowledge of the Scriptures and great oratorical skills—the perfect combination to pull many Anabaptists back in.

The Anabaptists, however, went too far. They demanded the impossible, but if even God does not do this, why should we? "They in their turn sin in that they go too far. For where the Lord demands meekness, they drop it altogether and give themselves over completely to an immoderate severity." Their perfectionism in regard to the Christian life and the church was unbiblical. Calvin tried to persuade them that Luther's view of the redeemed as *simul iustus et peccator*—that a believer remained a sinner—was true not only for the individual but also for the church. We do our best to live perfectly as Christians, but we know that we will never attain that level. In this way one does one's best without becoming anxious the minute things go wrong.

ORDO

The absence of ordered, structured thought among the Anabaptists and Libertines was another problem for Calvin. He simply could not put up with disorder. This was part of his personality, but it was also his theological conviction that God was a God of order. This was evident already in creation, and was shown again later in the exodus from Egypt, and in everything that followed thereafter. The salvation God accomplished through Christ was also effected with order, and the same was true for the *ordo salutis* of calling, repentance and salvation. In short, order was good because it was the way God himself worked. Chaos and disorder were introduced with sin, and for that reason must be countered. In that respect, Calvin would work his heart out in Geneva, since, as he saw it, there was a lot that needed to be done. Already in 1536, he established together with Farel a sort of church order, a project that surely benefited from Calvin's background in law. That first church order, the *Articles concernant l'organisation de l'église et du culte*, immediately introduced a theme for which Calvin would become famous: church discipline. To achieve order, and to maintain order once achieved, a form of discipline was required that Calvin argued Jesus himself had instituted in Matthew 18. Church discipline was to have the threefold goal of protecting the honor of Christ, of bringing to repentance those who transgress the order, and of protecting others from the bad influence of the sinner. To achieve this, the city was divided into wards, with each ward given a bishop in the original sense of the word, that is, an overseer or elder, to help the people stay on the narrow road, to admonish them, and, in extreme cases, to notify the council of those who violated Christian order as it was established in Geneva. Those who disrupted the order were to be punished, were they not? It was only logical that such people should be kept from the Lord's Supper, since participation signified a confession to live according to God's will. By being kept from the table, those who did not follow God's will were given a wake-up call, so that they could see where their sin might lead them. Eventually, an unrepentant person might also be expelled from the city. In short, no one was forced to live in Geneva, but those who wanted to live there were expected to keep the established rules as in every other city.

Confession

The aim of Calvin's discipline was not a sort of police-state, nor a set of bylaws to enforce civil norms and values; it sought rather to reach the heart. Not everyone, however, understood this at the time, and neither did many later Calvinists see this clearly. For this reason it was only natural that Calvin published a catechism along with this church order to teach young people the contents of the Christian faith in an orderly way. A third product also followed naturally, when a concise confession of faith was also added. All of the inhabitants of Geneva were to express their agreement with this so that they could be held accountable to it, given that with this confession they voluntarily submitted themselves to church discipline as well. As such, this was not too remarkable, since the practice of taking civic oaths was customary in the surrounding cities as well. Calvin thus already had a vision of a city that was fully faithful to the Scriptures, but there were others who saw things differently. The proposals for the confession were approved by

both the Little and the Great Council but only after a number of changes
had been made. It was decided that marriages were to be solemnized before
the magistrate, and the idea that discipline would be administered by the
church and not by the government was rejected as unacceptable.

At first the public confession of faith could not take place because there
were still too many heretics in the city, but on July 29, 1537, many people
made their profession at the St. Pierre Cathedral. There were many others,
however, who did not. In their minds, they had just escaped the downpour
of Catholicism; were they now to walk into the storm that was Calvin? Soon
it became clear that another thundercloud was about to break. The skies
darkened—think here of the adage *post tenebras lux!*—when the pastors insisted on mandatory agreement to the confession, which would have entailed
expulsion from the city for those who refused to express their agreement.
The council gave in to this demand and, on November 12, 1537, decided that
those who did not follow the path decided upon by the city were required to
leave. As it turned out, however, this group was so numerous that the council refrained from enforcing its decision. This could, of course, only mean
trouble for Calvin and his followers, so they berated the council from the
pulpit, and these actions made the people remark that the freedom Geneva
had just obtained was being sold to the preachers by the council. The Council
of Two Hundred thought it politically wise to listen to the voice of the people
and to reverse its earlier decisions, and on January 4, 1538, it decided that a
person could no longer be barred from the Lord's Supper.

It looked as if all hell would break loose, since the question had now
come down to this: is it the church or the state that controls the sacraments?
As we will see, during the next celebration of the Lord's Supper the storm
would break, and the forced departure of a number of people would result.
They were not, however, those whom Calvin and his followers had in
mind.

Heretic

It goes without saying that one ends up in a somewhat embarrassing and
difficult position if identified as a heretic, especially if it happens shortly

after one has devised regulations to counter heresy and do away with heretics. The stakes are heightened, though, when the accusation is not just of
any error, but of a denial of God's Trinity. In March 1537, Pierre Caroli, the
pastor of Lausanne, made this charge against Calvin. Caroli had gotten his
back up after being the leader at Lausanne during Pierre Viret's brief absence. At that time—apparently unsure whether he should be Catholic or
Reformed—Caroli set himself up as a sort of mediating party between
Rome and the Reformation. This was little appreciated. When Viret returned to Lausanne, Caroli had to take his old place once again. Having no
desire to step down, he accused Farel, Viret and Calvin of denying the doctrine of the Trinity on the basis that their works did not follow the terminology and concepts of the early church, whereby it had attempted to for-
mulate this doctrine in the first centuries of the Christian era. Thus Calvin
and his colleagues were made out to be Arians, an accusation even worse
than it sounds. Arius's followers were known as people who did not believe
Christ was fully God, and any such person was by definition an enemy of
the church and of the gospel. In Geneva, the penalty for denial of the Trinity
was death, as Servetus would later discover. Calvin could have responded
very simply to this accusation by subscribing to the three ecumenical confessions, but he was stubborn enough not to take the easy way out. He had
nothing against the substance of this confession, but he resisted speaking
about God using concepts that were not themselves found in Scripture. One
had to be very careful. An additional motive in all of this was, of course,
Calvin's refusal to let himself be pushed around by someone like Caroli.

Calvin wanted to defend himself properly, so he withdrew together with
Nicolas des Gallars to his brother's house in the Genevan countryside for
several days. Suddenly his documents appeared to be lost. Farel had sent
him all kinds of papers for the preparation of his defense, but they had seem-
ingly disappeared. Calvin immediately suspected theft and became enraged,
even though he very well may have lost them himself. In any case, the
greater issue was soon resolved, for Caroli was deposed, and Calvin was
vindicated of the charge of heresy. He continued to have a thorough dislike
for Caroli, however, and Caroli for his part continued to irritate Calvin.

Calvin did not react to these provocations and tried to give the impression that he was not bothered by Caroli's writing. Calvin claimed that Caroli was a swine, and that such animals were not to be honored with a letter. Caroli may have been nothing but a swine, but in 1545 when Calvin published a work against Caroli, it became clear that he was still a very irritating swine and that Calvin was not as stoic as he let on. The action he took was very weak, however, in that he put des Gallars' name on the piece to give the impression that he himself had let things ride and had maintained his emotionless attitude. Calvin later claimed that he published the work under des Gallars's name to deflect praise from himself, but it must be noted that the author of the work—Calvin himself!—praised Farel, Viret and Calvin, and cut Caroli to pieces. This was weak on Calvin's part, and not very bright either, since everyone who read the work immediately saw that it was Calvin's, even if des Gallars had taken it down in dictation. It can hardly be surprising that Viret remarked that the aforementioned trio received too much praise and Caroli too much criticism. Calvin thought this remark was nonsense: did Viret really think Calvin was so foolish as to praise himself and only give more reason for his critics to heap up blame against him? He had written nothing in reference to himself except to remark that he was renowned. Since this was indeed so, how could it be seen as a case of self-promotion?

GUEST AT THE TABLE

The cause for the conflict that eventually led to Calvin's expulsion from Geneva lay in the Lord's Supper. Calvin wanted it to be celebrated on a weekly basis. As the sign and seal of the Word, it was only to be expected that the Word would be followed by the sacrament. This had been a tradition established for centuries, so why should it be changed? The city council, however, considered this too radical a departure from what Bern and Zurich were accustomed to. They also thought it a little too "Romish," and feared the people might get the same impression. Calvin cleverly suggested instead that the Lord's Supper be celebrated once every four weeks, rotating among the four churches in Geneva. The council saw right through this proposal, however, and the syndics and councillors of Geneva decided that four celebrations per year would suffice. The millions of Reformed believers throughout the world who continue to uphold this practice are thus out of line with Calvin and are actually defending the position of the much less Reformed politicians of sixteenth-century Geneva.

Over time the Lord's Supper that was instituted to bind believers more and more to Christ and to each other developed a tradition of division. Exactly where unity ought to have been most visible, a division arose that keeps Protestant Christians from communion with each other to this very day. To be sure, the Lord's Supper is not just a social gathering, but a sacrament where many points of theology come together, including the doctrines of Christ, the Holy Spirit, faith, the church, discipline and the eschaton. The table is actually a microcosm of how things ought to be in society at large: everyone equal, yet not the same, united in their dependence on the grace God distributes and in their readiness to obey God according to his Word.

It is therefore no wonder that a city that wanted to live according to the gospel would run into trouble with inhabitants who would not have things regulated so strictly or who would perhaps desire things to be run in a completely different manner. These problems would become visible at the Lord's Supper. If, among other things, participation in the Lord's Supper signified the confession of a good life, those who claimed to, but did not actually, live such a life had to be kept from the table. This was Calvin's view, and it was where things went wrong in Geneva, just as they have so often throughout the world. It is one thing to keep common people from the table, but if one wants to do the same to those of high standing, problems are bound to arise. Calvin, however, made no such distinction; for him all were equal, and there was no way he could have imagined that some were more equal than others.

WAY

Things did not become any better for Calvin when the four new syndics elected in 1538 all came from the party that were fed up with the policies of this Frenchman. They were also more than ready for a showdown with the pastors and to extend their jurisdiction over the church. The pro-Farel quartet had been replaced by an anti-Farel foursome. Hostility toward the pastors in Geneva also had to do with the situations in the other Swiss Protestant regions where churches did not have independent power. Geneva now wanted to follow suit. Calvin and Farel noticed this when at the order of the government they were forced to participate in a synod in Lausanne at the end of March 1538. There it was decided that Geneva would also adopt the liturgical practices of Bern. Bernese practices still had a popish flavor, noticeable in the use of unleavened bread as a host at the Lord's Supper and the introduction of several feast days. Such things may have been open to discussion had the overall impression not been that they were in fact attempts to decrease the power of the Genevan church and increase the power of the city of Bern.

As noted before, the celebration of the Lord's Supper would clearly settle the question of the authority of the church. For Calvin there simply was no debate, and he would have refused the bread and wine to some with a clear conscience, because he thought it was within the church's power and even considered it the church's duty to protect the sacrament and awaken sinners from their slumber. Things never got that far, however. After the arrest of the pastor Elie Corault, who climbed into the pulpit to preach after loud protests against the council and in spite of a prohibition by that same council, the other pastors declared they would refuse to administer the Lord's Supper on Easter. For this they too were forbidden to preach. The high, or low, point of the controversy came on Easter Sunday. In spite of the council's prohibition, Calvin mounted the pulpit of St. Pierre, and Farel that of St. Gervais. From the pulpits they declared that they would neither preach nor administer the Lord's Supper, for in such a situation a meal that was to commemorate communion with Christ could not reasonably be celebrated. For the city council, this was the last straw, and the next day the Little and Great Councils decided that Calvin and the other pastors who refused to obey their authority were to leave the city within three days. Calvin actually appears to have wanted nothing more; he left immediately on the following morning along with the others. Their response to their banishment was along the lines of: "Very well, then. If we were serving men, this would indeed be a poor reward. But we have an almighty Lord who will reward us."

NO PROBLEM

From Geneva, they went together to Bern to explain the situation and from there to Zürich to tell under what circumstances they would be willing to return. The most important condition they laid down was church discipline. Geneva wanted nothing of it, and they did not want to see Calvin at all. When he was on his way to the city for some private discussions, he was refused entry. Thus he did everything he could and had to do, but without result. Geneva was now part of the past, and Calvin was glad to be finished with it. He left for Basel where he took up residence with Grynaeus.

It was actually a strange situation. Calvin instituted a confession to combat heresy, but ended up being accused of heresy himself. He instituted a church order to keep people from the table and, if need be, from the city, but ended up exiled from the city himself. For Calvin, however, this posed no problem. He was convinced that he had simply done what God had wanted and what the council itself had at first intended, and when things turned out as they did he could say that he was back where he had actually wanted to be in 1536: free to dedicate himself to scholarship. It would, of course, be scholarship in service of the church, but all the same, there was freedom from all the fuss of church members.

DOG

They chased me away, Calvin would say on his deathbed. Chased away like a dog, the way Calvin dealt with the question as to whether he himself was also to blame in the situation is worthy of notice. On the one hand, no trace of awareness of guilt for the situation can be found in Calvin. "There is no one at all who can lay even a little guilt on us." Although someone like Bucer thought Calvin was overly stubborn and hotheaded, Calvin could not understand how his demand for weekly—or at most monthly—celebration of the Lord's Supper was unreasonable. On the

REFUGEE

(1538-1541)

NEXT FATHER

Calvin had made two involuntary departures, first from France and then from Geneva, and now he would also involuntarily encounter a new father for the second time. When he had wanted to go from Basel to Strasbourg, he passed through Geneva where Farel had trapped him. Now that he wanted to go from Geneva to Basel, he passed through Strasbourg, where Bucer was already waiting for him. That Bucer still wanted him was a bit of a miracle, since the way Calvin had treated Bucer in a letter would have given him every right to hang Calvin out to dry. As recently as early January 1538 Bucer had gotten a faceful from this young French theologian, who, though but a greenhorn, berated the Alsatian master for being too long-winded when he wrote and too soft and not radical enough in his view of Rome. In line after line of that long letter, Calvin laid into Bucer and criticized his stance. When he stood in front of Bucer, however, and the latter forced him to stay in Strasbourg, Calvin lost all his earlier impudence. When Calvin had still been in Basel, Bucer had sent a letter of invitation, but once he had Calvin inside the city walls, he swore that his younger colleague would become the pastor of the French refugee church. This was not at all as Calvin intended things to be, for Strasbourg offered a scholar far more agreeable possibilities than to be saddled down with preaching and pastoral reponsibilities. Bucer, however, called down imprecations on Calvin should he not stay, pointing to the lot that fell to Jonah when he backed down from his preacher's task. That reference sounded awfully familiar to Calvin, and just as he had been unable to resist Farel two years earlier, he could now once again do nothing but reluctantly accept Bucer's invitation, which in fact was really no invitation at all. All the same, this was the beginning of a good relationship, where from 1538 on, the young know-it-all began to see Bucer more and more as a father figure to whom he would do well to listen. In October 1541, when Calvin was back in Geneva, he invited Bucer to admonish and discipline him, in short, to do "what a father is allowed with respect to his son."

The commandment to honor one's father and mother has the reward "that it may go well with you in the land the LORD your God is giving you," and for Calvin this became a reality. Obedient to Bucer, he immediately set himself to his task and passed some of the best years of his life in Strasbourg. This may also have had to do with Bucer's suggestion that Calvin avoid Farel, since the two would only stir each other up in their hotheadedness and all that came with it. Bucer knew Calvin all too well, and Calvin did what he was told. In this way he appears to have benefited from Bucer's influence; a year after that insolent letter referred to above, Calvin wrote that he would not hear any bad of Bucer, even though there were some things he would like to have changed in him. "However, we must not let ourselves be guided by personal biases, but listen to each other and make no decisions before we have so together arrived at the truth."

STRASBOURG

It was in Strasbourg that Calvin was born. Not actually, of course, but it was his birthplace as a theologian and church leader. Throughout the centuries so much seemed to come together in that city, and so it was in Strasbourg that virtually all the theological influences came together to form the Cal-

vin—and the Calvinism—known today. Only later did Calvin himself see
how his stay in Strasbourg helped him deepen his work and theology. Also
among the gains for which Calvin was indebted to both Strasbourg and
Bucer was his wife. Strasbourg banned the Mass in 1529 immediately after
this so-called imperial free city chose for the Reformation. Here too the
decision meant that the church had become Reformed, but as in other places
the politicians took power over it. The city's fine government caused Erasmus to remark that in Strasbourg the wisdom of Athens, the morality of
Sparta and the discipline of Rome went hand in hand. These and several
other factors ensured that it grew into the great refugee center of Europe.
Anyone and everyone with divergent opinions could find a place there, if
only they were not too heretical or rebellious. Aside from that, Strasbourg
had a strong tradition of preachers that stretched well back into the Middle
Ages, Matthias Zell and Martin Bucer being its reforming representatives.

In Strasbourg, Calvin had an excellent opportunity to do in a church
what he had been unable to do in a city, namely, to regulate everything as
much as possible according to the Scriptures. He began preaching there on
September 8, 1538. He preached twice per Sunday, and another four times
throughout the week. He ministered first in the St. Nicolai church, then in
the Magdalena church, and finally in the choir of the Dominican church, to
a congregation numbering some five hundred refugees, which was a nicely
manageable group. The congregation's status as refugee church meant that
it was actually a little enclave in the city, which gave Calvin more freedom
to model this experimental church after his own vision, and so as early as
September 1538, he began the exercise of church discipline. A month later
the Lord's Supper was celebrated for the first time following the Strasbourg
liturgy, which prescribed that it be held once a month. The table was at first
quite open, but shortly before Easter 1540, Calvin announced that the participation of too many people was lax, so that from then on everyone who
intended to join in had to report to Calvin first. Not all the French refugees
were happy with this announcement, since some felt as if they were being
placed under the yoke of penance again. Calvin's response is worthy of notice, because even today people throughout the world still experience its

consequences—or, more positively, its fruits—every week. Calvin replied that penance could only be done away with if a pastoral visit was set up in its place. According to Calvin, penance could not simply be discarded without a replacement, and the replacement he proposed was that conversation for admission to the Lord's Supper. Calvin envisioned those wishing to partake in the Lord's Supper dropping by to see him when the celebration was drawing near. This way, he could instruct those who had not been well instructed in the meaning of the Lord's Supper, or else admonish if necessary, and comfort those whose consciences were not at rest. Thus the home visit was instituted, which many Reformed church orders prescribe to be held in the members' homes at least once a year, and if at all possible, before each celebration of the Lord's Supper. To put it another way, the confessional was not thrown out but was relocated to the living room. The shepherds became mobile and visited the sheep rather than waiting for the sheep to come to them. Calvin intended these pastoral visits for instruction, admonition and comfort, but there was in fact little change from the older practices of penance, since both were concerned with how things stood between God and his people, and whether things were good enough to allow one a place at his table.

DISCIPLINE

When it came to discipline, Calvin learned from the way Martin Bucer did things. In contrast to Calvin, Bucer was responsible for the whole city and not just one church, and thus used some original methods. Bucer introduced a sort of home-group system, based on the assumption that a whole ward could be reached from a circle of several conscientious Christians. Bucer also established the office of elder as one who helped people live with and for God. He turned the office of deacon into something more than a collection agency, making them responsible for putting the mercy of Christ into practice. Other changes from which Calvin would greatly benefit were in the area of liturgical reform. With the abolition of the Mass, the altar was replaced by the pulpit, and the sacrament of the Lord's Supper was no longer an offering of the congregation to God, but rather a gift from God to the congregation. When it came to the doctrine of the Lord's Supper, Calvin had arrived in Strasbourg at the right time. For many years Bucer had attempted to combine the views of Zwingli and Luther, and in 1536 managed to effect an agreement with Wittenberg in which his efforts ensured that at least some of Zwingli could be retained, albeit in limited measure. That same year the first Reformed pastoral handbook was published, which was Bucer's *Von der waren Seelsorge* ("Concerning the True Care of Souls"). Although Calvin could not read German, the contents of this work were well known to him through personal contact with Bucer. Connected to this was another of Bucer's special insights: his conviction that the Anabaptists were dead wrong to deny infant baptism but correct in their insistence on discipline and sanctification. Calvin was to benefit from this vision too. There were further liturgical changes allowing church members to sing God's praises in their own language, which represented quite a change from the old ways, under which they only listened to a choir sing in Latin. Much more could be said, but since this book is not on Bucer and Strasbourg let it suffice to say that here Calvin found pretty much everything in terms of doctrine, church polity, liturgy, preaching and pastoral ministry that would turn him into Calvin as he has become known worldwide. Strasbourg turned into a huge success for Calvin, and this coincided perfectly with his view that God would bring good even out of things that are not good— in this case, Calvin's forced departure from Geneva. Calvin's teaching of providence meant that in the end all things work out for the good.

CHURCH

In Strasbourg, Calvin rediscovered the church. He had broken with Rome because he thought it was not a church after God's will, but found no answer as to how the church *should* be until his arrival in Strasbourg.

For Calvin, the church was so important that he consistently referred to it as mother. For Calvinism, with its emphasis not only on the independence of the local congregation but also of the individual member, Calvin's view of the church sometimes sounds a little too Catholic. Calvin knew the objections to his view. Cannot one pray or read the Scriptures by oneself?

Does one really have to go to church for that? These were not new questions Calvin was raising; he was merely formulating the questions of the people around him. He responded that it was not for nothing that God had instituted an office for instruction in the Scriptures, and that with it he clearly directed believers to the church's bosom. Speaking of the possibility of a faith exercised outside of the community and preaching of the church, Calvin argued we should not suppose that we can fly without wings. One can only fly with the church. Some may suppose the church to be constricting, but it is actually otherwise. Without the church, faith soon falls down and is dead.

SINGING

In other words, the church sets one free as a bird. One might say as free as a songbird, since it was in Strasbourg that Calvin learned about singing. He was impressed by the liturgy he found there and immediately implemented it in his own church, which means that the well-known "Genevan liturgy" actually had its origins in Strasbourg. In his French congregation, psalms were sung in French, and Calvin also devoted some time to rhyming this portion of the Scriptures. He found it difficult to do this well and consulted with his French colleagues. In Germany the Reformers had also attempted to reform liturgical singing with rhymed versions of the biblical message, but there was a difference. Calvin and company wanted to stay as close as possible to the biblical text and further chose to make exclusive use of the Psalms as the songbook given by God himself. The Germans, on the other hand, were as determined to be biblical but thought this could also be achieved with biblically-based hymns.

In 1539 the first Psalm book appeared with the title *Aulcuns pseaulmes et cantiques mys en chant*. It contained eighteen psalms and three hymns, the hymns comprising two Scripture passages put to rhyme (the song of Simeon and the Ten Commandments) and a rhymed version of the Apostles' Creed. Clément Marot, whom Calvin had met in Ferrara in 1536, was the greatest contributor to this collection. Calvin quickly saw that his own strengths were not in this area, and after only a limited contribution to the first edition, he did not involve himself with subsequent editions at all.

That Calvin and the members of his churches in Strasbourg and Geneva were so fond of the Psalms can easily be understood: they recognized themselves there. Calvin saw a lot of himself in David, and together with his congregation—almost all French refugees—he could identify with the nation Israel that wandered in the desert, experienced so many setbacks and yet was in God's care. The Psalms became existential pilgrim songs but also rhymed battle cries. The identification with Israel, however, was problematic for the Reformed, as well as for the Catholics, Anabaptists and Lutherans, both for themselves and with respect to their relationships to others. If the Reformed, or any of the other parties, understood themselves as the chosen nation, all others must be Egyptians or perhaps Philistines.

LITURGY

Calvin's stay in Strasbourg was extremely significant for his thought on liturgy. In 1540 he wrote a form for baptism, and intended to instruct the congregation in the meaning of baptism and in the biblical warrant for infant baptism as he conceived it. The idea to write such a form occurred to him when more and more former Anabaptists presented their children to him to be baptized. Aside from the instructional element, Calvin also reconsidered how baptism was to be administered in the liturgy. He thought children ought to be baptized during the public worship service, since it would be better for this solemn reception into the congregation to take place before more than just a few witnesses. "Unless it is really not possible, the fathers ought to be there with the godparents to answer the baptismal questions." Only men and women of the same confession should be chosen as godfathers and godmothers.

During the same time, Calvin wrote up a form for the Lord's Supper, and once back in Geneva, he added a form for marriage, again with the benefit of his Strasbourg experience. Calvin's liturgical views do not completely correspond with those of many of his later Reformed followers, however. Not only did Calvin promote weekly communion, he also led the first part of the service from behind the communion table, and only then did he climb into the pulpit. At this point the congregation sang the Ten Commandments as a confession of its desire to walk in God's ways; they were not read by the pastor to expose to the believers their sins. Calvin also advocated kneeling at prayer, while today the pews in most Reformed churches leave barely enough room for one's knees. That the elements of the Lord's Supper were not to be received while kneeling speaks for itself, since the impression could be left that one knelt for the same reason as in the papal Mass.

From Bucer, rightly considered the inventor of the "public confession of faith," Calvin also learned that there ought to be a definite moment of decision between baptism and the Lord's Supper. "No one may be allowed to Christ's Holy Supper who has not professed his or her faith." To this end, children were examined four times per year to trace their progress. "For although they in a certain manner actually profess their faith every Sunday in the catechism service, they may nevertheless not participate in the Lord's Supper until in the pastor's eyes it is clear that they have progressed far enough in the principal points of faith." To sum up, in Calvin's view one also needed flying lessons in order to fly. In his church, the final test could be taken during one's teenage years.

SYNAGOGUE

Calvin's appreciation for the Old Testament, the Hebrew language and rabbinic commentaries is well known. But what about his view of the Jews?

In 1536, Calvin had already spoken out in the *Institutes* against a mission aimed at converting Jews by force. He considered this not only inhumane but also out of line with predestination. Faith cannot be forced on anyone since it is a gift originating in God's choice. Force will bring no one to heaven, nor can we know which of the people who resist have nevertheless been chosen by God. The latter is also true for the Jews. Calvin believed, according to his reading of Romans, that the greatest part of the Jewish people was reprobate but that God would still keep a remnant for himself. Calvin himself appears to have had no, or almost no, close contact with Jews. During his stays at Frankfurt, Hagenau and Worms, he could have managed to get in touch with the rather large Jewish communities there, but it is not clear whether anything ever came of it. At first, his view of the Jews seems very negative. "I have often spoken with many Jews, but have never been able to find even a drop of piety, or a seed of truth and mental strength among them. Indeed, I have never been able to find something even resembling normal human intelligence in a Jew." Nevertheless, in Calvin's writings there is no trace of anti-Semitism, and here he distinguished himself from many of his contemporaries, including several Reformers. What he wrote of them is instead theological in character, and what is true for a Jew is true for everyone else. Without Christ, even a Jew is simply a lost person. As sharp as he was with the Jews, Calvin was equally as sharp with the Christians.

Everything centered around Christ, and this was also true when it came to Calvin's high regard for the arrangement of the tabernacle and temple. These structures were shadows, but now that Christ had come in full light, the church no longer needed these external arrangements. For this reason, Calvin found the Catholic liturgy and church layout little more than a return to the Old Testament, which also explains the rather plain character of Reformed churches. This has given rise to the misunderstanding that Reformed people, with Calvin in the lead, have launched in word and deed a virtual crusade against any expression of the visual arts in church buildings and services, with no other motive than the *sola Scriptura*. Calvin's own motive, however, was different. For him, it was just that simplicity marked the truth. Anything extra could only detract from the clarity of the message, and did not serve the edification of the people. Calvin simply saw no use in keeping all kinds of unnecessary traditions and practices "where we are after all free to have a purer, simpler structure in the worship service."

But Calvin was no absolute stickler in this, as became evident when the French congregation in Wesel asked him what they were to do when the city government forced them to adopt certain Lutheran practices that had a definite popish tinge. Just do it, Calvin wrote back. Would you allow the church to collapse for refusing to adapt to some liturgical customs?

LORD'S SUPPER

The table, which was intended by Christ as a sacrament of communion with him and with each other, had by that time almost fallen to pieces. Calvin had a strong urge to do something about this, and in Strasbourg he wrote a short treatise with the simple title *Short Treatise on the Holy Supper of Our Lord Jesus Christ*. Calvin fully understood that the mystery of this sacrament could not be understood. Luther would not back down from his belief in the real presence of Christ in the bread and wine, since for him it was yet another proof that salvation came not from inside of him but from outside. Zwingli, on the other hand, could not put up with that view, owing to his discovery that salvation did not consist in external things but was a spiritual, internal matter. Zwingli's view was, in turn, suspect for Luther because it made him think of the Peasants' War of 1525 and of what the Anabaptists had done in Münster of 1534 and 1535. Just the word *spiritual* would make Luther itch all over, and he immediately connected it with images of violent, murderous peasants and other radicals. Calvin was left with the pieces of this dispute and tried to resolve things by combining the elements that both Luther and Zwingli insisted on. He thus arrived at a belief in the real presence of Christ through his Spirit, a solution through which some kind of unity was established both with the Wittenbergers and with the Swiss. Unfortunately, a three-party consensus was never achieved. Calvin was honest enough to admit that he did not fully understand Christ's presence. "If someone were to question me as to its mode, I would without shame admit that the mystery is too great to be grasped by my understanding or to be expressed in words. To be very honest, I experience it more than I understand it."

Calvin wanted to keep things as simple as possible and thus had little use for Bucer's endless search for formulations that would satisfy Luther and the Lutherans. Luther was so intent on Christ's bodily presence in the bread and wine that he was willing to propose the omnipresence (or ubiquity) of Christ's body to explain it. This doctrine meant that Christ was present in many places—if need be, everywhere—not only spiritually but also bodily. For Calvin, this only confused heaven and earth. Since the ascension, Christ was simply in heaven and would return on the Last Day; in the meantime there was no going back and forth. Calvin himself was not ready to bring a little heaven down to earth, and found the invention of this doctrine unbiblical and a failed solution, but neither was he any more willing to twist Christ's words of institution to end up with Zwingli. Calvin wanted to bring light to the discussion, and wanted to do it simply. Christ is present through his Spirit. We should be content to leave it at that.

MONEY

As noted before, Bucer made much of the office of deacon, and Calvin followed him in this. Perhaps his own efforts can be explained from the fact that in Strasbourg he was not well off and on the verge of poverty. At first, his salary as pastor was paid by friends, but Calvin still had to sell a number of his books to support himself. Even when he was finally allotted a dwelling, he had to take in several students to make ends meet. All the same, he urged those students into the ministry, a vocation that is not pursued for the money anyway. Financial matters improved a little when he received a position at the school in Strasbourg for which he was paid fifty-two guilders per year. Jacob Sturm, the mayor of Strasbourg, did his best to procure a chaplaincy income for him, but as Calvin had earlier expressly distanced himself from this kind of financial arrangement, he would not accept. Calvin actually cared little for money, and even if there is some truth to the thesis linking Calvinism and capitalism, Calvin himself understood nothing of the practice of this economic theory. Even later in Geneva he was not exactly rich. In the best of times Calvin's expenses had to be managed carefully, and when things became more difficult, he would have to go into debt. Calvin related all of this not to complain, but rather because he thought God always provided enough for him. Calvin had no desire to become rich and actually hated having money. To prevent even the slightest appearance of financial indiscretion he refused to accept a sum of money bequeathed to him by someone who had very little time to live without a written proof of receipt. Calvin did not want to receive even a penny from that inheritance.

What he did want cleared up was the rumor alleging that he had procured some land for himself in Geneva at a high price. "All of Geneva and the surrounding areas know that I do not own even a square inch of property. For I have not made it this far, and in fact I use furniture that belongs to someone else. Neither the table from which we eat, nor the bed in which we sleep, is ours." Any who were still unconvinced would only need to await Calvin's death when the fact that he had no money would become more than clear.

Calvin himself was content with his limited finances, though it did trouble him when others suffered on account of his poverty, as when he had to ask the recipient of his letter to pay the courier. This also shows how quickly and deeply Calvin felt indebted. When a rich noble woman was offered to him as a bride, he refused, but in doing so he felt thankless and apologized for his refusal. In 1560, when he did have a bit of money, Calvin appears to have felt uneasy and immediately wrote to his childhood friend François Daniel, offering him all his possessions and enclosing two coins for Daniel's two daughters, explaining that he felt indebted for all that Daniel had done for him.

SCHOOL

Strasbourg's academy was instituted by Jean Sturm at the order of the Strasbourg government in 1538 and would later develop into a university. The post Calvin held there provided him with more than just a stable income. It also helped him gain in knowledge and experience, as well as providing the opportunity to further improve his use of the French language. The general tendency to find nothing positive to say about Calvin has meant that his important contribution to the French language is often forgotten. The elegance of his French can probably only be best appreciated by one who is French, though perhaps those who read, for example, his *Petit traicte de la sainte Cene de nostre Seigneur Iesus Christ* may appreciate not only its content but also its language and style. It is as if Calvin's style flourished only when he had come to an environment where French was not spoken. It was also in Strasbourg that he completed his translation of the second edition of the *Institutes*—published shortly after his return to Geneva in 1541—another example of immaculate French.

In January 1539, Calvin was also appointed to lecture and hold disputations on the New Testament. He began with the Gospel of John, and thereafter dealt with Paul's first epistle to the Corinthians, and possibly also the letters to the Philippians and the Romans. Calvin published his commentary on Romans in 1539, and because there were already several Reformed commentaries on it, his preface had to address those of Melanchthon, Bucer and Bullinger, even if only to justify the publication of yet another. In his work on Seneca's *De clementia,* Calvin had practiced this sort of self-justification, and once again he succumbed to the temptation to criticize those to whom he actually owed so much. With *De clementia* it had been Erasmus; now it was Bucer who had to pay for the long-windedness Calvin detected in his commentary. That Calvin had learned something in the meantime, or at least had become a little wiser, was evident when he added to his criticism that no one was more conscientious and diligent in explaining the Scriptures as Bucer.

In any case, Calvin's post in the Strasbourg academy was the beginning of a career as an expositor and commentator, during which he managed to write an exposition on almost every single book of the Bible, so that in the intervening centuries, pastors have been able to consult Calvin in their sermon preparations. Two biblical books stood out to him: the Psalms and Paul's epistle to the Romans. One could say that the Psalms were for the heart, Romans for the head. Calvin saw the Psalms as a reflection of everything that played in a person's heart, while the letter to the Romans was a goldmine of knowledge for the faithful. "Once we know the contents of this letter well, the doors are opened to the greatest treasures of the Scriptures." Calvin's view of these two books, which spoke to the head and the heart, tells us the most about what he thought and who he was.

COMMENTARY

Calvin was the sort of person who would not simply accept what others had already said without thinking he could add something to it. He had great esteem for the exegetical work of Luther, Melanchthon and Bucer, and he sounds very proper and modest writing that he has never even considered competing with them, never mind taking away from their fame. He immediately adds, however, that the quality of their work is not such that others who come after them—including Calvin himself, of course!—would have nothing to add. Calvin wrote politcly simply to say that the commentaries of his Reformed colleagues and predecessors were not definitive. This betrayed his conviction that thorough study of the Scriptures could always unearth new treasures that had not been noticed by others before. Calvin valued the work of others but wanted to progress beyond it, and thus it also followed that those who were to come after him should not simply rest content with what he had written, either.

Among his works there is a commentary on virtually every book of the Bible, but Revelation is one of the few he omitted. He himself gave no reason for this. Calvin scholars have proposed several hypotheses, though they do not fully agree with each other. One who simply reads Revelation, however, will soon enough understand why Calvin preferred to leave it alone.

One of the new features of Calvin's commentaries was the absence of doctrinal asides. For centuries, theologians had been in the habit of interrupting textual expositions with long asides on whatever topic suggested itself to the commentator from the particular Scripture text being treated. Calvin did not want such excursus to sidetrack either himself or his audience, and he wrote the *Institutes* as a sort of handbook to accompany the commentaries. In this way, when theological topics such as the church or creation appeared in the subject matter of his New Testament lectures, he could refer his students to the appropriate passage in the *Institutes,* should they want to know more and simply continue his textual exposition.

When one looks at how much Calvin wrote, it is almost impossible to understand how he could ever have done it. It is simply a fact of life that some people can accomplish more than others, and Calvin was one of those who could accomplish not just more, but a lot more. Calvin's time in Strasbourg was marked by a very high rate of productivity. Thus it is strange to read the frequent complaints about his laziness in his letters. It may seem a little less strange, however, when one considers Calvin's work ethic: a rest from labor after an eight-hour workday might seem reasonable to many, but for Calvin, who thought in terms of a twenty-four hour workday, even a half-hour break could appear as laziness.

Unity

Since the establishment of the European Union, Strasbourg has become a symbol of the unity sought in Europe. In recent centuries, this city has been German at one time, French at another, and has a language that is both and neither. The city, which has given refuge to so many different people throughout the ages, had also become a base of operations for Calvin in his efforts to unify the church in Europe—efforts that began with contact with Rome. In those years many were still convinced that restoration was possible; there had not yet been any ecclesiastical pronouncements on numerous topics that would soon close the doors on either side. It was the time before the Council of Trent and its anathemas on Reformed teachings, which would make even dialogue all but impossible, and the time before Protestant confessional documents took on a status of unchangeable doctrinal formulations. The possibility of restoration still existed; though Luther was rather skeptical, Bucer and Melanchthon were quite optimistic, and Calvin's hopes floated somewhere in between. In Strasbourg, however, people were convinced that Calvin was just the man to enter into dialogue with Rome.

The image of Calvin that has come down through the ages is one of a fierce doctrinal dragon, the last person one would imagine holding dialogue with those who held different views, and particularly with Rome. In Calvin's own time, however, people evidently had a different image of him. He was a man with knowledge of the Scriptures and tradition, with ingenuity for devising formulas that could bring people and factions together, with a gift for clarity of expression, and with a lawyer's education and skill in the art of disputing and convincing.

Sadoleto

All of these qualities were displayed in Calvin's letter to Jacopo Sadoleto. Sadoleto was the bishop of Carpentras and had written an open letter to the government and people of Geneva on behalf of a conference of bishops in March of 1539. When Calvin was banished, the Catholics had seen a perfect opportunity to reclaim Geneva for Rome. Sadoleto was known as a learned and upright man who devoted himself to improving the present situation of the church. He had the respect and confidence of many, and used this to impress upon the hearts of the Genevans that they should hasten to restore the unity of the church and return to the familiar, well-worn and centuries-old path of Catholicism. The doctrine of justification by faith, after all, had done nothing less than undermine morality and foster division among the citizens—this was the result of the Reformation. A return to Rome, therefore, was in all respects the best solution.

Bishop Sadoleto made one mistake in his plea. His accusation that Calvin had acted out of self-interest was like a red cape to a raging bull. Unlike a bull, however, Calvin (for once!) did not charge Sadoleto immediately. At first, he wanted to do, and in fact did, nothing. It was only later, when others forced(!) him that he diligently went to work writing a long open letter that tore Sadoleto to pieces more than any bull ever could have. Whether or not one agrees with the letter's contents, friend and foe alike have agreed that Calvin produced an absolute literary masterpiece. Calvin painstakingly laid out his vision of the unity of the church and could not but conclude that Rome had broken that unity by departing from divine truth. Is unity institutional? Isn't it rather to be found in the fact that believers are one in faith? The external, visible aspect of the church is present only where there is internal, spiritual unity with Christ, isn't it? There was also a personal side to Calvin's epistolary testimony: he appealed to God as his judge in defending himself against the accusation that he had acted in self-interest. The letter, therefore, says much not only about Calvin's view of Rome but also reveals a man so deeply hurt by this reproach that he appealed directly to God's courts. He had little fear of Geneva and certainly none of Sadoleto, but he was afraid for his eternal salvation. So the letter to Sadoleto was Calvin's appeal to Geneva on behalf of God, but also Calvin's appeal to God on behalf of Calvin.

DIALOGUE WITH ROME

Calvin had, in any case, shown that he knew the ropes and so he was delegated for dialogue with Rome. He had no desire to go and would later even remark that he went against his will. He wrote to Farel that he expected to be embroiled in the business of dialogue for the next while:

> They are dragging me to Regensburg although I do not want to go at all. First, because I know that the journey alone will be heavy; secondly, because I am afraid that it will take a long time, since such conferences often drag on for some ten months; and finally, because I do not consider myself fit for such dealings.

Though he had no desire to do so, Calvin went to Regensburg for the same reason he did and endured everything: "Yet I want to follow God, and he will surely know why he is putting such pressure on me." For Calvin, an order from a human superior was an order from God. As was typical, Calvin would rather have done something else. He did not want to go but went nevertheless, believing divine authority required it of him.

Dialogues had already been held in France between political and ecclesiastical leaders of the two parties, but these yielded no results except promises to continue the dialogue. This was one of the reasons why Bucer made sure Calvin attended the next round of talks held in Hagenau, some six miles from Strasbourg. Toward the end of 1540 the dialogue was continued at Worms but got off to a very slow start. When it initially seemed that nothing would happen, Calvin was ready to depart, but Melanchthon held him back. "When I tried to make objections, he said that he could not care less about my excuses." Melanchthon must have said something along the lines of, "I don't care—you're staying." So Calvin stayed, and felt like a soldier ready for battle with nothing to do but to wait. "We are in our camp with nothing to do because the enemy gives us so little to do battle with." To kill some time around New Year's, Calvin wrote "a short song for the sake of pleasure." It was to be his only poem, a "Song of Victory Sung to Christ by John Calvin on the First Day of January in the Year 1541." When the dialogues finally had begun in earnest, a message came from the em-

peror ordering that they be continued a few months later at the Diet of
Regensburg.

WITHOUT HOPE

At Regensburg there was real cause for hope. Calvin wrote to Farel that a
statement on justification had been formulated on which both Catholics and
Reformed could agree. Calvin admitted that the Reformed position should
have been expressed a little more clearly, but, considering the opposition,
one ought to be pleased with the results achieved. These first words of good
news were soon eclipsed by issues on which no unifying position could be
found. No agreement could be reached on questions of whether or not the
pope held the highest position in the church, and whether bread and wine
were really changed into the body and blood of Jesus. By this point, Calvin
decided he had seen enough. He did not stay for the end of the dialogue and
returned to Strasbourg in spite of the protests of Bucer and Melanchthon.
He could better use his time serving the many needs of the church in Strasbourg. New refugees had come to Strasbourg from France, adding to Calvin's regular workload; his replacement had left; and Capito had fallen ill,
causing the work of the academy to stagnate. Calvin left Rome for what it
was. His departure from Regensburg was his last farewell to Rome, and he
made no effort to hide this in his works. In this respect, Calvin had a different view than Luther, who still held on to the hope of a single church. Calvin was of the opinion that matters could never be reconciled with Rome.
The time of unity had passed, a fact that had to be reckoned with. Calvin
may have been an idealist in many things, but in this matter he was more of
a realist.

It thus need not be said that Calvin was not all that fond of Rome. In ac-
cordance with the customs of the time, his characterizations of anything
and everything to do with Rome were as colorful as they were direct. On
the other hand, the Catholic side was none too happy with Calvin, either.
Even two years after his death, the Sorbonne theologians would claim that
there had never been such an infectious and dangerous error as the doctrine
of Calvin. With forty-nine titles, Calvin also topped the charts of forbidden

works. "O Calvin, how bitterly kind you were!" wrote the Parisian theologian René Benoist. "How did you ever manage to lead and lure the unstable souls, and win over that simple and ignorant people?" In Calvin, Rome saw an even more formidable danger than Luther.

In addition to his difficulties with many Catholic teachings, Calvin also had a low opinion of monasticism, even though he himself would probably have done well in a monastery. "There is no order of people that is so contaminated with all kinds of sins." Only one in ten monasteries was not a whorehouse. Monks were fools, false prophets and good-for-nothings. There may well have been some decent clergymen among them, but the majority suffered from pharisaical pride, hypocrisy and ignorance. They were on the whole a corrupt lot, and only a careful search would unearth a few pious exceptions.

In contrast, Calvin had no problem recognizing the legitimacy of Catholic baptisms. Some Christians of the Reformed persuasion, either because there was no Reformed church nearby, or else—just to be on the safe side—had allowed Catholic priests to baptize their children. As Calvin saw it, this entailed sin, and yet it did not mean that the children were not really baptized. "The papal baptism maintains its efficacy even though it overflows with a thousand laughable follies." Despite all the Roman mutilations, baptism retained something of the divine, just as the power of circumcision was maintained in spite of all the godlessness in the temple. Thus, in spite of the break with Rome, there was still a bond.

Friends for Life

There was, though, no break in the bond with Luther and Melanchthon. Late in February 1539, Calvin traveled to Frankfurt on his own initiative after hearing from Bucer, who was already there for religious dialogue, that little had been accomplished for the persecuted Protestants in France. Calvin wanted to do something about this, and set out for Frankfurt hoping that he could convince the German princes to assist the Reformed believers in France. He also saw this trip as a nice opportunity to speak to Melanchthon. The conversation Calvin sought and realized was, in fact, a

great success: thereafter, even though they did not always agree on everything, dialogue would never break down between these two skinny Reformers. Like Luther, Calvin disliked Melanchthon's *Leisetreterei,* his tip-
toeing or softness in regards to Rome. The main thrust of Calvin's letters
was: why not simply say what one thinks? He was just about driven crazy
by Melanchthon's ability to keep silent, a talent he did not share. Calvin
referred to this as Melanchthon's weakness, "that not even the greatest
need can bring him to speak frankly." He would have been glad had
Melanchthon been more resolute once in a while.

It also bothered him that Melanchthon was afraid to show his colors and
involve himself in the Eucharistic controversy that broke out after Luther's
death. It would have been better for Melanchthon to be taken out of his all
too Lutheran surroundings. Calvin and Melanchthon also differed on the
question of free will and predestination. Calvin dedicated his work against
Pighius on this topic to Melanchthon, for which the latter was most grate-
ful. Melanchthon had a positive regard for this book, but he still rejected
Calvin's so-called determinism. Calvin suggested that the cause of their
dispute was that the Wittenberg theologian was too accommodating of human reason, more of a philosopher than a theologian. Nevertheless, Calvin
claimed no one could set them in opposition on the basis of this difference.
Their friendship was heartfelt, owing partly to the fact that they were both
humanists. There was room for public disagreement precisely because they
were bound to each other through mutual esteem. In light of their friendship, Calvin regretted that they did not live closer together, writing that it
was a burden on him that they were separated by so great a distance. If
Melanchthon lived closer, he and Calvin would have been able to discuss
more because "in a three-hour conversation I would get further with him
than in a hundred letters." In Calvin's estimation, Melanchthon belonged
among the best of the Bible commentators. He advised Farel to read
Melanchthon's book on the authority of the church, and when Calvin met
Melanchthon at Worms in 1540, he told Farel he would be illumined after
listening to Melanchthon for even half an hour. Since they did not live
close together, Calvin thought to comfort himself and Melanchthon with

the expectation that they would better enjoy their mutual love and friendship in heaven, where they would live together forever.

LUTHER

Calvin never had a personal conversation with Luther, and Melanchthon holds part of the blame. Melanchthon held back a letter Calvin had written to Luther, fearing that Luther would be angered by it. Calvin wanted a personal meeting because Luther meant a lot to him. Calvin mentioned Luther for the first time in a letter to Bucer on January 12, 1538. He wrote that he was convinced of Luther's piety, but was still not quite sure what to make of him. Calvin thought that Luther's resolute commitment to his own doctrine of the Lord's Supper was hindering any chance at Protestant unity. The fact is that Calvin had greater trouble with Luther's character than with his teachings, since he thought that his own view agreed with that of Luther in substance. Calvin's French pamphlet on the Lord's Supper shows him trying to approach the hotheaded Luther. Luther too appears to have noticed the agreement between himself and Calvin, for Melanchthon reported that when someone tried to incite Luther to attack Calvin's teaching on the Lord's Supper as formulated in his letter to Sadoleto, Luther actually praised Calvin after reading the relevant passages. Although Calvin knew no German, and Luther knew no French, both read and wrote in Latin, so fortunately they could benefit fully from each other's work.

The significance Luther held for Calvin can best be illustrated in a remark Calvin made in 1556 during the Lutheran Eucharistic controversy. He wrote that when he began to "liberate himself from the darkness of the papacy" he was so influenced by Luther that he distanced himself from the writings of Oecolampadius and Zwingli. These words indicate Calvin's independence from, as well as his closeness to, Luther over Zwingli. Calvin did not want to compare Luther to Elijah as if there was no prophet of equal standing after him, but he did say that "the Gospel went out from Wittenberg." For him, Luther was the one who first made the papacy waver. In the letter Melanchthon held back, Calvin addressed Luther as his "most learned father in the Lord." He wished he could fly to Luther to be with him and discuss several matters, but if this was impossible on earth, he hoped it would still be possible later in God's Kingdom.

Calvin was thrilled when Bucer brought him personal greetings from Luther, along with a report that their German colleague had been pleased with Calvin's writings. Calvin even felt it should be added to the preface of his commentary on Romans that he had written something that had met with Luther's satisfaction.

At times, however, Calvin also expressed discontentment with Luther's attitude. He was a great spiritual leader, but also a great problem, and Calvin was one of many who attempted to reckon with both aspects of Luther. To Bullinger, Calvin wrote that his Wittenberg colleague was "immoderately ardent and violent in character." Luther should have better controlled his temper and been more aware of his shortcomings. To Melanchthon, Calvin wrote that Luther lacked self-control and allowed himself to be worked up into a rage far too quickly. Behaving like this, Luther was a danger to the church, and it appeared no one would dare to counter this behavior. Respect remained, however, and—according to Calvin himself—even if Luther were to call him a devil, Calvin would still show him honor and tell him he was a most special servant of God. In 1554 the Swiss reformers accused Calvin of being too lenient with Luther. He defended the German's fierceness by saying that this was simply part of Luther's character and that malicious men were consciously provoking him. In Calvin's estimation, Luther remained a superb servant of Christ to whom all were indebted. His wrongs ought only to be reproached in such a way that room remained for appreciation of his great giftedness. Calvin's defense of Luther's turbulent character should come as no surprise; he was like that himself.

CAROLI ONCE MORE

Just as the bonds of some friendships do not break, neither do the bonds of some enmities. This was the case for Calvin and Caroli, who met once again in the streets of Strasbourg. Trying to escape arrest in Bern, Caroli had come to Strasbourg seeking refuge. When the Strasbourg theologians discussed the matter among themselves, Bucer thought it best to exclude Calvin because of his history with Caroli, or at least because of the character traits he had displayed in that history. Here the focus is not on the issue between Calvin and Caroli, but on Calvin's attitude and what it reveals about him as a person. Calvin was called in after the initial meeting with Caroli and asked to give his opinion of him. An agreement was then drafted that left room to accommodate Caroli. The document included a clause that was unacceptable to Calvin—as would soon become clear. In it the blame for Caroli's departure from true doctrine was laid not so much on Caroli himself, as on others. Calvin, however, had already returned to his home by the time this passage was drafted, and it was not delivered to him until shortly before he was to go to bed. What happened next is best described in the account he provided to Farel:

> The articles were delivered to me very late at night, and when I read them I was more shocked by one clause than I have to my knowledge ever been this entire year. Early the next morning I called Sturm to my house and poured out my pains to him. He in turn told Bucer, and they settled on a time for me to come to the house of Matthias Zell where I could relate what it was that anguished me so. And there I gravely sinned *[graviter peccavi],* for I could not restrain myself. I was so galled that I just burst out with bitterness spilling over on all sides.

Calvin let himself go completely after feeling he had been misled. He had the impression that the others were trying to settle things quickly behind his back. He continued:

> I ended with the words: I stand resolute, I would rather die than sign. By that point in time, however, our anger had become so heated that I could not have been sharper with Caroli had he been there himself. Finally I stormed from the room. Bucer came after me, brought me around and calmed me, and then we walked back into the room. I said that I wanted to think things over very carefully before giving my final response. When I returned home, I was suddenly completely overwhelmed. I could find no comfort, and only sighed and cried.

Calvin was a very emotional man, a person very different from what we

would expect on the basis of the image that has come down to us. He wrote
as a man aware of his stubbornness, one who could hardly be moved from it
even by the mildness of others, but above all one who could get so worked
up over injustice and unfairness that he became sick. Yet his character was
such that he remained straightforward and honest. In 1540, when the same
Caroli complained to him that he was unable to find work, Calvin wrote
him a long letter exhorting him to an attitude of humility and conciliation.
If only Caroli would stop accusing others who had done no wrong simply to
maintain his own innocence, he would be making a good start. "We would
be glad to forget everything and forgive, if only you cooperate normally
once again. . . . I wish that you could look into my heart, since there is nothing I desire more than that you first reconcile with God so that thereafter
you can once again be bound with us." Calvin was evidently concerned for
Caroli, and continually urged him not to give up hope. If Caroli would only
stop being so arrogant, everything could be resolved. Calvin said he was
ready to reconcile, but things turned out differently for Caroli, and especially for Calvin himself.

ON THE HORIZON

One cannot see Geneva even from the top of the Strasbourg cathedral on a
clear day. Nevertheless, the city remained constantly within Calvin's sight.
He closely followed the developments there, but would not have gone back
for all the gold in the world. When Viret suggested he return there, Calvin
could only laugh.

> I could not help but laugh at that part of your letter in which you so kindly
> looked to my well-being. Am I to go to Geneva for my good? Why not di-
> rectly to the cross? It would be better to die at once than to suffer repeatedly
> on that torture rack. In short, my dear Viret, if you want me to get better,
> you should drop your plan.

Calvin, though, did return to Geneva. He went there once again, completely against his own will, and yet completely sure that his return was in
keeping with God's way—a way of which he was so convinced and which

he appears to have known so well. It is clear that Calvin experienced doubts and trials, but according to him they were never so strong that he no longer knew God's way. Calvin was not self-assured in his decisions, and he certainly did not think he was faultless in them, but it was still clear to him where he ought to go. As the Genevans would soon discover, it was also clear to him which road others ought to take.

5

PREACHER

(1541-1546)

ELEVATION

The fact that pulpits are elevated above pews has less to do with the pastor's stature than with the importance of the message. The message comes from above, and the preacher only passes along the Word. The preacher's importance is, therefore, both great and limited. It is for the sake of hearing that the pulpit is raised. According to the Scriptures, Jesus preached from a fishing boat to crowds on the shore. This was not merely to keep distance, but to better reach his hearers. Calvin's pulpit was also at a distance so that he might come closer, elevated so that the Word might descend.

Calvin took his task as a preacher seriously. He saw the preacher as God's ambassador to the church. Calvin thought that when he spoke as a preacher, it was God himself who spoke. This also meant that Calvin would have to account for every word he uttered. It was for this reason that Calvin could not ascend the pulpit without careful consideration, because he thought of it as "the throne of God, and from that throne he wants to govern our souls." The presence of the pulpit meant that at church the congregation would come face to face with God's judgment seat, where guilt must be confessed and where forgiveness would be obtained. For the preacher it meant speaking only after first listening respectfully to his Taskmaster. This was true not only for Calvin but also for every other preacher. If a pastor did not first become a student of the Word, "it would be better if he were to break his neck while climbing into the pulpit." "For God there is nothing higher than the preaching of the gospel . . . because it is the means to lead people to salvation." Calvin had enough self-knowledge to realize that he himself had to be subject to the Word as well. "When I climb into the pulpit, it is not simply to instruct others. I do not exclude myself, since I myself must remain a student as well, and the words that come from my mouth are to serve me as much as others. If not, woe to me!" According to Calvin, the power of the Word of God to change people was twofold: first it changed God's enemies into his children, and second, it taught God's children to honor their Father more and more.

MOUTH OF GOD

Calvin wanted to be the mouth of God: "For of myself I have nothing to say, but I speak as if the mouth of the Teacher." This was a lofty claim, and it also came with a risk. One needed to be most careful with what one said to avoid presenting one's own word as the Word of God. Calvin, however, wanted to maintain a high view of the preacher's office, and once again this was rooted in his concept of fatherhood.

> It ought to be a hard and fast rule for you to consider as fathers those who have the office of ministers of the Word, as long as the care of your souls is entrusted to them. . . . With that I do not mean to rob you of the right that God has given to you and all his people, to examine all preachers so as to be able to distinguish the good from the bad, and to turn away those who, disguised as shepherds, are as wolves on the prowl. I only want you to act in a Christian manner toward those who make a good job of their duty as preachers.

And what a duty those preachers had to carry out! Geneva was divided into three church districts, each with its own building: St. Pierre, St. Gervais and St. Madeleine. On Sundays each church held three services, the first at sunrise, the second at nine o'clock and a third at three o'clock. At twelve noon, there was a children's service, where the catechism was taught. Throughout the week additional services were held in each church every Monday, Wednesday and Friday. In short, there was more than enough work for a pastor seeking it. Calvin not only sought it, he was compelled to work hard as well. In October 1549, the city council decided that there should be more preaching, and expanded the schedule to include sermons on every day of the workweek instead of only(!) three days a week. From then on, Calvin preached twice each Sunday and, every other week, on all workdays as well, which made for an average total of ten new sermons every fourteen days. In spite of his heavy schedule, Calvin wanted to prepare well, and as a rule he withdrew after dinner to prepare for the next day. He said he would have been a "conceited prig" if he were to ascend the pulpit without first studying the Scriptures, expecting God would lay some words on his heart at that time. Still, Calvin complained constantly that he did not have enough time for thorough preparation.

PREACHING STYLE

Calvin preached in a style that was easy for people to follow, using short, clear sentences. This was apparently so remarkable at the time that he is considered the inventor of modern French sentence structure. Without using any gimmicks, he drew greater crowds than his colleagues. He simply preached through the books of the Bible from beginning to end, passage by passage, closely following the text, explaining important Hebrew and Greek concepts, and making short applications. This also meant one had to look up the appropriate passage of Scripture if one wanted to know Calvin's view on any given topic; one would never catch him expounding what did not arise from the text. Calvin's strength lay in the way he applied the text to the situation of his listeners. His sermons built bridges between the past and the present. Calvin could do this very well as a trained orator, but even more so as a theologian: he saw that throughout the centuries there had simply been one history, one church, one chosen people, and above all one God who remained and remains the same, and whose nature and plan did and do not change. This, by definition, was precisely how the Word of the Scriptures remained relevant. Calvin preached at St. Pierre on Sundays, usually elsewhere in the city during the week. His sermons lasted at least one hour, and the time was measured using an hourglass. Thus, short sentences did not mean short sermons, and Calvin's oft-praised *brevitas* ("brevity") had nothing to do with the length of his sermons or writings, but with his ability to explain clearly using only a few words.

Calvin, however, complained that people did not always pay attention. He remarked, for example, that "when we administer baptism there are people who just walk about a bit and others who talk business." Even worse, some did not really attend to the sacrament at all, waiting by the door for the sermon or baptism to be completed since they were really there only to recognize the baptized child. For Calvin such people were like "swine who peek their heads around the corner and then turn around without coming in. . . . Baptism and sermon do not at all interest them."

Speaking of swine, it should be noted that Calvin frequently compared people with animals or gave them animal names, but this was not just intended to be insulting. Calvin saw the human ability to distinguish between good and evil as a crucial difference between people and animals. He saw, however, that many people disregarded the good and indulged in all kinds of iniquities, and these he simply called animals. "Let everyone thus be on guard, and not be led like a mindless animal as if unable to distinguish even which is the safest path to take." Calvin's ideal believer could use the Bible to make decisions independently, to see and to do what was good, and to abandon what was evil. Thus he emphasized knowledge—not a knowledge that was merely intellectual or rational, but an existential knowledge that enabled one to serve God and neighbor, to live and to die well.

COMPLAINTS

Criticism of his sermons would occasionally come while Calvin was still preaching and often had as much to do with his policies in general as it did with any particular sermon. In 1547 a poster was found attached to his pulpit warning that Calvin and company would soon meet their end—something that obviously did not happen. In November of the same year, a complaint was registered against Philibert Berthelier, secretary of the Little Council, who had tried to disturb Calvin's preaching with loud coughing. When confronted, Berthelier responded by remarking that his body could produce other sounds that would be even more irritating.

From the pulpit, Calvin could lash out vociferously against abuses and improper behavior, but he claimed to aim at moderation in such rebukes. He expected the same of the others pastors, instructing them as to how they might best attain that goal. Admonition was necessary, but it had to be done carefully "so as not to bruise the souls with immoderate harshness." Above all, the pastors should not insult people or give the impression that they enjoy their admonitory task. The people were to be able to feel that the pastor's concern was for the congregation's welfare. A kind heart, not yelling, would help people. Calvin also felt there was no room in the church for cold pastors. Pastors were not only to bring God's Word to the people, they were also to plead before God on their behalf. Taking his cues from the Bible, Calvin saw the preachers as the friends of the bridegroom whose duty was to ensure the welfare of the marriage between Christ and his church. They could only do this if they dearly loved both Christ and their congregations. "So get rid of all coldness and indifference in it, because one who is cold is not cut out for this office!" A pastor's warmth must be sensed in his preaching. Boring preaching styles were likewise to be done away with. Calvin called sermons that were more like lectures "dead." In spite of criticism, Calvin always addressed his listeners as believers, as people with an unbreakable bond with God. On that basis, he called them to be mission-minded: the church was to grow in numbers, and each member of the congregation was to work in word and deed to bring others to faith.

IMAGES

Calvin may be known as a fierce opponent of images in churches, but he was nevertheless a fervent proponent of images in preaching.

Let those who want to do well in carrying out the task of the ministry of the Word learn not only to converse and to speak publicly, but especially to penetrate through into the conscience so that people can see the crucified Christ and his very blood as it flows. If the church has that kind of artists, it will need neither wood nor stone, that is to say dead representations, and will in fact not need any images any more at all.

Calvin demanded rhetorical efforts from the pastors that would make matters of faith visible for their hearers.

Calvin's preaching had a strong teaching element, and he frequently spoke of the church as the school of God *(l'escole de Dieu)*. God was the pedagogue or teacher, the Bible was "the school of the Holy Spirit," and the believer was a "student in God's church." As mother the church not only gave birth but also nourished and educated her children. Instruction was a lifelong affair, and even at the edge of the grave "God calls us to his school." Human beings, after all, have a short memory, forget quickly and have a constant tendency to seek out all kinds of new things. Frequent repetition of the curriculum was best. Just as teachers and parents had to repeat their instructions, so also in the church, teaching had to be reiterated again and again, yet in a fresh manner. Sin would constantly lead men and women from the right path *(droit chemin)*, and this fact alone made constant education a necessity; A thorough knowledge of the Bible would help reveal the wanderings with which humanity had to be confronted. Left unchecked, such strayings could be a poison that would make people sick, even to the point of death. Instruction in the Scriptures would result in knowing what God wanted and how he could and must be worshiped. One also needed to pay attention during the sermon, however, "for we do not come to the preaching to say 'I was there,' but to reflect on the Word that we have heard." For Calvin, the sermon was to last beyond the service. By now it should also be more than clear why the Reformed life has for centuries centered around preaching.

BACK BUT NEVER GONE

In the pulpit, Calvin stood alone, over against the people. He wanted to be there only and completely for their sake. From 1541 onward, the people he served in this way were the people of Geneva. He had actually not wanted to go, but—as every good Calvinist knows—this was exactly the reason he had to go. Just as one should curb one's enjoyment, so one should also do what one actually did not want to do. Calvin said so himself: "The more I balked at returning, the more suspicious I became of myself."

In a sense, though, Calvin had never really left Geneva when he returned there on September 13, 1541. Three years earlier he had indeed been forced to leave the city in body, but in spirit he had remained bound to it. During his absence, Calvin wrote several pastoral letters addressing escalating tensions that threatened to produce a schism within the Genevan church. In these letters, Calvin's tone was full of interest in and concern for the affairs of his former congregation. From this, it is perfectly clear that deep in his heart it was not at all true that he wanted nothing more to do with that awful city. Within Geneva, people had seen that the situation had not improved during Calvin's absence. He was, in fact, vindicated in 1539 when with his help a new conflict over the Lord's Supper was settled in the nick of time, even though he was not present. Another step toward his return was taken with his letter to Jacopo Sadoleto. Though his reply to Sadoleto was formally a letter to Rome and the Catholic world, it was in fact also a letter to Geneva. Though it was never intended as a cover letter for an application to return to their city, Calvin's letter greatly pleased the Genevans when they saw that the Frenchman they had expelled was putting forth such efforts on their behalf. They were, in fact, so pleased that several attempts were made to get Calvin back. "Come and help us," was a cry that went up from other Swiss as well. Calvin, however, had no desire to go back at all: "Should I be looking for a way to go back to that hell?" He even said that he would rather die a hundred other deaths than return to that Genevan cross, where he was sure to meet his end a thousand times a day. Calvin was exaggerating, of course, but clearly he had no desire whatsoever to return to that awful place. He knew that life could be a struggle, but in light of the mental anguish he had endured during his time in Geneva, one would be hard pressed not to pardon him for supposing a return would end in nothing but more harm. God was his witness that he had put up with the previous hardships only because he had felt the yoke of God's call; when he departed he experienced it as deliverance by God's own hand. It would only be foolish to return. Even if there were no danger, he would still be unable to make any difference whatsoever: "the way the people are there, they will not be able to put up with me, nor I with them." Just as Saul (1 Sam 10:22), Calvin hid for a time among the baggage. He claimed that he was, after all, very busy with the religious dialogues that allowed him to serve more churches than just the one in Geneva. Similarly, the church at Strasbourg would not want to see him go, either. In the end, however, Calvin submitted once more to Farel's powerful and authoritative words when the latter again called him to account before God's judgment seat. "If I were able to choose, I would do anything but obey you. But since I know that I am not my own master, I offer my heart to the Lord as a sacrifice." Calvin claimed that he wanted only to follow God's voice, and thus he had more tears than words when a meeting with delegates from Geneva took place. "Two times a flow of tears interrupted me as I spoke so that I had to take a quick break outside."

SACRIFICE

The decision had been made, and after wrapping things up in Strasbourg, Calvin arrived in Geneva on September 13 with an apology for being a little late. He presented a proposal for the organization of the church and further announced his desire to be a pastor to Geneva for the rest of his life, adding that this resolve had met with Strasbourg's approval. It is as if fear of another accusation of self-interest led Calvin to make clear in word and deed, and as soon as possible, that he wanted nothing more than to follow God. "But since I know that I am not my own master, I offer my heart to the Lord as a sacrifice." He preferred the cross of Geneva to the judgment of God—and to the judgment of other people. Calvin never did his work unwillingly, even when he would have preferred to decline the task, and so he acted as if nothing had happened, though he knew full well that he could have done things differently. "I could have laid into that entire pack that had insulted us, but I let it go." Calvin wanted to make his enemies into his friends and tried to accomplish this through self-restraint. He knew this would demand his best efforts, and therefore immediately followed it up with a prayer: "May God cause me to be resolute in my resolve." Bucer said that Geneva ought to be glad that Calvin was back and wrote to the city council that they had better listen to him, or rather to Jesus Christ in him, because he would establish his teaching and discipline in the city through Calvin. Thus not only Calvin, but others as well, were convinced of his divine mission. He took up residence near the St. Pierre cathedral in the rue de Calvin, which of course had a different name at that time, the rue des Chanoines.

MORE THAN PREACHING

So Calvin began to preach again, simply picking up with the text of his first sermon where he had left off three years earlier. It was a sermon that bore no grudge or traces of criticism, and it was as if nothing unpleasant had ever happened. At least, that was how Calvin saw it:

> When I went to preach again for the first time, there was not a soul that did not sit up straight, full of curiosity. However, I completely passed over everything that had happened and that they surely were curious to hear about, and devoted a few words to explaining the essence of my ministry. Thereafter I gave a short testimony of my faith and the sincerity of my intentions. Then I chose to expound on the passage to which I had come before my banishment. In this way I hoped to show that I had not put down my teaching office, but had only interrupted it for a while.

The true Calvinist never looks back for long, and simply goes on ahead.

During Calvin's first stay in Geneva, he thought little was being done in the church there aside from preaching, so he now eagerly grasped the opportunity to do more. Organization of the church was first on the agenda, and so in 1541 Calvin wrote a piece titled *Ordonnances ecclésiastiques,* which became the basis for an ecclesiastical structure that has by now been managed with reasonable success throughout the world for several centuries. Officially it was the product of a seven-member committee, but in fact the other six men had hardly any say. On one central point, however, Calvin was the one who had hardly any say, since the council wanted to maintain its jurisdiction over ecclesiastical affairs while he sought a free church having the right to exercise discipline autonomously. His inability to accomplish this resulted in numerous problems and disputes, which were for the largest part not resolved until 1555, when Calvin's supporters were finally elected and could give him room to shape his free church concept. In 1541, however, things had not progressed nearly so far, and thus the *Ordonnances* read that "pastors have no civil judicial authority whatsoever, but only wield the spiritual sword of the Word of God." These words sound nice, and indeed they are nice, but if a church really wants to get anything done, these words are of course worthless. It should also be noted that it was the council that solemnly pronounced them on November 20. The implication of this small fact is that the supposedly scandalous things of which Calvin has been accused for centuries were nothing other than the results of laws enacted by the government of Geneva and received by its citizens. The introduction to the church order thus also read as follows: "In the name of Almighty God. We syndics, Little and Great Council, assembled with our people at the sound of the trumpet and the great bell, according to our ancient traditions . . ." This was followed by regulations concerning the offices, home visits, care for the sick and poor, administration of baptism, admission to the Lord's Supper, exercise of discipline, church attendance—the whole set of measures for which Geneva has become so famous, and—dare we say—by which it also became so important as well.

PULLING

Within three months of Calvin's return, the consistory of Geneva—famous and infamous to this very day—began to meet. Calvin was actually the inventor of the consistory, although his conception included many elements he had learned from others, especially Bucer. Calvin did, however, give the consistory its final form and its two particularly notable structural features: attention to church discipline and organization of church offices. In the consistory, these two aspects of church life are most closely related. Throughout subsequent centuries, Calvin and his followers have been given a bad rap over church discipline. It is fitting, therefore, to consider first Calvin's conception of discipline and its exercise.

According to Calvin, the Bible makes it clear that God demands a Christian lifestyle and that he uses means to stimulate it. One of these means is discipline. Interestingly, in Bucer's language (German) the word for "discipline" was *Zucht,* derived from the verb *zuchten,* meaning "to pull in." Thus discipline was not meant to exclude, but to draw in, to draw people back to Christ and the church. The task of pulling in fell especially to the elders of the church, whose biblical task was to comfort and encourage. Discipline was encouragement, but encouragement of a kind that at times needed reinforcement in the form of exclusion from the table of the Lord's Supper and, if need be, from the congregation itself. Not only was the church to be kept as pure as possible, but those who strayed onto the wrong path had to be shaken from their slumber so that they might turn back in time. In later years, church discipline was also used to vent frustrations or get rid of difficult people, but this cannot be blamed on Calvin; he would be the first to say that abuses of discipline could not invalidate its proper use. In Calvin's time, the debate over discipline did not revolve around whether or not it was needed—everyone was more or less agreed on its necessity. Long before Calvin had come to Geneva, the people wanted the city to be characterized by Christian living. Toward that end Calvin was doing nothing but contributing to what the citizens of Geneva already wanted, assisting them in the creation of a city that was as Christian as possible. The great matter of debate in Calvin's time was not discipline per se, but rather whether the church should exercise discipline, or whether this was a matter for the civil government. The government itself wanted control over these matters, even if only to prevent the church from regaining the position of dominance it had held until the Reformation. The church, on the other hand, claimed that by definition the disciplinary dimension of the Christian life belonged to it. There was fear that a civil government exercising Christian discipline might be tempted to let itself be persuaded by nonbiblical motives.

UNWILLINGNESS

Calvin himself was of the opinion that Christian discipline belonged not in the hands of the government but under the control of the church. He immediately communicated this to the magistrate and submitted a church order that reflected his position. To his dismay, however, the magistrate would not allow all of Calvin's proposals, and his hope for a church that was fully free was unattained. There was, at least, some form of church government, which Calvin saw as necessary in order to work out what was being preached. Interestingly, in the years 1541-1546, Calvin was also Geneva's most important juridical advisor. He was not only making rules in ecclesiastical affairs but also drawing up new legislation for civil matters when his services were requested. In none of this, however, was Calvin a great innovator. He went to work carefully, making just a few changes to the episcopal charter of 1387. Some penalties were softened and steps were made to ensure that everyone would be given equal treatment. Some were soon to discover firsthand that from then on the wealthy and prominent would be punished in the same measure as those less well-off. It was to be very significant for further developments in Geneva that Calvin, who had been given a solid juridical training, received reinforcements in Theodore Beza and Nicolas Colladon, two French refugees who had completed the same course of study. Colladon had even taught law for eleven years (1531-1542) at the university of Bourges and thereafter had worked as lawyer.

Calvin's attempt to put all of the above into effect collided with the will of Genevan people and met with heavy resistance. Calvin saw this as nothing less than resistance to God's Word, while from Geneva's perspective Calvin was showing a neglect of Genevan traditions and circumstances. It was another round in the old conflict between Christianity and culture, faith and tradition, conversion and preservation. Calvin never said he was unwilling to take account of Genevan customs, but he did maintain that the Scriptures were above and, in this case, against them. In short, Calvin and Geneva made for an odd couple: they didn't seem able to live with or without one another. Calvin thought God would not allow him to leave Geneva, and the people of Geneva knew they could not afford to lose Calvin. Though they never actually said so, the Genevans had more than enough opportunity, and perhaps even cause, to banish Calvin again after his return in 1541—but they never did.

CONSISTORY

Calvin's church order listed four offices: deacon, elder, pastor and doctor. Calvin thought these four were all found in Scripture and were fully directed to the holiness of the congregation, the salvation of the people and the glory of God. That Calvin saw the four reflected in Scripture should not be taken to mean that they were really all there: no trace can actually be found of Calvin's offices of pastor and doctor. When it comes to the pastor, the case could be made that this was an elder with a special task and training for preaching the Word, but hardly any biblical support at all can be found for the doctor. Whatever the case may actually be, Calvin saw four offices, and this was how he implemented them.

Perhaps the most remarkable feature was the office of the elder. Elders were clearly mentioned in Scripture, but the way Calvin gave interpretive shape to the pertinent biblical passages was still unique. For Calvin elders were the real shepherds since they oversaw the flock, brought comfort in adversity, pointed out the way of faith, and dealt out blows with the rod of discipline to those who wandered too far from God's flock in doctrine or manner of life. During his stay in Strasbourg with Bucer, Calvin had already seen how this system could work, and considered it *the* instrument for turning Geneva into a God-pleasing city. If Calvin had had his way, the elder's office would have been exercised fully within the fold of the church, but the council thought this went too far and instead Genevan elders became semi-public servants. As a result, the body of elders came to have something of the feel of a police force, and this had been exactly what Calvin wanted to avoid. The perception that Calvin was to blame for the criminalization of church discipline is, therefore, wrong. It was the council that did not pass up the opportunity to crown the elders as "servants or deputies for the magistracy in the consistory." Thus the consistory became another avenue of the government's greater control of the city, and the matters of church discipline treated on Thursdays came to acquire a more legal character. For Calvin, however, what was meant to have been of primary importance was not so much discipline and public order, but one's life with and for God. "The strictness must not be such that people are only weighed down by it, and the punishments must likewise not be anything but remedies to bring sinners back to our Lord." Twelve council members were appointed as elders and met together with the pastors every Thursday.

Calvin described two, or actually three, types of deacons. The first two were official, and consisted first of those who looked after the financial matters of the church, and second of a group entrusted with the task of visiting the sick and the poor. The third type of deacon was the congregation itself, which was also to be active in the care of the sick and the poor. The doctors existed to ensure that the preachers were well-instructed in doctrine and were intended especially to prevent the pure gospel from being obscured by human opinions. The doctors were also appointed to the city council in consultation with the pastors. All of the church offices, therefore, were intended to fit together: elders were to help people stay with God and on their way in adversity and in prosperity. Pastors expounded God's way from the Scriptures; doctors educated the pastors and further guarded the purity of doctrine.

AT THE TABLE

The whole team and affairs of church discipline came together at the Lord's Supper where God, the officers of the church and the congregation sat at one table. At that table it became clear that Calvin had developed a church order that was characterized by qualities that would be welcomed as revolutionary by a great number of other Frenchmen some two-and-a-half centuries later: *égalité, liberté* and *fraternité*. At Calvin's table all were equally sinful and righteous, all were free of guilt and free from all masters except Christ, and all were bound together as brothers and sisters. It was the consistory's task to guard these revolutionary fruits.

The Genevan consistory was to become world-renowned, especially be-

cause of the concept of discipline it embodied. There were also councils that
dealt with ethical matters in Bern, Zürich, Strasbourg and Basel, but what
was new in Geneva was the consistory's right of excommunication that Calvin demanded, and managed to obtain. The consistory, however, was in no
way a court of law; it was rather an advisory body that judged disputes and
dealt out admonition rather than punishment. Calvin himself acted particularly in the role of a mediator, something that is evident from the minutes of
many cases. One example of this occurred early in 1548 when the young
man Jean Frochet was summoned before the council. Instead of going to
work, Frochet had hung around with a bunch of ne'er-do-wells who spent
most of the day drinking. Calvin told him that a young man such as himself
ought to live a chaste and modest life, to honor and care for his father and
mother; he ought not to spend his time with a group of alcoholics. Later, on
March 1, the hatmaker Marquet and his wife were called to appear before
the council because of a marital dispute. Marquet had hit his wife when she
did not obey what he claimed was his clear instruction not to spend so much
time with the wife of a certain Phocasse. Marquet's wife claimed never to
have heard such a demand. Furthermore, her husband had hit her so hard
that she had fallen ill because of it. Calvin admonished Marquet, saying that
"it is not fitting for a Christian man to treat his wife in this way." He also
admonished Marquet's wife not to go to the Phocasse house if her husband
did not really want her there. A week later Claude, the widow of André
Dhatena, came before the council because she had committed adultery with
a young man who had by then already left the city. Earlier, she had already
spent eight days in jail for a similar error. Calvin addressed her, told her that
a woman who did such a thing was to show contrition before God, and let
her go with the warning that she should not let herself be tempted like that
again. These were just a few of the cases that clearly show how Calvin and
the consistory aimed at reconciliation and peace between God and humanity. Those who were summoned to Calvin's consistory did not appear before
a court of law, but before a confessional, and likewise did not leave with a
penalty, but with an *absolvo te*.

PROJECT

Given his ideals, a huge project lay before Calvin, and he had a long and difficult journey ahead of him to organize affairs in Geneva as he thought God wanted them to be and as the city itself had asked him and pledged itself to do. He began by gradually replacing the pastors—a matter he considered highly necessary. "Our colleagues are more an obstacle than a help: they are rough and conceited, show no initiative, and even less knowledge. But the worst is that I cannot trust them." This, of course, was Calvin's side of the story, but the archives confirm that as things stood in 1538, the group of pastors hardly knew their business, and in varying degrees were guilty of the usual sins involving alcohol, money and sex. Calvin claimed that at the time of his return he had had the opportunity to replace them all at once. He refrained from doing so, however, because he wanted to do whatever was possible to keep the peace of the church of Christ and also avoid the reproach that he was acting too forcefully.

If things are to go well in the church as a whole, they had better first go well among the pastors. Several of Calvin's colleagues were friendly enough to him, but others were outright hostile. Nevertheless, Calvin tried to work for reconciliation by staying friendly, even though he knew this would be difficult for him given his own character. As it turned out, he did manage the task, "for it happens daily that those who once were enemies now become friends."

In the process, his enemies not only became his friends, but by 1546 Calvin also managed to have replaced the old guard of 1538 with pastors from France. Not everyone in Geneva was as happy as he was with this accomplishment. A group averaging between nine and twelve pastors met once a week to guard the unity of doctrine and to resolve or avoid differences of opinion. Two important institutions were established in Geneva to facilitate this. At seven o'clock on Friday mornings the *Congrégation* assembled in the *Auditoire*. Consisting of the pastors of Geneva and the outlying areas together with their assistants (and later also the professors of the Academy), this body effectually took over the functions that had belonged to the bishop. One member of the group would provide an introduction to a passage from the Bible, which would then be discussed by the group. Calvin also always participated with a lecture of sorts. Regular members of the congregation were also welcome to participate, and not only as listeners. This Bible study was intended as something of a development course for members, and as continuing education for pastors. There was room for discussion, for the treatment of new insights, but always within the context of guarding the true teaching.

Immediately following the meeting of the *Congrégation,* the *Compagnie des Pasteurs* met in a closed session. Here only the pastors participated in order to discuss the course of events and to keep oversight of one another by a variety of means, one of which was holding a *censura morum* once per quarter. This was an open conversation where each pastor was free to say whether he had any problems with the life or doctrine of a colleague, and if so, what the problems were, so that they could be resolved. Stipulated within Calvin's church order was a list of sins that ought not to be found in pastors. These naturally included quarreling, drunkenness, adherence to errors, but also such things as using the Bible in an irritating manner, lack of effort and too much interest in useless questions. In short, the list contained a broad catalog of many of the all-too-common shortcomings that have always been easily found in pastors, even though they are intended to be role models of Christian virtue to their congregations. It was in the context of this *Compagnie* and its rules that the phenomenon of the typical Reformed pastor was born.

REFORM

It was clear to Calvin that the church was in need of some major reconstruction and that a complete overhaul would be unavoidable. Exactly what he meant can be most clearly seen in a letter he wrote to the pastor of Cernex in Savoy in September 1543. Calvin wrote that so many superstitions, customs and beliefs had by now infiltrated the church that faith had become too complicated and God's honor was diminished. Within the unreformed church, people spoke to the dead and worshiped images of wood and stone. Not only were such practices unnecessary, they also dishonored God. Take, for instance, a comparison between the Mass and the Last Supper. Was there not a world of difference between them? Wasn't it a terrible sin not to accept God's grace—which is free, no less!—as one should, and instead to trouble the conscience by claiming that salvation depended in part on human effort, and that further help was to be sought from saints and the like? With all that was going on, people had heaped up all kinds of inventions and traditions, burying true worship under them. These were like dead weight. Calvin added that he understood it was difficult to do away with things to which one had become accustomed, but what had to happen simply had to happen. If one wanted to serve God well, one had to reject whatever customs had crept in and return to what God had actually demanded. Some customs were long-standing, but they would have to be done away with if they hindered God's glory. Things could not be permitted to continue as they were in the church at the time, because, as Calvin put it, a Babel of confusion had arisen for which there was no other remedy than full-blown renewal. The sacraments were not administered as they were instituted by the Lord Jesus. Numerous foolish practices had arisen around baptism, and now confirmation—which was not even a sacrament—was even seen as more important than baptism. And then there was the Lord's Supper! It had been given as Christ's gift to us, but it had been turned into an offering from us to God. The priest separated himself from the congregation to partake of the Eucharist by himself all the while incomprehensibly muttering all kinds of formulas as if he were some kind of sorcerer. When the time came for the congregation to partake, they participated in only half of the sacrament since the cup was withheld from them. Given the state of things, said Calvin, there was clearly no choice but to perform a complete overhaul.

Reformed DDR

These days, Calvin is seen less as the leader of a renewal movement and more often as a tyrant. It is imagined that it must have been horrible to live in a city like Geneva, where one was observed on all sides and where it was a civic duty to report the sins of one's neighbor. The image is something like a Reformed DDR, with Calvin as the party leader who saw

everything and overlooked nothing. This image has in its turn stood behind all kinds of other horror stories and has nourished a deep loathing for
Calvin, Calvinists, church discipline, consistories—in short, for anything
Reformed. The one tremendous problem, however, is that the popular
image has no connection with historical reality. Calvin was certainly not
the big boss of Geneva, and in fact had no political power at all. He was
indeed the chief pastor, but that got him very little in a city where the
government made all of the final decisions, even in the church, and it got
him nothing at all when that government was not particularly well-
disposed toward him. Furthermore, the ideal of a Christian state had
been adopted by the Genevans even before Calvin walked their streets.
Geneva's tough ethical norms were not exclusively theological; they also
had a strong social and political character since they were intended to
maintain peace and quiet and to cultivate an appealing social and economic climate. It is also particularly striking that many of the things long
decried as Calvinist horrors are now considered positive attributes of developed Western culture. For an example of this, one need only think of
advertisements on television and on large roadside billboards encouraging
the duty of reporting crime with cash incentives, which is intended to
promote a certain kind of civil morality. Other examples are present in
government policies that aim to intentionally cultivate civil norms and
values. Many of the same things contemporary people find horrifying and
worthy of rejection in Calvin are warmly welcomed, or at any rate, accepted without criticism in their own cultural settings.

In Geneva, as in other cities of that time, the agenda was not so much to
impose a particular religion on the population but rather to promote unity
among the people, which would also contribute to their economic and social welfare. Behind efforts to maintain one religion often lay the fear of
losing independence. United, a city could resist any threat. More prominent than the fear of losing independence, however, was another that was
felt throughout Europe: the possibility of a repeat of Münster. The disaster
of the Anabaptist kingdom, of a religiously divided city that ended in a
bloodbath and was transferred back under the power of the bishop, was the

last thing the Genevans wanted—and Calvin was a perfect fit for a city that was so inclined. Geneva's moral climate had already begun to take clear shape well before Calvin's arrival. As early as 1490, gambling in the streets and taverns was forbidden during the Mass. Two years before Calvin's arrival, the magistracy forbade all dancing in the city's streets, and in February of 1536—still prior to Calvin's arrival in May—card and dice playing were prohibited during the time of preaching and after nine o'clock at night. The civic duty to report the crimes of one's neighbor was common in the majority of cities and had been adopted in Geneva during the late Middle Ages. Geneva also generally followed the principle of *principiis obsta* (literally, "resist the beginnings," more colloquially, "nip it in the bud"), and while complaints that were made against these measures are fully understandable, they are really no different from today's complaints about speed traps and parking tickets.

In any case the number of cases treated by the consistory—which in actual fact was not a church council but a semigovernmental body—grew steadily over the years. Marital cases, for example, increased from 182 in 1546 to 323 in 1557. The increase was a result of population growth as well as a more active intervention by the council. During this period spiritual punishments became stricter. In 1546 it was mainly admonitions that were doled out, but over the years exclusion from the Lord's Supper steadily increased from 5 instances in 1546, to 36 in 1552 and 114 in 1557.

Calvin's motto, "Improve the world, begin with Geneva," largely coincided with what the city wanted for itself. Those who had no desire to place themselves under this yoke with Calvin were free to build their own city elsewhere, as Calvin wrote to the Favre family, who thought that things were becoming all too Christianized. "As long as you live in Geneva, every effort not to obey God's law is completely useless."

Calvin knew that things would never be fully perfect there, but thought people should unite in their efforts to make the church as good as it could be. This also explains the extent of his labors. Perfection would never be attained, but Geneva could still do its best to come as close to it as possible.

BICKERING

While Calvin was not fully satisfied with the way the church was organized, he was at any rate glad that there was a consistory and some form of
discipline. He would have preferred to see things as they had been in ancient Israel, where the king and the priest, the palace and the temple, had
cooperated closely though each left to the other its own area of jurisdiction. Calvin was not the only one who felt this way; many Reformers had
dreamed of the same ideal, one that is, in fact, probably to be expected in
any society where virtually everyone is baptized. The hope that Geneva
could have become a temporary new Jerusalem was thwarted by the council, which thought it was too soon for such a city, and Calvin just had to live
with it. The resultant situation, however, caused much bickering and frustration, not only between pastors and council members but also among the
pastors themselves, who were not always in agreement. This meant that
between the moment when the *Ordonnances ecclésiastiques* were solemnly
introduced with the sounding of the trumpet and the tolling of the church
bells on November 20, 1541, and the proclamation of the independence of
the consistory on January 24, 1555, there were many, many conflicts and
disputes. Public life may well have been under the supervision of the consistory, and there may well have been elders and deacons in every city
quarter, but the consistory decisions meant nothing without the backing of
the city council, and exactly therein was the problem. Calvin was no push-
over, and he had no desire to be chased from the city once again, but the
council also stayed resolute in its decision and had no desire to have its laws
prescribed by a foreigner. Thus, some interesting anecdotes still await the
reader of this book.

Things began in such a nice way. On November 21, the day after the
celebration, Calvin and several others were given the task of reforming the
Genevan law code. Calvin's gifts in the area of law were recognized, and he
put great effort into the project. The Genevans were pleased with the results, and upon completion of the new law code Calvin received a barrel of
aged wine as a reward for his efforts on behalf of the city—a reward Calvin
did not mind at all! But isn't this how it so often goes for pastors? In the

beginning everyone is happy, but soon the time comes when even sweet wine is turned into bitter gall.

What made people begin to be suspicious was the steady increase in the number of French pastors. In 1543 Calvin added four new ones, followed by two more in 1544 and another two in 1545. With a total of eight new Frenchmen in influential positions under the leadership of another Frenchman, there was sure to be tension among the native citizens.

HEARING

Calvin's most faithful listener was Denis Raguenier, but he was paid to go to church. Raguenier was the appointed recorder of sermons, and he was expected to make word-for-word transcripts of Calvin's sermons, if possible. Raguenier made a good job of it, sometimes with the help of others, and as a result about 2,300 of the 5,000-odd sermons Calvin preached were recorded. It would be nice if it could be written that records of those 2,300 sermons still exist today, but this is not the case. For a variety of reasons, among which was the pervading idea that the *Institutes* contained everything that Calvin had to say of any significance, his sermons were neglected, left lying around, and even thrown out. The latter was actually done by a librarian in Geneva who, in order to free up some room, cleaned out the Calvin section in 1805. Fortunately Raguenier did not know this would be the end of his painstaking efforts, and so in the summer of 1549, he began to take down Calvin's sermons on Acts and Jeremiah in shorthand. Raguenier took down 6,000 words per hour, which were then dictated—after the service, naturally—to a number of secretaries who wrote the texts out in full. For his work, Raguenier received half of a pastor's salary. This task soon turned into more of a business when he was joined by several additional colleagues. Of all his sermons, Calvin himself published only four, and the rest all passed through the hands of the Raguenier team first. Following Calvin's directions, the sermons were sold and any profits were directed to the *Bourse des pauvres étrangers,* that is, the fund to support French refugees. This was another way in which the Word supported the people.

LISTENING

If Calvin is to be believed, Raguenier was the only one who really listened to him at church. Calvin was rather critical of his listeners. Or was listeners to generous a term? He actually doubted whether they listened at all. The gospel was indeed being preached in Geneva, "but of what use is that when no one does anything with it?" People went to church only out of custom, and it had become a mere ritual so that "they leave just as they came in." Calvin had the impression that his congregation treated sermons just like fairytales. No wonder the people knew nothing. If around Christmas you were to ask them "whether they know what it means that God appeared in the flesh, you will be hard pressed to find one in ten who can repeat even what he had learned as a child." They are like animals that reflexively amble over to the feeding trough, "for as soon as they come to church for Lord's Supper, baptism or marriage, they do not even remember what they are asking for." The bells tolled every day, but the people ignored them. Every Sunday the bells were sounded four times to summon them, but they thought it enough to come once. "In short, by far the majority live according to the old saying: close to church, far from God." They covered their lack of effort and diligence with all kinds of idle questions, "and then they want to know why God has elected some and reprobated others." When the topic of God's judgment came up, everyone had an escape and no one was guilty. In short, "they are eager to explore the rooms in Paradise, but do not do their best to arrive there." Calvin considered it ridiculous that Muslims, Jews, heathens and papists were more diligent in their superstitions than we Christians in our service to the gospel. The use of *we* here is significant; Calvin included himself. As the preacher, he stood above the people, but as a human being he stood among them. Throughout all of the applications he drew, Calvin always stayed close to the text. This was probably the result of his humanism, according to which one could not stay close enough to the source text. A more personal reason, however, would have been his constant search for security. The Word was the only fixed point of certainty in a world in which Calvin saw all things as turbulent, in flux and in confusion. One seeking a firm handhold always did well to stay as close as possible to the text of that Word.

BATTLE SONGS

In Reformed churches people sing a lot, and what strikes outsiders is that they bring their own songbooks to the service. That many mothers have a stack of them to take to church every Sunday can be blamed on Calvin. God must be given praise, and those who know him do nothing more readily. God's Word demands a response, and singing is one means of response, preferably using God's own hymnbook, the Psalms. Calvin appealed to Augustine, who also thought there were no better songs than the psalms of David. For Calvin there was an existential element in them as well, because he saw many parallels between his own life and that of David. In the same way, he saw similar kinds of parallels between the Protestants in France and the Israelites in Egypt, the church militant and Israel in the desert, and scattered Protestants and Jews in the Diaspora. Such parallels were just too evident and suggestive not to invite comparisons and connections, and so the Psalms were understood with clear reference to the circumstances in which Calvin and the members of his congregation found themselves. The Psalms became songs for a pilgrim church, for believers who knew heaven to be their home country and were at home nowhere on earth. The Reformed became so attached to this collection that they sang from it in prosperity and adversity, while sailing the seas, fighting on battlefields, and while waiting on their deathbeds.

Behind this high view of singing there was a fear of at least two problems. The first was the problem of the silent congregation. As the Reformers saw it, Rome had muzzled the congregation. The priest sang in incomprehensible Latin, and if there was a choir, it took responsibility for what the congregation should actually do. Thus, Calvin wanted to do away with clergy and choirs that took the place of the congregation. If the Scriptures said that God was praised even from the mouths of infants (Ps 8:2), young and old should sing, should be taught to sing, and should be given something to sing from. In short, a songbook was needed. There was, however, a second problem as well. It was through song that errors could come into the church. Songs were more memorable than sermons, and since there were many songs containing unbiblical elements, Calvin thought one should not go beyond the Scriptures. On the one hand, music could strengthen the work of the Word. When Isaiah said that he wanted to sing to God (Is 5:1), Calvin commented that teaching was more readily communicated in song than in a "less lustrous" manner. On the other hand, however, because melody was like a funnel whereby wine could be poured into a barrel, poison and corruption could also quickly enter one's heart if the wrong words were set to music. Why would one run the risk of singing human interpretations when a divinely-approved, ready-made songbook could be found within the Scriptures? It is, after all, the understanding of what one is singing that constitutes the difference between a singing bird and a singing person. The heart seeks understanding, and understanding delights the heart. The heart wants to pray; music and song stimulate prayer; and so it comes full circle for Calvin.

MUSIC

Calvin had great appreciation for music and thought it striking that God had caused Jubal—a descendant of Cain, no less!—to invent it. Evidence of God's grace was to be seen even here in that the cursing of Cain did not mean that God would withhold remarkable gifts from his descendants. For Calvin this illustrated that rays of God's grace could be found even among unbelievers, and he cited as particular examples the areas of astrology, medicine and politics.

God had given humanity the gift of music in order to praise him (cf. Is 28:29), but music was unfortunately always liable to human abuse when it served nothing but pleasure and futility, when it was performed only for enjoyment, and when it kept people from more useful activities. Just as Calvin thought that idleness was a sin, he also thought making music simply for the sake of entertainment was not good. Any human activity should be directed toward a good goal. It was actually a matter of faith, for one who had once tasted God's grace would never again even think of singing simply for the sake of pleasure (Is 42:12). Perhaps Calvin had seen too much of wine, women and song to believe it was still possible to make music for pure enjoyment. Along these lines, he claimed that tambourines had a nice sound only when it came to useless, or even shameless, activities in which people would lose control of themselves and do the weirdest things. For someone who constantly sought to restrain himself and to fight all immorality, this was of course a serious matter. Similarly, Calvin did not think it was David's music that calmed Saul. Though music could help in melancholy moods, though it could refresh and lift the spirits of a depressed person, music itself was not the actual and lasting remedy; it was God's will that gave music this healing capacity. Calvin did not intend to undermine the value of music with this statement. He simply wanted to recognize God's hand behind it in order to avoid any suggestion that there were powers operating outside of God's control.

Luther too had recognized the power of music, but he used it to chase the devil away. Calvin, on the other hand, cited Plato and said that music "has a mysterious and almost unbelievable power . . . to turn hearts in one, or exactly the opposite, way." When it came to music, Calvin did not really make much of a connection with the devil. Luther sang to stand firm against the temptations of Satan; Calvin sang to warm himself against the coldness of the human heart. The virtually unbelievable power of music scared the devil from Luther's heart, but it invited warmth into Calvin's. Calvin was also the one who initiated the youth choir that sang the Psalms in harmony under the direction of well-paid cantors. As early as 1537, Calvin had suggested that the choir could help to teach the congregation to sing the Psalms again, a plan that was realized shortly after his return from Strasbourg in 1541. Zwingli had thought it impossible, but Calvin managed to introduce large-scale congregational singing that was disciplined and could also move people to greater depths of worship. Calvin furthermore thought that the Psalms ought to be sung not only in church "but also at home and in the fields."

CLARITY

The widespread notion that Calvin was an enemy of the arts, and limited the role of music in church for that reason, is thus simply nonsense. When Calvin came to Geneva, no music could be heard in the churches at all, and he was the one who actually reintroduced it in the form of singing.

That he promoted singing in unison rather than in harmony, and without musical accompaniment, can readily be explained and has nothing to do with a supposed hostility to the arts. For those who had fallen out of the habit of singing, it was only logical to begin again without complicated harmonies. Moreover, because the essence of song was the Word and the melody, instruments could only distract. Organ and multiple-part harmonies were left to the side because Calvin feared that the ear would receive more attention than the heart. "One needs to be very careful that the ear not pay closer attention to the melody than the mind to the spiritual meaning of the words." "What suffices are the simple and pure songs of praise that come from heart and mouth, in the normal language." Luther's preaching about the *claritas scripturae* became a commitment to the *claritas canticorum* in Calvin: God's praise must resound in the church with clarity, and harmony could distort that clarity. Furthermore, Calvin saw song and prayer as being so close that musical instruments could run the risk of detracting from that dialogue with God. Thus singing was not for human amusement, but for God's praise. If people were to sing in church only for the pleasure of listening, it would neither befit the majesty of the church nor please God.

CHURCH BOOK

In 1542, Calvin presented a draft of a songbook *(La forme des prieres et chantz ecclesiastiques)* composed of prayers, a series of forms for baptism, the Lord's Supper and marriage, and a number of rhymed psalms. This book had a number of characteristics that would become typical of Reformed worship books. The first was the appearance of the liturgical forms. God's people were destroyed from lack of knowledge, said the prophet (Hos 4:6), and to avoid this, Calvin thought they should be taught to know what they were doing in worship. The forms briefly summarized what the Bible says about baptism, the Lord's Supper and marriage, and before one of these was celebrated, the relevant form was read. They were constantly repeated lessons meant to ensure the reaping of even greater fruit and blessing from such events, and were also meant to prevent the mishandling of these acts to

God's dishonor as well as the detriment of oneself and others. In other words, the forms presented the knowledge of faith geared to the experience of faith. The other typical inclusion was the Psalms. Calvin's view and use of the Psalms could be treated as a subject on its own. The first songbook (*Aulcuns pseaumes et chantz ecclésiastiques*) he had published in 1539 in Strasbourg contained his own rhyming settings of Psalms 25, 36, 46, 90 and 138. Calvin, however, saw that his strengths did not lie here and recruited others for the project, including Clément Marot. As a result, the psalms of the 1541 collection were better in both text and melody. Calvin was just as concerned with melody as he was with text because he thought the melody ought to reflect the greatness and majesty of God. Calvin did not want to praise God using the melodies of street music, folk songs or bar tunes. A different style had to be created. It was to be a style with style, and with melodies of high quality, because the songs were directed to God for whom nothing but the best would do. One should be able to hear, even to feel, God's majesty in the notes, especially because God and his angels are present: "There is thus a big difference between the music people make for their enjoyment at home around the table, and the Psalms that are sung in church in the presence of God and his angels."

The order of service was rooted in Calvin's idea that the service was a meeting between God and his people, just as had been the case with the tabernacle and the temple. The separate elements of the liturgy should therefore be ordered logically, alternating between God's speech and the congregation's response. God's Word would always come first, and then the congregation would respond. God's greeting at the beginning was answered with the people's confession of sin. The sermon as proclamation of God's Word found a reply in the singing of the Ten Commandments or the Creed, whereby the congregation expressed its desire to walk in God's way, and to believe in and confess him. God then strengthened that faith in turn with the sacrament of the Lord's Supper, to which the congregation responded in praise with song and offerings of thanksgiving. For Calvin, however, God would always have to have the last Word, and so the service ended with his blessing.

PLAGUE

That blessing did not depend on the Genevan pastors, who certainly did not make a good impression when the plague broke out in Geneva in 1542. The city's magistrate had to order that the victims of the plague be given pastoral care. This order had to be given when the director of the hospital made it known that the clergyman who had provided pastoral care to plague victims had himself fallen victim to the plague. In light of the shortage of pastoral care, the duty of caring for the sick was given to Pierre Blanchet. Should he too become sick, it would be Calvin's turn. Calvin thought that some kind of agreement should be worked out among the pastors. It seemed to him inappropriate to leave off caring for one's whole congregation to attend only to the needs of one portion of it. He also maintained, however, that it was part of the pastor's office to support people in their distress, and there was no excuse for flight from one's duty out of fear of infection. Nevertheless, it was decided that Calvin should be relieved of this duty because he was considered too important for the church as a whole. With Calvin exempted from this duty, it fell to the others simply to face the plague, though they did not want to. Their initial refusal sounded very pious, for they claimed that God had not yet given them the power and determination to enter the hospital. In other words, they were saying it was actually God who held them back! Whatever may have been the case, one pastor appears to have received the necessary grace, and he eventually went to work. The harm, however, had been done. The weakness of the pastors, most of whom had come from France, caused more bad blood between them and the Genevans, widening the gap that was already there. Calvin too was reproached for his weakness, for, among other reasons, having admitted being afraid to face the danger. If one considers all the facts, however, one cannot but arrive at a different conclusion. It had already been clear in Strasbourg that Calvin was not afraid of the plague, and in Geneva it was actually the council that decided that he should be kept safe from this threat. Furthermore, Calvin's admission that he was afraid of infection does not mean he was unwilling to do his part in providing pastoral care to plague victims.

There was no lack of clarity at that time about the cause of the plague's return. Like his Catholic and Reformed colleagues, Calvin saw the plague as God's punishment meted out to all of Europe. The Catholics considered it divine punishment, specifically for the errors that had arisen through the Reformation. The Reformers interpreted the same plague as divine punishment for failing to be more avid in their work with those same errors, although they of course saw them as rediscovered truths. Calvin wrote a letter to a priest who had told him that the plague was raging in Geneva as a manifestation of God's wrath and that the people should be called to repent. Calvin replied that he was in complete agreement; God did indeed punish us for our sins and shortcomings, and it was high time that we repented and begged God for his mercy and grace. Calvin added, however, that God made no distinction between Catholic and Reformed in this respect. The Catholics were being punished for their idolatry and superstition, and the Reformed, who knew how things should actually be done, were being punished because they were not going far enough with the truth that they did have. The one side was being punished for its unbelief, the other for its thanklessness. For Calvin, nobody got off scot-free, and God was always just.

WITCHES

Plagues and witches were perceived as closely related. In Geneva, the search for a reason for the plague led to the identification of people who were believed to have entered into a pact with the devil, seeking to do as much evil as possible. Calvin reported the following:

> Recently a conspiracy of men and women was discovered that for three years had been spreading the plague with some sort of poison mix. Although fifteen women were burned, several men punished even more cruelly, some committed suicide in jail and another twenty-five remain in prison, they do not stop daily smearing their ointments on the front door locks.

There were indeed people who sought to willfully spread the disease, some of whom, for example, acted out of jealousy that others had not fallen victim to the plague. The actual number of these people, however, was quite small compared to that of the people charged with witchcraft. Between January 1545 and March 1546, a total of thirty-seven people were condemned for spreading the plague. The majority had made confessions, which is not all that surprising considering the heavy tortures they were made to endure. However much some have attempted to blame Calvin for these unseemly—by today's standards—policies, the methods used in Geneva were actually no different than what was then considered normal elsewhere as well. Furthermore, Calvin actually had nothing to say in the matter. It is not enough, however, just to say that Calvin was simply a man of his time; someone who lived and thought from the Scriptures as he did could and ought to have come to other conclusions. It is true that the minutes of the proceedings note that "Mr. Calvin, pastor, made an urgent request on behalf of the poor souls condemned to death, even for the poisoners, namely, that care be taken that they not be tortured for a long time." It remains disappointing, however, that Calvin believed in the existence of such witchcraft and even promoted punishment for it.

BREASTS

In the delicate situation, both among themselves and in their relationship to the city in which Calvin and his colleagues found themselves, the last thing they needed was a scandal concerning biblical nudity. Nevertheless, this became the reason behind Sebastian Castellio's departure from Geneva. Calvin had met Castellio (1515-1563) in Strasbourg, and out of esteem for his expertise in the classical languages he offered him a position at the gymnasium there. In the summer of 1541, Castellio became principal of the Latin school in Geneva upon Farel's recommendation, and was thus already in Geneva before Calvin's return. In 1543 Castellio made it known that he wanted to become a pastor, but at his examination it became clear—as had actually already been known—that he diverged on two points from Calvin and his colleagues. The first had to do with his interpretation of the Song of Songs, a book that has been among the most loved literature of young Bible readers for centuries because it speaks so cogently and openly about the beauty of physical love, describing the breasts of women as clusters of grapes and strong towers. For centuries theologians had considered such descriptive subject matter a little too graphic and hardly imagined that God could have intended this material to be taken with reference to its physical sense. Faced with the difficulty of removing the Song of Songs from the canon, they chose instead to apply a more chaste hermeneutic, taking the whole book as a spiritual analogy of the love of Christ for his church. Even the reference to breasts was invested with spiritual significance. Castellio had little use for such an interpretation and saw the Song of Songs as a love poem written by the young Solomon. Most Reformed exegetes today would prefer this to Calvin's view, but at the time Castellio made this claim, it was seen as nothing less than a departure from the tradition and an attack on the authority of Scripture. It can thus be no wonder that Castellio's view was unacceptable to Calvin, and not only because of the issue itself but also because the last thing he wanted then was another internal dispute. Wouldn't it plunge the people into confusion? The second issue was Castellio's disagreement with Calvin on Christ's descent into hell, a matter on which Castellio wanted to hold a public debate with Calvin. In addition to all this, the council was not very keen on the idea of appointing Castellio to a place in the ministry, either, and thus there was all in all enough reason to turn him down.

TOLERANT

Calvin, however, did not consider Castellio a heretic, on the grounds that the differences between them were not profound enough. As a result, he also had no difficulty providing the departing Castellio with a recommendation stressing his suitability as schoolmaster. "As I said, I wish we would find a way to care for Sebastian. I on my part will do what I can to help. Believe me, when I think of the future that threatens him, it greatly oppresses me." Calvin knew that Castellio did not hold him in very high regard, and for his own part, Calvin found him a little overambitious and belligerent, though not of an absolutely miserable character. Above all, Calvin considered Castellio a fine scholar. In fact, he had earlier even supported a raise for Castellio. Nevertheless, Castellio was left with a bitter taste in his mouth and accused Calvin of intolerance—an accusation that has made

Castellio the father of modern tolerance, especially after his later attack on Calvin's involvement in the Servetus affair. This raises the question of Calvin's tolerance, or rather of his intolerance. We, who consider ourselves so tolerant these days, find that we can only agree with Castellio, but in Calvin's time people thought differently. People whose views diverged widely from the beaten path were considered a danger to society. Furthermore, the tolerance Castellio promoted flew directly in the face of Calvin's efforts to cultivate ecclesiastical unity, which were based on unity in doctrine.

At any rate, Castellio resigned as principal and moved to Lausanne, but after a short time he came back to Geneva. His stay after returning was also short, since he gave free rein to himself while criticizing Calvin during one of the latter's lectures. There appears not to have been enough room in that town for two who were so alike in character, and Castellio had to leave the city again after Calvin registered a complaint against him with the council. Castellio became a professor of Greek in Basel and put his gifts to work as a Bible translator (French Bible 1555). His departure from Geneva, however, did not mean the end of contact between the two. Ten years later he would once again oppose Calvin in the Servetus affair.

BATTLE

The years 1541-1546 were characterized by battle, and Calvin launched some formidable assaults. In 1543 he published a number of forceful writings against the Roman Catholic Church, including a short piece against relics, a book on free will, and a work devoted to the question as to how a Reformed Christian was to live in the midst of Catholics. The treatise against relics was full of satire and expressly addressed to more than just theologians because Calvin wanted to make clear just how unbiblical and ludicrous it was to worship human remains. If one were to make a list of all the remains floating around Europe, he wrote, it would quickly be discovered that each apostle must have had around four bodies. Other saints, too, must have had two or three bodies each. The Nicodemites and Libertines did not escape Calvin's attacks, either. Calvin battled against the latter group all his life because he thought he saw them always and everywhere.

He identified as "Libertines," for instance, the group that had gathered itself around Ami Perrin and the Children of Geneva and who resisted Calvin's attempt at moral reform. The same term, however, was also used for other groups. Hypocrites, those who denied the resurrection of the dead, those who did not acknowledge the authority of the Scriptures, those who blurred the distinction between good and evil—all of these were Libertines. Calvin's Libertines were not really a single unified group with a particular shared identity—the only thing some of them had in common with one another was that they had departed from Calvin's ideals in different aspects of doctrine and conduct. Calvin recognized them as far away as the Netherlands, where he found them in the person of Dirck Volckertsz Coornhert, against whom he wrote his "Response to a Certain Dutchman." Coornhert argued that religion was not an external matter and that obedience was a matter more of the inner, rather than the outer, life. Coornhert was also among the defenders of Nicodemism, the other group against whom Calvin had turned earlier, and against whom he once again wrote in the period of 1541-1546. Calvin had nothing good to say about them and could not understand how anyone could so insult God by participating in the Mass, all the while knowing full well that it was idolatry. The Mass was not just a corruption of the Lord's Supper, but "its removal, destruction and abolition. . . . The Mass is full of all kinds of unbelief, sacrilege, idolatry and desecration." Calvin could be rather sharp in his criticism, something noted not only by later readers but by his contemporaries as well. He wrote to Melanchthon that he had heard that some found him too harsh on the matter of Nicodemism, but added that he did not understand this criticism. If religion were no more than a philosophical theory, it would not matter. But why would those who virtuously feared God want to be hypocrites and participate in this papal ceremony? The reaction of Antoine Fumée, a former study partner and a member of the church in Paris, was understandable: "Most people find your message extremely depressing. They complain of your heartlessness and strictness against those who live under pressure. From where you are it is easy to preach and admonish, but if you were here, you would maybe think differently of it."

APPEARANCE OF QUIET

Calvin did not think differently of it, however, and he remained as resolute and battle-ready as ever. He encountered opposition and hostility particularly within Geneva itself. As Calvin saw it, this came from an unwillingness on the part of the Genevans to conform themselves to the Scriptures, but those against whom this charge was directed saw it as a matter of resistance against the arrogance of the French pastors. Both parties were right. On the one hand, Calvin was actually only seeking to accomplish that to which Geneva had already committed itself. On the other hand, however, Calvin and his French colleagues did not always remember that Geneva had a longstanding anticlerical streak, and that they were foreigners from a country that posed a constant threat. Added to all these tumults were the plague and its consequences, the complex relationship with Bern and the internal tensions among the pastors. In short, during this period there was more than enough that foreboded a steady supply of new battles and recurrent crises. Toward the end of 1546, things appeared to quiet down a little, but that lasted only for a season.

VICTIM

(1546-1549)

DEVOTION

Calvin and Geneva were not exactly on the same wavelength. As the Reformer saw things, this city did not know what it wanted, and so he in turn did not know what to hope for or expect: "They appeal to Christ but want to govern without him." Geneva's attitude had nothing in common with Calvin's all-or-nothing style. Whatever he did, he did well, and this mindset became typical for many Reformed people after him. They do their best, no matter the time and cost. Calvin gave his all, and although he based his work on biblical norms, he had no desire to return to biblical times, simply because he knew this was impossible. Calvin had biblical ideals, but also tried to stay realistic. Nevertheless, he expected to see the devotion that marked his own life in the lives of others as well, and such expectations were bound to bring him problems, even if he did not cause them himself. Calvin suffered from an inability to accept that not everyone was as enthusiastic as he was. This was also the source of his self-defense against the charge that he and his colleagues were trying to be the big bosses of Geneva. "We brought you a message from God, and still you complain that we ask you to accept our authority over you, but it is God who wants to rule over you." The prophet Jeremiah had been resented by the people of Israel because he announced God's judgment to them. Calvin likened his situation in Geneva to that of Jeremiah among the people of Israel, "and behold, they are doing the same thing today."

All of this landed Calvin in an unfortunate and isolated position. He saw himself as a *peregrinus* (sojourner), as he wrote in 1546. He remarked to Viret early in 1546, "I am a foreigner in this city." At times he would refer to himself as a *hospes,* that is, a guest seeking temporary shelter. The Bible also spoke of believers this way: the children of God who were only guests on this earth. These two notions confirmed each other in Calvin's mind and would later build up and strengthen a Reformed restlessness in his spiritual offspring, a willingness to go wherever God called, and especially to build a church there. This feeling of being a foreigner or guest would remain with Calvin. Ten years later, when his situation had considerably improved and he had even become a citizen, Calvin again referred to himself as a sojourner in Geneva *(peregrinus in hac urbe).*

PROBLEM

The image of Calvin as one whose experiences were limited to problems, many of which he instigated, is partly his own making but owes more to some historians. Calvin immediately interpreted resistance to his policies by framing it in biblical terms as resistance to the gospel, but the level of resistance was actually not as high as he liked to believe. Historians, however, have eagerly latched on to Calvin's interpretation, concentrating on a number of specific instances, which they in turn blew out of proportion. Through their frequent and exhaustive discussions, an image of Calvin arose as one who simply made his way from one controversy to another. Once again, there were significant differences between what actually happened and the ways in which Calvin experienced it and historians after him described it. Nevertheless, Calvin once found life so difficult in Geneva that he wrote: "Today I urgently prayed and begged God at least twenty times that he might let me die." Calvin also knew, however, that God did not answer every prayer in the affirmative, and so he was to stay in Geneva, and to stay there alive.

It is high time to overturn another image: that of Calvin as the mayor of Geneva. He actually kept his distance from politics, claiming that it was because he was not suited to it and that it only brought him more hatred from certain quarters. Thus he attempted to keep away from political issues, but had to admit that he let himself get embroiled in them from time to time. He managed, though, to control himself in such a way as not to have any regrets afterward. He was glad to give up the power that others said he so eagerly sought—something that actually contributed to his sense of living as a stranger in the city. He noticed this particularly when he overheard conversations on political issues of which he himself knew nothing. Calvin felt he would have to be crazy to involve himself in political issues.

There were, of course, many political issues, both internal and external. The German emperor had begun a war against the German Protestants, a conflict that would become known as the Schmalkaldic War. Tensions increased, and Strasbourg was forced by imperial decree to reintroduce the Mass. There were rumors that the Pope was making his way to Geneva with an army of 25,000 soldiers. This fostered panic within the city. The Genevan politicians knew that internal differences and strife would only endanger the city's safety, so they pursued internal unity. In March 1547 the pastors were summoned before the Little Council and told to reconcile with one another, which—as will become clear later on—was highly necessary. Geneva's internal calm was seriously threatened by the fact that the city, in view of its location and politics, had become a particularly attractive haven for French refugees. Some of the remaining statistics are very illustrative. Between October 1538 and October 1539 a total of 10,657 refugees were given aid as they passed through Geneva; during the same period the entire population of the city was about 12,000 residents. From 1546 onward, an antirefugee sentiment arose among the citizens of Geneva, and the reasons behind this are not hard to grasp. Fewer and fewer refugees passed through, preferring instead to remain in the city. The great majority of these were French, and their arrivals were further complicated by precisely coinciding with a considerable cooling in the relationship between the Genevan government and the French pastors. The state and rumors of war also meant that every refugee was viewed as a potential enemy. This was the situation of the time, and it did not particularly work to Calvin's advantage as he attempted to realize his plans.

AMEAUX

Pierre Ameaux was one who would experience Calvin's plans firsthand. Ameaux, captain of the artillery and overseer of the city's weaponry, was a man of Protestant convictions and an early follower of Calvin. This did not last long, however, since Calvin was none too pleased with Ameaux's choice of occupation. He happened to be a manufacturer of playing cards, a product related to gambling and wild parties, to excessive eating and drinking, in short to anything and everything that was seen as a threat to social, cultural and religious life in Geneva. An injunction was soon levied against the production of playing cards, and what made it even more vexing to Ameaux was the fact that it came in the same year as his divorce. His wife Benoite was of the conviction that she could sleep with men other than her husband. She was, of course, not the first to think so, but her motivation was less common than most—and, for that matter, more interesting. Since all believers were one body and thus shared all in common, it would be unchristian to keep one's husband or wife for oneself, wouldn't it? Madame Ameaux even claimed that God himself had revealed this interpretation of the Scriptures to her. There were, evidently, enough people in Geneva who had doubts about her qualifications as a recipient of divine revelation that she ended up in jail where she was interrogated. Benoite seems to have realized that, if things were to continue as they were, she would probably never sleep with any man again, so she recanted and reconciled with Pierre. The reconciled marriage, however, did not last. Her husband soon had had enough of her and they split up. In her new difficulties, Benoite expected to receive help from Calvin and so went to visit him. She had a thing for educated men and suggested to Calvin—at that time still married—that she would be glad to move in with him. Calvin had a rather different conception of the communion of saints and tried to get her out the door as quickly as possible. Benoite was again arrested and was condemned in January 1545 to a life sentence behind bars for adultery and blasphemy. Her sentence, however, was short-lived, and ended within a few months. She was freed but had to remain under house arrest for the rest of her life.

Once lawfully divorced, Pierre remarried, but ended up in jail himself in January 1546 for libel of Calvin, which was considered as menace of the authorities. He had no job and no wife, but plenty of alcohol in him, when he aired his opinions on Calvin at a small dinner party with friends. He charged that Calvin was not only an unwanted foreigner but also a heretical pastor. In this inebriated state—which is sometimes conducive to getting something off one's chest—Pierre clearly announced that he considered Calvin to be proclaiming false doctrine. Furthermore, Calvin was preventing the city's children from learning Latin so that they could not see his doctrine was false. Calvin was also a no-good Picardian, and the French refugees who were streaming to him were set to take power. These statements were just too politically charged for Ameaux to continue to go free.

Calvin himself did not react. "In silence did I take these things in, and told the judges that I preferred it if they were not too harsh with him. I wanted to visit him in prison, but a decision taken by the council denied me entry." The friends of Ameaux asked Calvin to put in a good word for him, which he was willing to do on the condition that the suspicion that he was behind all of this would be dropped. Calvin did his best to advocate for Ameaux and then had to await the decision of the council. The city council was not sure how to handle this case because it involved a citizen of Geneva. Part of the council was of the opinion that it would be enough for Ameaux to apologize, but the party that together with Calvin and the consistory sought a more severe penalty gained the upper hand. Thus Ameaux had to parade through the city in a hair shirt and with a torch, begging God, the council and Calvin for forgiveness. Understandably, this outcome hardly contributed to Calvin's popularity, and it is incomprehensible that Calvin himself did not understand this at all. As a foreigner Calvin contributed to the humiliation of a respected citizen; there ought to have been no surprise when all kinds of disliking and hostility were suddenly directed against him. The situation became so tense in Geneva that the council was forced to set up a gallows in front of the church of St. Gervais. It was never used, but there were many people who were very irritated and even enraged with Calvin and his supporters.

SEED

"As I said before, in this city we are dealing with an internal seed of division." As Calvin saw it, he was not to be blamed for Geneva's many internal disputes; they were rooted in the very make-up of the city. This was not too far from the truth. Geneva had already suffered for some time under the internal rivalries of the city's old families with their marriage alliances, their friendships and their enmities. There was even more cause for conflict when Genevan patriotism was fueled by the many Reformed refugees who were coming from France—from the enemy! It was not for nothing that Calvin's opponents called themselves the Children of Geneva (Enfants de Genève), and aligned themselves against the group that organized itself around "that Frenchman." A look at the numbers will help to show why these sentiments arose. In 1536 Geneva had some 10,000 inhabitants, but it had grown to 13,000 in 1550, and even 21,000 in 1560, particularly on account of the waves of refugees that came into the city from France. France remained a threat, and the same was true for Bern, which would gladly have taken Geneva under its jurisdiction. There was also Basel and, of course, Emperor Charles V. In the midst of this complex of adversity, it was Calvin who gave Geneva its strength, but he would remain an outsider. Furthermore, his efforts on behalf of the city also gave many the impression that he wanted to take control, and this fear caused the magistrates to express their unease by opposing many of Calvin's proposals. Added to the mix was the lingering issue as to who would hold power in the church. In short, many elements were headed for a collision, and as it turned out, things would explode in 1546.

CHILDREN OF GENEVA

The Ameaux affair strengthened an important faction of the Genevan families in its resolve against the consistory. The so-called Children of Geneva were fed up with having to bow before a consistory made up mainly of foreigners, and the conflict should be seen not so much as one between competing interpretations of Scripture but as one between longtime citizens and new intruders. Evidence of this is also provided by the decision made by Ami Perrin. He belonged to one of the old Genevan families but was also the man who was charged by the city to try to bring Calvin back to Geneva in 1540. Six years later, however, Calvin referred to him as "that little Caesar," and, surrounded by his family, Perrin became Calvin's critic. As noted before, Calvin referred to the Children of Geneva as Libertines and thereby gave the impression that they wanted to be bound by nothing and no one. The fact of the matter was, however, that this group simply did not want to have its laws prescribed to it by Calvin, although Calvin was, in fact, only attempting to give shape to the very plans and decisions they had first set up and introduced. As so often happens in the church, this was more a matter of psychology than of theology, and looking back on the situation it is hard to overlook the childish behavior on both sides. The Children of Geneva accused the consistory of abusing their power but then refused to appear before it to substantiate their claims. When they were forced to appear, they made no attempt to hide their contempt. A ban on dancing had already been introduced before Calvin's time, but it is true that the regulations were being tightened. Calvin thought that since the way people touch each other in dance is nothing less than a first step to adultery, the purity of the body would be better safeguarded by the complete avoidance of dancing. Even if nothing untoward was to happen, it was still a rather tricky business—or, in Calvin's words, "an invitation to Satan." Dancing was thus forbidden, and once forbidden all the more interesting. It is therefore no great surprise that the Children of Geneva liked to hold dances in secret. They did the same with dice and other forbidden games, but also made sure to let everyone know that they were secretly doing these things.

Calvin told Perrin that his return to Geneva a few years earlier had not been for the fun of it. "For I did not come back to Geneva to find rest or to make money, and it would also not bother me if I had to pack up and leave again." Calvin stayed because he saw it as God's call, and claimed simply to do his duty and to seek the welfare of the church and state. As a result, he would not let anyone chase him from the city. "To my dying day I will not abandon my diligence for the city, and God is my witness!" After the elections of November 1548, the group allied with Perrin gained the majority, and in February 1549 Perrin became the mayor of Geneva. This was to be the beginning of Calvin's seven lean years.

BAPTISM

Absolutely unimaginable, today and at any time, was the practice of preachers who gave new names to children at baptism. Out of fervor for God and his honor, the idea arose that children should not be named after saints, and without any sort of discussion this policy was put into practice by the pastors. Catholic parents had named children after saints in the hope that they would come under their protection. The pastors wanted to do away with this "superstition," and so opposed names such as those of the three wise men from the East, as well as those of local (e.g., Martin, Claude), national or international saints. Calvin was lucky enough that his father had named him John and thus could easily speak out, but for many other parents the situation was not so. It could and did happen that a name chosen by parents was disregarded when the pastor decided at the baptismal font to give the child a different one. It is not difficult to imagine how parents would react when they presented their baby Claude for baptism, and the pastor solemnly said, "Abraham, I baptize you in the name of the . . ." This actually happened! From that moment on, baptismal services became even more exciting than usual, because more than once a pastor changed the baby's name. When Michael Cop, already known as a hardliner, rejected the name Balthasar and took it upon himself to assign a nice biblical name, Balthasar's father quickly took back his son, refused to recognize the baptism and angrily shouted that the foreigners were throwing everything into turmoil. The same thing happened on August 26, 1546, when the barber Ami Chappuis presented his son, also named Claude, and the pastor calmly baptized him as "Abraham." This father also took his child back, said the baptism was not legitimate, and claimed he would delay the baptism of his son until he turned fifteen, and could choose his own baptismal name. In the midst of the uproar caused by these events, and after the father of Claude—or Abraham, if you like—brought a complaint before the council, Calvin asked the council to make a decision on baptismal names. After much discussion, a list of forbidden names was drawn up, consisting primarily of the names of saints that had a longstanding connection with Geneva, the most popular being Claude, to whom was dedicated a tomb close to the city.

This whole business of baptismal names was a prime example of ill-conceived missionary activity, of mission work without regard for local history and customs. Now that the pastors wanted even to name the city's children, many in Geneva had had enough. They were fed up with it, and the protests of the most prominent inhabitants were not to be laughed at. They would no longer allow their laws to be prescribed for them and had no inclination to allow some French newcomers to overturn their long tradition of naming. Thus the new naming policy only served to increase the tensions between the inhabitants of Geneva and the refugees, aggravating the immigrant problem. Many would have agreed with that individual who prayed out loud in church that Satan might take away all the foreigners. When Calvin had to appear before the Little Council once again and was admonished for being too harsh in his preaching against the sin in Geneva, he should have realized that he had asked for this opposition with what he was doing. As an aside, however, it should be remarked that the policy was a success: the number of children named after saints dropped from almost one half in 1536, to an average of one in forty in the 1560s. By that time, some 97 percent of newborn infants were given biblical names. Nevertheless, if we are to believe what Calvin says in his sermons, this did not make the people themselves any more biblical.

THE LORD'S SUPPER

As is so often the case, it also happened that problems arose within the Protestant camp once the common enemy had been disposed of. When Luther and Zwingli had liberated themselves from Rome, they turned on each other over the bodily presence of Christ in the Lord's Supper. Their battle has configured the Protestant map even to this very day. Bucer may have called out loudly and frequently that there was no real issue between Wittenberg and Zürich, that what was at stake was more a matter of terminology than anything else, but this did not help. The issue was discussed willingly, without ceasing, and at times also without common decency. The unedifying discussions that took place particularly between the Lutherans and the Zwinglians also broke the political power of the Reformation and confirmed the Catholic supposition that Luther's message would only cause one church rift after another. The Swiss were deathly afraid of any view of the Supper that maintained even the semblance of Christ's presence, but after Zwingli's death the debate lost its sharp edges, as his successor, Bullinger, was more open to discussion.

This possibility of new dialogue between the factions was also needed because shortly before his death Luther had published a treatise against the Swiss in which, with his usual forthrightness, he identified them as nothing less than heretics. In this too it was to Calvin's advantage that he was a Reformer of the second generation. He was in a position to survey the existing range of opinions, and had the gift of being able to extract the advantages of each and to combine them into a palatable whole. Here too he was more flexible than the usual image of Calvin would lead us to think. Calvin engaged in an intensive correspondence with Bullinger in which he sought formulas that could both satisfy the Swiss and yet also justify the Lutheran standpoint. Thus Calvin arrived at a formula that spoke of Christ as present and not present at the Lord's Supper. He was not present physically, but he was fully present spiritually. Calvin made use of what he read in the Scriptures especially about the Holy Spirit and ensured that he could both relativize as well as uphold the importance of the external aspects of the Christian faith, such as baptism, preaching and the church. Calvin also understood, however, that the real presence of Christ was of enormous significance, and he therefore sought a way to combine the Lutheran and Swiss views, not merely as a tactical measure, but rather out of his conviction that they were

both partly right, and that what was right in each of them could be combined into a complementary whole.

   That whole would also benefit the Reformed cause, since by the end of
the 1540s things were not easy for them. In France, king Henry II initiated
unparalleled persecution of the Protestants; the preparations for the anti-
Reformation Council of Trent were in high gear; the Lutheran princes were
defeated in the Schmalkaldic War (1546/1547), and the Reform movement
was rewarded with the imperial Interim (1548) which, under threat of
plunder and attack, forced the reintroduction of the Mass in many cities.
For Calvin, all of this misery was added to by the fact that, since 1548, the
majority of the Geneva council had been made up of his opponents. In the
midst of all of this, Calvin thought he could make a start by doing something to address at least the division that raged within Switzerland. It was
also his hope that reaching an agreement with Zürich in the controversy
over the Lord's Supper might also help Bern become more mildly disposed.
Calvin had faith in his plan and once again gave it is his all. He trekked from
Geneva to Zürich as many as five times, and even though Bullinger did not
always receive him warmly, Calvin did not give up, because "we have the
same Christ and are one in him." The fifth trip brought success. When he
went to Zürich for a discussion with Bullinger once more in May of 1549,
the matter was settled within two hours, and a consensus was reached on
the Lord's Supper that would later carry the name of Zwingli's city: *Consensus Tigurinus*. Since the whole issue was a rather sensitive one both nationally
and internationally, the consensus document was not published and released
until 1551. Most Swiss cities could agree with it, but not Bern, of course,
since it always did whatever it could to make life difficult for Geneva.

DISAPPOINTMENT

A greater disappointment for Calvin was that Bullinger was not convinced
that this consensus would form a good basis for discussion with the Lutherans. The Lutherans themselves agreed with Bullinger, as is most evident in
their uncommonly bitter reactions to the consensus. A further problem had
arisen with Luther's death in 1546, when a significant portion of his follow-

ers wanted to be more Catholic than the pope and pushed Luther's views to their extremes. Calvin called them a bunch of apes because their work amounted to nothing more than some poor efforts to copy Luther. Poor Melanchthon, who was physically as frail as Calvin, could do nothing against the Lutheran fanatics. This was in part too because he always sought a way to unity. In Wittenberg Melanchthon lived a few doors down from Luther, but after Luther's death the so-called Lutherans tucked him in a theological corner far away from his former colleague, placing him among those suspicious Calvinists. A Hamburg pastor, Joachim Westphal, came out swinging against the entire Reformed camp. He tried to show how the likes of Bullinger, Bucer and Calvin disagreed with one another and were united only in their common departure from biblical truth. Calvin countered, emphasizing above all the difference between how Luther himself had spoken and the way his spiritual offspring did. The Lutherans almost choked on this charge, and Bullinger almost did the same; he thought Calvin spoke too positively of Luther. To make a long story short, there remained a Lutheran church and a Reformed church. The Reformed had little esteem for the Luther in Calvin, and the Lutherans hardly realized that on several essential points they were less in line with Luther than they thought or wanted to think.

POLITICS

In the meantime the conflicts in Geneva gradually progressed beyond psychology and theology, and came to have a strong political character. In the spring of 1546 a certain Favre came into conflict with the consistory because he accused the council of going beyond its jurisdiction. He thought that it was unjust that the consistory sent sinners to the city council, which would, in cases of hardening in sin, send them back to the consistory so that the latter could exercise discipline. In reality things worked differently than this, as Favre was fully aware, and so his complaint seemed likely only to rouse the public sentiment. For the consistory this was enough cause to ask the city council to demand that Favre reconcile with it. The city council, however, preferred a middle road and admonished

Favre to appear before the consistory but ordered the consistory to do nothing more than admonish him. This event is illustrative of the situation within Geneva: there were pastors who tried to carry out the policy drawn up by the city, citizens who wanted no part in that, and a council that tried to remain friendly with both parties.

Criticism of the pastors increased and became more vocal as well. Madame Froment complained of the tyranny of Calvin and company, which, for her, had gone so far in Geneva that one could no longer speak freely. The dispute caused by this became so fierce that Calvin noted, as far as he was concerned, the Lord's Supper could be celebrated without him the next time. He was sick of it all and was ready to crawl to Farel in Neuchâtel on hands and feet. After Favre's complaint, his daughter—who happened to be the wife of Ami Perrin—was summoned before the consistory for secretly dancing, and during the proceedings she called one of the pastors a lying pig. This was not the most complimentary thing to say, and so the consistory felt obligated to drag her outside by force. What a scene that must have been! The level of violence increased when a letter was attached to the pulpit, threatening the pastors with death should they not soon change their preaching. An investigation brought to light that this was the work of a former monk, Jacques Gruet, and in his home other similar documents were discovered. In an interrogation he revealed under torture that in the group gathered around Favre there was so much resentment against the French pastors that a rebellion was not unlikely. It was felt among them that something simply had to be done to prevent these foreigners from putting their feet to the throats of the citizens. Gruet was condemned to death on the grounds of blasphemy and of threatening the magistrate and pastors, and this punishment was administered on July 26, 1547. Calvin had nothing to do with the affair and kept out of it. In a sense, Gruet's condemnation was nothing remarkable: one who so openly threatened the civil order and the Christian faith would have received the death penalty elsewhere as well. That it happened in Geneva, however, and in Calvin's time, meant that for his contemporaries, as well as his later image, this would become yet another black mark against him. Calvin understood little of the commotion surrounding the events in the city and wondered why there was so much talk about it outside of Geneva. "They talk about it as if we all are lost. Particularly about me it is said that I am already dead or severely wounded. I myself have clearly not noticed this."

Yet another stage on the road of conflict was the return of Ami Perrin from a stay at the French royal court. There he had been able to round up a contingent of French soldiers who would be stationed in Geneva for the sake of the city's safety. Furthermore, plans were made public according to which Geneva would adopt an anti-imperial, pro-France politics. This made Bern uneasy, and so the Genevan government split into two factions: one for, the other against, close bonds with France. Illustrative of the high tension was the quarrel that broke out in December of 1547 in the Council of Two Hundred—among the Children of Geneva!—where it was Calvin himself who threw his frail body between the two parties: "I cried out, 'If blood is to be shed, let it be mine.'" The chance to do away with Calvin at his own invitation appears to have been so surprising that it was passed up; Calvin reports that tempers cooled sufficiently, and that everyone agreed that his action had avoided considerable bloodshed.

Swiss Tensions

These internal tensions, together with the constant external threats of Bern and Savoy, provide a partial explanation of the rather rigid implementation of a number of drastic measures. In 1546, dancing, dice, card and ball games were prohibited. The city council regulated how much cutlery and how many plates were allowed to be used at the table and also prescribed the clothes that could be worn. It was a sort of martial law where strict measures served good supervision and where close control served in turn to better identify other potentially dangerous intruders or developments. Calvin, for his part, was glad that leisurely pursuits and excessive meals—which were, in his opinion, sinful—were curbed.

Geneva also departed considerably from Bern in terms of liturgy, spurred on by the initiatives of both the city and Calvin, though with different motives. Calvin undoubtedly did the things he did on the basis of his conviction that it was biblical; the politicians will have supported Calvin's policies because they would send a strong signal of independence. While the feasts of the church calendar were celebrated in Bern even when they fell on a regular workday, in Geneva Sunday was the only feast maintained. Even Christmas Day was abolished and turned into a regular workday, which ruffled the feathers of Bern. Until 1605 Bern used wafers at the Lord's Supper, while Geneva opted for unleavened bread. In Bern virginal brides were allowed to adorn their hair for their weddings, but Calvin refused this as unbiblical. In Bern the names of those who had passed away during the preceding week were read out, but Geneva did not allow this for fear that it could instigate the practice of praying for the dead.

Relations with other Swiss cities were not all that great, either. According to Calvin the problem was what some called "strong character," but which was in fact simple stubbornness. Although an agreement was reached on the Lord's Supper, Calvin had difficulties with Bullinger's decision *cum suis* to forbid the students in Strasbourg who had come there from Zürich to participate in the Lord's Supper. "I really do not understand why they are tearing the church apart over this." In Zürich, on the other hand, they thought Calvin had been influenced too much by Bucer, who in turn had worked for agreement with the Lutherans. All of this tired Calvin out. "How can they reproach me for being a friend of someone who assures me that it is not his fault that he is not your friend and brother?"

Zürich, however, had to be won over, particularly since Bern was a constant source of trouble. During these years, Calvin spoke to Bullinger and others of a French covenant *(foedus gallicum)*. The aim was to unite all that was both French and Reformed and to go out from a strong Geneva to conquer all of Europe for God via France. The plan was intriguing, but Calvin's negotiations for tolerance with Henry II delivered no results.

STAGE

For centuries, stage, theater and cinema have had a bad reputation among Calvinists, and anyone who falls into such sins is expected to be left with at least an uneasy conscience over it. Calvin, however, spoke of creation as the theater of God's glory, and further referred to the church as the stage on which God shows who he is. The 1546 dispute about a certain theater production is therefore interesting. The play in question was based on the book of Acts. Calvin had seen the piece and had found nothing wrong with it, but several of his colleagues did. Thus Calvin had to report to the city council that there was nothing wrong with the play as such but that its production was sure to cause division and therefore had best be cancelled. The council had other thoughts, however, and gave not only approval but a subsidy as well. At this the pastor Michael Cop, Calvin's old friend, lashed out so fiercely from the pulpit against the play and the council that a crowd was waiting for him outside the church, and he had to be escorted home under police protection. Calvin too thought that Cop had gone too far, and when it was his turn to preach in the afternoon he tried to smooth things over. On the morning of Sunday, July 4, the play was performed. Calvin did not attend, not because he was against it, nor because it was a Sunday, but because, out of consideration for his colleagues, it was simply better not to go. Viret, however, did go, and reported on it to Calvin. After this the council decided not to allow any similar productions for the time being.

A further limit on entertainment was imposed with the experiment that closed the city cafeterias and opened a sort of alternative restaurant-like establishment in every quarter, supervised by a council member, where the bartender was to make sure that everyone prayed before their meals. The experiment was a complete flop. The restaurant business wanted nothing to do with it, nor did the people. Thus it was not easy to turn Geneva into a Christian city, but the above does make two things clear: first, that Calvin was not the only one who stood behind the project of city reform, and second, that at times he was more lenient than his colleagues.

ORA ET LABORA

One could easily get the impression that Calvin just moved from one crisis to the next and started his every day thinking of how he could resolve the previous day's conflict, only to start another. The reality, however, was very different. He experienced no more than did others with similar fame and position. If the disputes in which he was involved are taken out of their context and isolated, what remains is an image of a man whose anxiety to push his own project through brought him into collision with everyone and everything. Compared with the number of conflicts experienced by his colleagues during the same years, in similarly tense situations between church and state, and in cities of comparable size, Calvin's particularity is revealed in the nature, not the number or intensity, of the conflicts in which he became embroiled.

If Calvin was not always battling someone, what did he do during the day? What did a typical day look like for him? Calvin began each day with prayer. He prayed a lot because he expected so much from it. Thus a fact unknown to many also speaks for itself: the longest chapter by far of the *Institutes* is devoted to prayer. The Bible calls us to pray continually, but in Calvin's opinion nothing would come of this if you did not establish a regular regimen. Prayer too ought to be done in good order and, as with so many other things, with moderation and directly from the heart. Calvin thus established what was virtually a monastic rule: "we pray when we get up in the morning, before we begin our daily work, when we come to the table to eat, after we have eaten under God's blessing and when we get ready to go back to bed again." The worldwide Reformed practice of praying before and after every meal, at home and elsewhere, had its origin in Calvin.

After his return from Strasbourg in 1541, Calvin also introduced a weekly day of prayer. Wednesday was a day of prayer, and a prayer meeting was held every week from eight to ten in the morning. "The prayers that belong to it I wrote myself." Calvin began this practice when Germany was beset with plague and war, but evidently it pleased him so much that he kept it up after as well.

Between morning and evening prayer the largest part of the day was devoted to writing letters, preparing lectures and sermons, finalizing publications, making visits and hosting visitors, preaching, and meetings. If Calvin had really spent all day in conflict, he would never have been able to publish what he did. A quick look at his bibliography will show that these years were among the most productive of his life. Between 1546 and 1549, aside from a number of other works, Calvin published five commentaries on New Testament books and their French translations, wrote many long letters, and further delivered sermons that he also prepared for sale.

PESSIMIST

This chapter has a somewhat negative title, and so it seems a fitting place to deal with Calvin's pessimism. Calvin has often been viewed as a first class pessimist. That Calvinists make their way through life as if it is nothing but a vale of tears, bent double under their burdens, has also in turn been largely attributed to him. Additionally, Calvin's anthropology, or view of the human condition, was as dark as his view of the world! One needs, however, to ask how much light there actually was in Calvin's time. How much cause for optimism was there really? Calvin's time was one of high infant mortality and great political and social uncertainty. Europe was ready to buckle under a refugee crisis, poverty and threats of religious wars. It is no wonder that Calvin was so gloomy at times. What is remarkable, in fact, is that he still had a lot to say about the goodness of this life. What else could he have done? He believed that God had created the world with no other goal than the happiness of humanity, and this implied, among other things, the enjoyment of good food and fine wine. Although we can make do with water, God has also given us wine to make us glad. Calvin knew the dangers of alcohol, "but if wine is a poison to the drunkard, does that mean we are to have an aversion to it? Please, no. We do not let that spoil the taste for us, for on the contrary, we delight in the taste of wine!"

Nevertheless, we find in Calvin continual references to the reality of sin. He thought that Rome undermined its seriousness, giving the impression that doing penance once would suffice to blot out the sins of an entire year, though in reality an abyss of sin separates us from God. Calvin understood not only that we sin without end throughout the entire course of this life but also that we will never comprehend the scope and depth of our sin and guilt. The most fundamental sin is that of arrogance *(superbia),* which marks our entire existence. Through our arrogance we offend God. Through it we offend our neighbor. Through it we also even offend creation, which suffers under our sin. "Through a sort of natural instruction, the earth—which has no feeling or understanding at all—grieves when God is dishonored. Just the same, it rejoices when it sees God is worshiped as he should be." Calvin, who enjoyed finding rest outdoors in nature, appreciated the beauty of plants and animals. The earth was not our own, and so all these things were to be handled with care. "The earth demands vengeance when it is polluted," and it is sin that mars and pollutes creation.

From an awareness of sin, however, Calvin wanted to move to the message of grace. The teaching that only confessed sins were forgiven would lead to desperation among those who knew they might never know all of their sins let alone confess them. The only remedy was the fullness of God's grace. This grace, however, did not imply the end of God's punishment. Calvin's reflection on the Bible brought him to the conviction that there was a direct link between sin and punishment, and he did not hesitate to make very concrete connections.

> There was a man who, during the Sunday sermon, went down into the cellar of a café to get some wine, stumbled and fell onto his sword that had slipped from its sheath, so that they carried him away as a dying man. Last September, someone else, on a day on which the Lord's Supper was being celebrated, in his drunkenness wanted secretly to enter the home of a prostitute through her window, but in the process fell so badly that he was carried away with multiple fractures. I concluded: before hell swallows you and your households, you will refuse to believe in God who stretches out his hand.

Such conclusions were meant to incite people to live a Christian life, but the question is whether they succeeded. The point of Calvin's criticism was that, as he saw it, the majority of the people did not take their faith very seriously. There were innumerable hypocrites, and hardly anything irritated Calvin more than those who called themselves Christians but in the meantime offended both God and neighbor with their sins. For Calvin, things were very simple. Those who knew the holiness and grace of God would do all and leave all to worship and honor him. Those who knew his wrath would avoid sin. Those who knew his love would devote themselves completely to him. It all came down to a way of life that reached to the heart and came up out of it. Calvin admonished those who thought it was good enough just to go to church and who thought that grace was cheap. Some seemed to think that if there was forgiveness, there was no need to concern oneself with living a careful life. "The people want to make a little pact with God. They think they are square with him if they simply say *mea culpa*." As Calvin saw it, such things had nothing to do with being a Christian. Apart from inward examination and the experience and confession of one's guilt and lost state, the Christian life had not even begun.

ORATOR

Calvin felt like a victim at times, but with his pen he could also make victims of his own. With Erasmus he shared an artistic gift for mockery, and he felt it should be allowed as a constituent part of polemics. In the preface to a satirical work from Pierre Viret, Calvin considered whether mockery was permissible in a debate on theological issues. He replied in the affirmative, though he maintained a need for moderation. A theologian should be able to combine seriousness with humor in order to entertain his readers, but above all to convince them. Such humor consisted largely in poking fun at errors to show how ridiculous they really were. It should still be based on good arguments, and ought not devolve into idle talk, but given these safeguards it was certainly to be allowed. Christian doctrine ought to be laid out carefully and seriously. There is nothing lighthearted in that. To expose superstition and other theological nonsense, however, descriptions should make the reader burst out laughing. Although Calvinists are not known for their laughter, Calvin wanted nothing less for his readers, and led the way.

Calvin could be ironic particularly with Rome, as in a letter to Bullinger in which he mocked the Council of Trent.

> Although you must know that I am passing through Zürich on the way to Trent, I find it unfriendly on your part that you did not invite us even for a day. But you are surely awaiting another papal bull inviting us to Trent. Well, unfortunately we do not belong to those who by right, custom or

special privilege can before the holy papal chair lay claim to a place there. And so we can remain quietly at home, where there are also things to do. Christ gives us plenty of work, and also Satan makes sure that we are not bored.

Calvin also made fun of what Rome had made of the office of deacon.

> Those papists do that just as someone who says he wants to appoint apostles and goes on to give them the commission of burning incense, polishing images, sweeping church buildings, catching mice and chasing away dogs! Who would allow such people to be called "apostles" and be compared with Christ's apostles? Let them from now on no longer lie by speaking there of "deacons," for they are only put to work for their theater pieces.

Elsewhere Calvin explained why the Catholics attacked the Protestants so fanatically. "Do you know why they fight so fanatically for the Mass, purgatory, pilgrimages and other such nonsense? . . . Because God is their stomach, and religion their kitchen. The more someone in those circles becomes worried for his stomach, the fiercer his battle for his faith."

There is a clear distinction between the Calvin of the letters and the Calvin of personal conversation. He was like a scholar who dealt best with people when he did not see them. What he could not do effectively in actual conversation, he was able to do when putting things on paper, and this was true both for people who needed comfort and for theological opponents who needed a firm shake every once in a while. He thus saw his letters as "the living image of my soul," so that the real Calvin is to be found in his correspondence.

SICK OF IT ALL

Calvin wrote so much, however, that at times he was completely sick of it all. "I get so tired from that endless writing that I at times have a loathing for it, and actually hate writing." In reality he had little choice. Though he rarely left the city in body, he was present throughout Europe in his letters. It was yet another kind of *presentia realis*.

Calvin would have been delighted to study and write books in quiet.

When Bucer was forced to leave Strasbourg in 1549 and found refuge in England, Calvin wrote that he could only envy him because Bucer now had time and quiet to write for his beloved Germans, "while I, swamped with all kinds of work and plagued by poor health, will not have much time for that anymore." Bucer, however, had other things to do in England besides writing books in peace, and he died within two years of this letter. Calvin was to have plenty of time left, with another fifteen busy years ahead of him.

WIDOWER

(1549-1551)

A WIFE

Although Calvin was always occupied with marital questions and marital law, in his own life there was more emphasis on his unmarried state than on his marriage. We address his marriage, therefore, at the point at which he became a widower. That he did not much care for women can almost be seen in his appearance. As far as he was concerned, marriage was unnecessary, although he did oppose required celibacy. If he were to marry, he wrote, it would not be because he needed an excuse for sex, but to free himself from some of his troubles and thereby be able to better devote himself to God. He never said what these troubles were, but they would probably have been all sorts of household chores. Calvin, therefore, needed a housekeeper more than a wife. He said of himself that he was not one of "those mad lovers, who praise even the shortcomings of their loved one as soon as they are completely taken up in her." He was very clear on what attracted him in a woman. She was to be hard-working, obedient, not proud, thrifty, and if on top of that she took good care of you in bad health, you were a lucky man. For Calvin real beauty came from within.

Clearly, Calvin was not really looking for marriage. Early in 1540, he was introduced to a young woman of German nobility, but would have none of it. "I was presented with a girl of noble origins, and with a dowry that exceeds my station. But there were two things that kept me from a marriage with her: she did not speak our language, and I was afraid that she would rather too often think back to her origins and upbringing." He added that her brother urged this marriage on him because he was a strong supporter of Calvin. His wife, who was to be Calvin's sister-in-law, pressed him even more, so that Calvin almost felt obligated to take the hand of this young girl offered to him as wife. He also felt he was almost wronging her family by not marrying her. This time, however, Calvin for once did not do what his betters told him to do and announced he would not even begin to consider this marriage "unless the Lord takes away all of my reason." The Lord apparently left his reason intact, and Calvin saw it as God's deliverance that he had not given in. The extent to which God's hand was directly involved is questionable. Calvin himself wrote that he had told the girl she was to learn French as a condition for marriage. When she asked for some time to consider, Calvin saw his chance. "I immediately sent my brother and another trusted man out to find another woman for me, and this is one who, if the positive reports about her are true, will bring much into the marriage even without money, for everyone who knows her recommends her to me." From this we learn two things about Calvin's second marriage candidate: first, that she was not wealthy, and second, that she was of a good character. The third thing, however, is that she did not become his wife, either. Calvin's brother and his partner had found her, and a marriage was in the works, but when they came back and reported on her to Calvin, their information was evidently such that Calvin sent the two of them back out, this time to put an end to the matter. Calvin stayed single and thought he did well to do so, but this would last only two months.

Idelette

Martin Bucer, as renowned as a matchmaker as he was notorious for his liberal view on divorce, had other plans. He thought Calvin would do well to have a wife, and so it was that in Strasbourg early in August 1540 Calvin married Idelette van Buren, a woman from Liège who had fled for the sake of her faith. She was a good-looking woman, according to Farel. She was several years older than Calvin but looked young. The widow of an Anabaptist, she had two children, a girl called Judith and a boy whose name we do not know. She was a woman of considerable experience and thus had intimate knowledge of marriage, children and heresy. Calvin had no firsthand knowledge with any of these three experiences, but did have a connection with refugees. Besides, Calvin said, she was a woman of special qualities *(singularis exempli femina)*, and that was an added bonus. Of course any woman who was to marry Calvin would have to have special qualities.

It appears the marriage did not agree with either Calvin or his wife, since two weeks after their wedding the two of them were very sick. Calvin immediately attributed this to God ensuring that no one would take too much delight in something as beautiful as marriage, and this statement encouraged many later Calvinists to curb their enjoyment themselves before God had a chance to do it for them. Better to moderate one's own pleasure than to be afflicted by God with a sickness for it.

Calvin and his wife faced more difficulties several months later when in Regensburg Calvin heard that the plague was making its rounds in Strasbourg, and that two members of his own household were infected. Idelette had fled the house, and on April 2, 1541, Calvin wrote to Farel about his worries. "My wife is in my thoughts day and night, where she, now that I am not there, does not really know what to do." He felt helpless because he could do nothing for her. Once again, this is a far cry from the supposedly stoic Calvin.

Calvin and his wife also experienced pleasant things together as well. On July 28, 1542, Idelette gave birth to a son who was baptized with the name of Calvin's uncle, Jacques. Jacques, the equivalent of James, was thus a biblical name and not a saint's name. The birth was not without its dangers; the boy was born premature. He died premature as well, passing away after only twenty-two days. "The LORD has given me a son, but he has also taken him away." There were no further children, and when three years before his death Calvin was reproached for having remained childless, he remembered Jacques with sorrow, but comforted himself with the thought that he had spiritual children throughout the Christian world. As a further note, all of this also suffices to destroy once for all the myth that Calvin approved of a death-sentence passed upon his daughter-in-law when she was caught in adultery. It should go without saying that it is somewhat difficult to agree to such a thing, especially when one does not even have a daughter-in-law.

BEAUTY

Even when married, Calvin was not oblivious to a woman's beauty. This is evident from his remark that he knew of a widow in Geneva whom he found very well-suited for another—a certain Sieur de Fallais. "I would be glad to have her as my own wife, should God have afflicted me with the death of my wife and I would need to marry again." The death of Calvin's wife was not just a remote possibility; Idelette's already rather weak health had been further assaulted by her inability to get over the death of Jacques. Calvin's letters are full of references to her illnesses, and he often writes that she was confined to bed because of them. "My wife is recovering slowly. Now she also has hemorrhoids. Added to that are her coughing fits, which increase her pain. Nor has she shaken her fever." Once she traveled to Lausanne to help Viret's wife who had just given birth, but Calvin had to offer apologies upon her return. "I am very sorry that my wife was such a burden on you and, I suspect, was not able to help your wife that much, since she herself constantly needs to be helped by others because of her own illness."

A letter from 1545 makes clear how serious her health problems were. Calvin wrote that she had recovered a little, and that it was as if he had received her back from the dead. This went on for years, but around eight o'clock in the morning on March 29, 1549, death would no longer be denied. Several months before, Calvin had already written that Idelette was once again confined to her bed because of a long-lasting sickness, and it appears that she never recovered. "She was no longer able to speak, but could still indicate how she was doing. I spoke to her of the grace of Christ and the hope of eternal life. . . . And I withdrew to pray. With a quiet heart she listened to the prayers and clearly heard the words of comfort."

Calvin's announcement of the death of his wife to Farel speaks of his great love, care and grief.

> Because she never spoke of her children, I was afraid that she worried about them in her heart but did not really dare to say this even though this worry tormented her more than her illness did. So I told her in the presence of the brothers that I would care for her children as if they were my own. She answered, "I have already committed them to God." When I said, "But that does not mean that I am not ready to do my part for them," she responded, "If God cares for them, then I know that they are commended to you as well." Her willpower was so strong that she already appeared to be beyond this world.

Calvin related the same story to Viret some five days later, which attests to his great concern for Idelette's worry about her children. Calvin described Idelette's last hours to Farel, how he time and again came back to her throughout the night to encourage her with God's grace, and then would withdraw to pray. The end came in the morning: "Shortly before eight she quietly breathed her last, so that those who were present barely noticed her passage from life to death."

HALF A MAN

Calvin claimed that he had lost his best friend, adding that she had been extremely faithful in helping him in his ministry. These are nice testimonies, but Calvin felt the need to add also that she never hindered him in his work. For one as truly afraid as Calvin was of the possibility that marriage could do this, this is, of course, a positive observation. Still, although it is to be hoped that everyone might claim his or her partner was no hindrance, we might also wish that Calvin had simply dropped this remark. Here, however, he was as open as he was everywhere else, as is also true of his remark that he tried to deal with his grief in such a way "that I continue my ministry without a break." His work had been given to him before the woman, and his work also continued without her, and working hard did indeed help him overcome his grief. Nevertheless, Calvin would have to continue life as half a man: "I am no more than half a man, since God recently took my wife home to himself." That Idelette was more to him than just a helper and no hindrance is all the more clear from the letter of comfort Calvin sent several years later to a colleague at a French church in Frankfurt when he had also lost his wife: "What a terrible injury, what a pain the death of your wife has caused you, and I speak from my own experience. For even now I fully know how difficult it was, seven years ago now, to deal with such grief."

SHAME

Calvin chose to go on as a widower, but not everyone was pleased with this resolve. He found criticism of his decision hard to bear—so hard, in fact, that he defended himself in public and claimed to have a clear conscience before God and man. He had been careful to make sure that nothing unbefitting of marital decency would come up, but noted that his reason for not marrying was not that he thought himself more virtuous than others. Calvin claimed that he could simply serve God better single than he could married, and that it was not to his merit, but rather out of weakness, that he remained unmarried. If he had still been a Catholic it would have been to his merit, for there it was considered a virtue for a widower to control his desires and not remarry. Calvin, however, was more aware of his weaknesses than his merits and also believed that a woman would hardly be happy with him. Unless Idelette herself were to find a way to voice her opinion and persuade otherwise, few would contradict Calvin on this even to the present day. Concerning Idelette, Calvin wrote that she would have gone with him into exile, into misery and even into death. Things had turned out differently, though. Calvin was once again alone, and once again alone he had to continue on his way. He did, of course, now have stepchildren, the son of Idelette whose name remains unknown, as well as her daughter Judith. We know very little of either of them, and the little we do know is hardly positive. The son was spotted in Strasbourg, and Calvin tried in vain to get him to come to Geneva.Concerning Judith he wrote in 1562 that she had brought shame to the family, and that this had so moved him that he withdrew into solitude for several days. What the shame was we do not know. What we do know is that Calvin received no support from either of them.

WOMEN

Many people may not expect it, but Calvin's view of women is actually notable in a positive sense. Aristotle, the highly praised philosopher, considered a woman only half a man. Calvin, on the other hand, said that without a woman, a man was only half of what he was meant to be. He was critical of what he thought were typical womanly faults such as endless chatter, a fault he thought only increased with age. According to Calvin most women were also obsessed with clothing, taking matters so far that "they sometimes leave dinner standing, and cheat their appetite so as to be able to dress even more elegantly and lavishly." He even knew of women who refused to breastfeed their children so that they could continue to wear certain clothes.

What dominates, however, is Calvin's respect for women. For him, every woman was deserving of respect, and men were to honor them following the example of Christ. Calvin argued this in a very straightforward manner. The Bible's teaching to "honor your mother" was to be extended to include honoring all women, and any men who fell short in this were liable to punishment. This view stood behind Calvin's warning against the nobleman who had come to ask de Fallais for the hand of his niece. Calvin knew that this man had contracted a venereal disease in his youth, and also knew that such things were so common that many made no point of it. Nevertheless, Calvin thought the girl ought to be protected, and that she would be wronged if he were to keep quiet.

Another example of Calvin's respect for women can be seen in his treatment of Renée de France, in whose Ferrara residence Calvin once stayed for several weeks. She supported the Reformation, but under pressure from the Inquisition she had acknowledged her "errors" and returned to Rome, not only participating once again in penance and Mass, but even entering a monastery in 1554. In Calvin's view one could hardly have done anything worse, but he apparently had a soft spot for this woman. He told her she need not feel guilty if she stayed in contact with him, even though under oath she had sworn that she would no longer do this. Just a few months before his death, Calvin wrote a letter to her, this time because her son-in-law, the duke of Guise and a fanatical Catholic, had been murdered. Reformed France rejoiced, but Calvin understood that the loss grieved Renée. Calvin told her that, unlike others, he did not see the murder as confirmation of God's rejection of the duke, and added that he had attempted to avert the plot. Calvin tried to console Renée with a reminder that it was not up to us to decide whether or not someone is saved.

No Women

For all of this, however, Calvin was no proponent of women having a decisive voice in the church and in politics. He wrote to Bullinger that times of women being in power—as were sometimes the case even in the Bible—were to be understood both as divine judgment as well as a sign of God's grace. Calvin cited Deborah as an example, adding that her leadership contravened the natural order and that God sometimes brought such things about to admonish men for their weakness. On the other hand, he was not at all happy with John Knox's infamous "The First Blast of the Trumpet Against the Monstrous Regiment of Women" that was published in Geneva in 1558. Calvin felt embarrassed by Knox's misogynistic arguments, even though he understood that for Knox it was more about the Catholicism of the two Queen Marys than about their being women as such.

Calvin held the same view on the authority of women as it pertained to their function in the church. When Renée de France wanted to attend a synodical gathering, Calvin reminded her that Paul had forbidden women to speak in the Christian assembly. He added another argument relating to the particular circumstances of his time, fearing that yet another Reformed departure from a commonly accepted rule would put them under even greater suspicion: how the papists and Anabaptists will mock us if they see that a woman is our master!

Calvin's view of the women to whom he wrote in 1557 was very different. These were the wives of a number of French Protestants who were jailed in September of that year. Calvin tried to encourage the women, pointing them to the women who "conducted themselves forcefully and with determination at the death of our Lord Jesus Christ," precisely at a moment when the disciples had given up hope. Calvin did not, however, intend to encourage the wives to take these biblical women as their example, for his argument went in the other direction. If God had helped those women at that time, he was sure to do the same for women today. This, of course, was fully in line with Calvin's theology: he did not point to humans as examples but rather to God as a source of strength.

Sister-in-Law

One woman who became a problem for Calvin was his sister-in-law, Anne le Fert, the wife of his younger brother Antoine (ca. 1511-1573). Antoine constantly shadowed his brother, and remained in his shadow as well, spending a considerable amount of time in Geneva. Antoine is said to have been Calvin's closest friend, and this appears to be correct, considering that when Calvin grieved the death of his friend Claude Féray, he wrote that Féray had been almost as close to him as he was to his brother. Antoine became a bourgeois of Geneva in 1546, without the usual payment, as reward for what his brother had done for the city—even though Calvin himself had to wait another few years before he would be granted this privilege. At any rate, Antoine's family lived with Calvin in his house where things could not have been easy for Anne. Her husband ran a flourishing, but time-consuming, business, and her life became even busier with the care of her children, as well as the students who came to board in the house. After the death of Idelette, everything was left up to her. Trouble reared its ugly head in the fall of 1548 when Anne came under suspicion of adultery. An attempt was made to reconcile the marriage, and it managed to stay afloat until it was dissolved at Antoine's request in 1557. Anne was banished after being named the chief offender by reason of adultery. Martin Bucer would have asked whether Antoine's conduct had not driven her into the arms of another man, but in Geneva such questions were not raised.

This was partly because of Calvin's view that a marriage could in fact only be dissolved in cases of adultery and the so-called Pauline Privilege (cf. 1 Cor 7:15). He did not differ here from any of the other Reformers except Martin Bucer, who found so many grounds for divorce in the Bible that it shamed his contemporaries. All the same, Bucer agreed with almost the entire Christian world of that time, Calvin included, that adultery was to be punished with death. After 1555, when Calvin exercised greater control, Geneva began to punish adultery with death. It should be noted, however, that neither Calvin nor the consistory were responsible for these decisions. Most cases were dealt with by the city lieutenant and the Little Council, often without even informing the consistory. When the consistory was informed, its involvement in such matters was only marginal.

CARACIOLLO

Calvin's view on the legitimacy of divorce in the case of one partner turning from Catholicism to the Reformation while the other did not becomes interesting in this context. Galeazzo Caraciollo's story is well-known. This rich noble from Naples went over to the Reformation in 1542 and was so happy about this change that, as the situation was becoming more and more difficult for non-Catholics in Italy, he gave up everything for the sake of his faith and left Naples to come to Geneva in 1551. His wife Vittoria, however, did not want to leave, and stayed behind firmly rooted in her Catholic faith. The couple lived in separation for eight years. During that time, Caraciollo's family made multiple trips to Geneva to try to turn him from his decision. Likewise, he made several journeys to Naples to try to convince his wife and children to join him in Geneva. On both sides these efforts were futile, and Vittoria even turned down her husband's proposal to move to a more neutral place. She remained in Naples and added that even if he were to return, she could not live with him in a normal marriage because the church had declared him a heretic. It was at this point that Caraciollo decided to apply for a divorce. Calvin did not immediately acquiesce but consulted his colleagues. They wanted to grant a divorce on the basis of the Pauline Privilege. Calvin, however, wanted

Caraciollo to make one more attempt at reconciliation. When it failed, Calvin finally did give his consent, but only after the normal procedures for divorce had been followed. The divorce was pronounced, and soon thereafter Caraciollo married a woman who wanted to be Reformed. From the large amount of information that remains from this case, it is clear that Calvin tried to proceed objectively and to investigate all aspects carefully before coming to a decision.

MARRIAGE

As noted previously Calvin occupied himself with many marital questions, and he had some interesting ideas. He was, for example, unable to understand a marriage between two partners who were separated by a large gap in age. He thought that an old man simply did not make a good match for a young woman, nor an old woman for a young man. Such cases had to be about something other than love, which was not good because the younger partner would always be shortchanged. "If a frail old man falls in love with a young woman, it must be from shameful lust. If he marries her, he will in fact deceive her." Something just had to be wrong; perhaps the younger partner was crazy, perhaps the older partner was lustful. Calvin's astonishment and indignation were hardly contained in a letter in which he discussed the case of a younger man who was to marry an older woman. He could hardly believe it. "It already seemed like a fable from the old poets that a woman of sixty could still get excited, but this woman is already seventy!" If she were to marry a man of her own age, one could still imagine that she was after something other than sexual gratification, but in this case no one would believe her.

Calvin had nothing against sexual intercourse as such; he thought the notion that one became stained with sin by it was an invention of Satan. It was the whole person, intellect and will and soul and spirit, that was stained with sin, and so it was foolish to look for sin only in physical desires. Calvin thus claimed that those who campaigned against sex and promoted celibacy were clearly going against God's will. Within marriage, sex was something holy, and husband and wife were not to deny each other—Calvin did not believe in spiritual marriages where the only intercourse was spiritual. This also implies that, for Calvin, sexual intercourse remained an essential element of a healthy marriage even after the possibility of procreation and childbearing had come to an end.

Even worse than a marriage between two people of vastly different ages was a marriage between a Reformed and a Catholic. A Christian man was to marry only that woman who would help him fulfill every duty of the life of faith. "For that reason a marriage in which this goal is even temporarily lost sight of is to be reproached. And is it not a desecration if one brings into one's home a woman who is still attached to the papal superstitions?" Here, Calvin wanted to distinguish between a girl who had not yet dared to break with Rome out of fear, and one who was a real enemy of true religion. When he was asked whether marriage with a Catholic was just as bad as marriage with a Muslim, Calvin answered in the negative. There was clearly a difference between the two, and yet there is one and the same kind of difficulty. Calvin had too often seen that such mixed marriages could lead to a weakening in faith. Still, he was unwilling to make a set rule as to how attached to Rome a viable marriage partner was allowed to be. Moreover, it was clear that a mixed marriage was still a fully legal marriage. Such mixed marriages could be denounced, but once the vows of faithfulness had been made, they remained valid.

Calvin, who had Bucer to thank for his own wife, took on the role of matchmaker for Viret. Calvin told him that although there were enough women where he was, he was not fully satisfied that any of them would be a good match for Viret. Thus he wrote to de Fallais: "If you see one in Strasbourg who would be suitable for Viret, let me know." This appeal seems to have been successful: a little over a week later Calvin wrote to Viret that he should make his decision quickly because Calvin wanted to speak with the father of a woman who seemed to be particularly suitable. "I think it best if you permit me to ask for her hand. I have already seen her twice. From her face it is easy to see that she is very modest, and on top of that she has a nice form." Calvin seems to have known what he was talking about.

MARITAL LAW

Calvin was like an architect who, after the extravagance of the baroque era, wanted a return to straight lines, simplicity and efficiency. This was also true of his policies in marital law. Thus it was decided that weddings were to be sober affairs, consisting of an exchange of vows, a blessing and a sermon. There was little to see or to hear. No kneeling, no kisses, no exchange of rings and no music, just God, the church and the bridal couple listening together to God's Word after making their vows. Marriages were usually held on Sundays, or another weekday when the congregation regularly assembled for preaching. On Sundays, when the Lord's Supper was celebrated, no weddings were to be held so to prevent any overshadowing of the sacrament. Any celebration that followed was also to be sober, which was nevertheless something other than boring. Calvin was not merely afraid of sinful extravagances, but also feared the waste of food, drink and money in a world full of poverty. Marriage should of course be celebrated, Calvin thought, and the Scriptures even provided examples for that. Neither was there anything wrong with having a big dinner, even an expensive banquet, but it ought not go too far. Calvin worried especially about the drinking, and said he hardly knew of any party where that did not get out of hand. When people drank too much, the topic of conversation degenerated, and with that the door was left wide open to all kinds of sin. This was what had happened when John the Baptist was decapitated during a dinner party gone wrong (Mt 14:1-12). For this reason Calvin was more than ready to prevent such mishaps by legal means, but it should also be added that the law limiting dancing to weddings had already been introduced in 1539, when Calvin was not even in Geneva, but still in Strasbourg. After Calvin's return, the rules governing weddings were slowly tightened, so that in 1549 all dancing was prohibited, and in 1558 it was determined that the dinner could consist of no more than three courses, each course having no more than four different dishes. Control over such matters reached their height with the ordinance of 1560: from that point on, all excess in food, drink and clothing was prohibited, as well as gold or silver necklaces and other jewelry. Those who were accustomed to wearing these items had to cover them up or leave them behind. Standing behind this ordinance was the idea that such things would only arouse desire and jealousy, and perhaps even lead to quarreling. The result was that those who wanted nothing to do with Calvin and his followers simply kept their parties behind closed doors.

QUARRELS

Quarreling couples were to appear before the consistory and were admonished "to live in peace and harmony with one another." Husbands were forbidden to hit their wives, and the fact that such a prohibition was made suggests that it addressed a fairly common occurrence. In the course of time, sanctions against the mistreatment of one's spouse were also sharpened, though in Geneva this never became grounds for divorce. Calvin maintained there were only two reasons for divorce: adultery and the Pauline Privilege. As long as a domestic situation was not life-threatening, a woman who was beaten by her husband—or a man who was beaten by his wife, as also happened—was to bear that cross in faith.

Prostitution was once viewed as a necessary evil against rapists or a useful institution that provided the venue for a little practice before marriage. Even before the Reformation, however, prostitution had been abolished in Geneva. A number of professional prostitutes were kindly requested to leave the city, and had their travel costs reimbursed as added enticement. Married women who prostituted themselves to make some extra cash were heavily punished, facing the death penalty after 1560, simply because people wanted Geneva to be prostitution-free. For the same reason, adultery was also treated seriously, including adultery before marriage. Remarkably, Calvin departed from both the Bible and tradition in arguing that the sexual sins of men were to be punished just as severely as those of women, and that a man who slept with another woman during his engagement period was no less culpable than a woman who did the same. Calvin knew that if the city council did not punish such men and women, then God himself would. Calvin recounted the story of a man, one of the Children of Geneva and already known as a blasphemer and drunkard, who left his wife and family when the plague came to Geneva even though the pastor had admonished him to stay and care for them. God rewarded him for his behavior by striking him with the plague too. Shortly afterward he was urged to confess his sins, but like a madman he jumped from his bed, ran out the door and drowned himself in the river. That was what happened to those who abandoned their families! God punished immediately, and according to Calvin there was no need to pity such people.

COURTSHIP

Calvin also had clear opinions on what could, or more correctly, what could not be done during courtship: no sexy clothing; no make-up; no naughty poems, off-color jokes or suggestive songs; no going to the bar; no excessive eating or drinking; no going out without chaperones; no bathing or swimming together; and, of course, no sexual intercourse. The background of his prohibitions against intercourse for those who were courting or engaged was Calvin's view of all sexual activity outside of marriage as adultery. In short, there was little for couples to do except read the *Institutes* together.

As any Reformed worship service will make clear, Calvin loved external simplicity and internal solidity, and the same was true for the way he thought about a marriage partner. The most important thing about a woman was her heart and spirituality, but since the eye also has its desires, Calvin did not think it wrong "that men in the choice of a wife take into account their beauty." It was not inherently sinful to choose a woman because she was beautiful. Neither was it wrong for women to consider men's looks, that is, when the choice of a marriage partner was concerned. Calvin advised that one should carefully consider another's beauty, but not for too long because of the danger of ending up with sinful thoughts. He also thought that couples should spend some quality time together to gauge their compatibility. This was very different from the customary practice under canon law, where two young people could make their vows without knowing each other at all. Calvin was therefore also a fierce opponent of parents who arranged marriages against the wishes of their their sons or daughters, and herein he sought the same protection for girls as for boys. A marriage ought not circumvent parental permission but should be based on the consent of all parties. "If the man and the woman do not agree and do not love each other, it is a desecration of marriage and actually is no marriage at all. For the most important bond is that they both want it." Unlike other Reformers, Calvin did not base the need for parental permission on the fifth commandment ("Honor your father and your mother") but on the natural order recognized by all nations. A marriage was such a significant event in a person's life that it was only natural that one should listen to the advice of one's parents. There were, moreover, a number of biblical examples of people who first consulted with their parents before marrying. Somewhat peculiar is Calvin's view that the role of the father was more significant than that of the mother. Also remarkable is Calvin's claim that it was nonsense for a man to insist that the woman he married be a virgin. Calvin did not condone sex before marriage, but he was no less an opponent of the virginity cult of the Middle Ages. This, as Calvin saw it, would only lead to a girl claiming to be a virgin and lying about it. If this was later discovered by her husband not to have been the case, it was sure to be a situation from which marital problems would arise.

Calvin, of course, disapproved of marriages with Catholics, Jews or Muslims. Those who desired such marriages were to be strongly admonished, but of course they could not be kept from making their own decisions. It was sinful but not prohibited. The same was true for marriage to an unbeliever. Here Calvin's rule was that "the piety of the believer sanctifies the marriage more than the impiety of the unbeliever desecrates it." Ideally, however, it was hoped that this would be especially true with respect to marriages entered into by two unbelievers, one of whom was subsequently converted. That a believer should enter into marriage with an unbeliever was thus denounced by both Scripture and Calvin.

All of Calvin's views on marriage were rooted in his conviction that marriage was a reflection of the covenant between God and humanity. Thus a mutual relationship of love and devotion, of readiness for and meaningful interaction with the other, was of utmost importance. For Calvin, marriage was not a contract, but a covenant wherein each partner was fully present for the other—for the benefit, and not to the detriment, of the other.

CHILDREN

When Calvin was ridiculed because he had no children and the child he did have had passed away early, he responded that he had tens of thousands of children throughout the Christian church. That may sound like a good and quick response, but it cannot hide Calvin's sorrow over not having children of his own, especially when he cared so much for them. Did he perhaps intend to make up for what he himself had lacked as child? Calvin thought children were very important and for that reason insisted on the duties of parents, particularly for the spiritual education of their children. It was a bad thing when parents were only concerned that their children should make it as high as possible on the social ladder. Often such parents only sought their own benefit from the luxury and wealth such success would bring. Parents were so proud when their children could say a few words in Latin, but there was little attention given to education in the knowledge of the Lord. Calvin, though, managed to connect these two kinds of knowledge rather cleverly with the appearance of several primers that taught children how to read using the confession of faith.

Parents were to invest in their children. This did not mean excusing everything they did, for without punishment and correction no learning would take place. If a child ended up on the wrong path, parents should not hesitate to take firm action. If, however, parental efforts at correction did not work, parents were not to abandon their child but to patiently try to win him or her back for God. Calvin advised parents to find a middle road between coddling and sternness.

LEARNING

Calvin wanted to look after the church and the child, and so sought to renew the old Catholic practice of confirmation, administered to children as a sacrament around the age of twelve. Children who had been taken up into God's covenant, who had received his promises and lived out of his love and grace, had the right to be told what all of this meant from the time they were children. One of the first things Calvin did on his return to Geneva was to write a catechism for the instruction of children, since "without a catechism the church will never remain." Calvin wanted to guide children toward the Lord's Supper, and toward that end they had to understand its meaning. He agreed with Bucer that the Anabaptists had a point in their criticism of infant baptism. They argued that there was a danger that the necessity of a conscious choice for the faith could fall into the background. Thus the public profession of one's faith was introduced to replace confirmation. Calvin thought that a profession of faith, which would serve as the door from baptism to the Lord's Supper, could best be made when a child reached the teenage years upon having received a solid catechetical instruction. So Calvin arranged for catechetical instruction for children and servants in each of the three churches every Sunday afternoon around twelve o'clock. Both parents and instructors were to ensure that the children attended. Four times per year an oral examination was held before the celebration of the Lord's Supper, when children were required to recite from memory or to summarize sections of the catechism. This was accepted as their own confession of faith and gave them access to the Lord's Supper. Instruction was aimed at both the hearts and the minds of the children, because the goal was to bring them to know Christ by teaching them the facts of salvation. The focus was on growth in the Spirit and in the unity of faith, and for Calvin it made no difference whether there were one or more catechisms. Calvin himself wrote some as well, first in 1537, and a second in 1542, in which he divided the material into fifty-five sections arranged in question-and-answer format, which allowed all the biblical themes to be treated year by year. Calvin also wrote an accompanying handbook for pastors. Already during his lifetime, the booklet was translated into Greek, Hebrew, German, Italian and Spanish and thus enjoyed a wide reading. The Latin translation of 1545 has become especially renowned as a confessional document. As a catechism, it would become clear that the one from Heidelberg (1563) was even better, and it became the Reformed textbook *par excellence*. There was, however, still much of Calvin to be found in it.

Calvin also gave children another significant place in the church. He mobilized them for singing, having them lead the new rhymed psalms. Calvin was convinced that parents could learn something from their children.

School

Another of Calvin's great concerns was proper schooling. He regularly came before the council to make sure that good teachers were appointed, to recommend salary increases for them or else to take action against those doing a poor job. Education was divided into two stages, the second of which was the *schola publica,* the ancestor of the academy that would later become the university of Geneva. This will be dealt with later on. The first stage of education in Geneva was the *schola privata,* divided into seven classes, where students in the sixth and seventh grade mostly read a lot of French and Latin literature and for which a foundation had been laid in the earlier years. The style and order of this institution also owe much to Calvin. There was to be quiet and harmony in the classroom, one sermon on Wednesday, two on Sunday, the memorization of psalms, and from the fourth year on, only Latin was to be spoken. Discipline was strict, and it was completely legal and even seen as useful to deal out blows for correction. At the end of each week, three students had to recite the Lord's Prayer, the catechism and the Ten Commandments. When a new school building was being constructed in 1558, Calvin himself went to inspect the building and location together with some masons and carpenters and several members of the council. Calvin thought the school should be built in a sound location, where the children would have enough room to walk around a bit. Children needed such space. They also needed to be protected, and Calvin recommended to the city council that all windows and balconies in the city's public buildings be provided with railings for the sake of their safety.

Friends

In spite of the fact that Calvin walked a lonely road in many things, he did have friends outside of his family. For him, friendship was a greater good than any familial bond. Thus on his birthday he wrote to his friend Laurent de Normandie who had since taken up residence in Geneva: "There are different kinds of internal bonds that tie people together, but no blood relationship nor any other type can surpass our love."

Friendship is a broad concept based on different kinds of values in differ-

ent cultures. In the United States you can become friends within a matter
of seconds, while in Europe it generally takes longer. In the sixteenth century, friendship was a rather popular concept among humanists but had
more to do with agreement in conviction than an emotional bond. This
makes it somewhat problematic to see Calvin as a man of friendships, though
there clearly were some people with whom he had friendly relations, particularly Farel and Viret, as was also remarked by those who referred to
them as the three patriarchs. Calvin himself spoke of their relationship
openly in the preface to his commentary on Paul's letter to Titus, which he
dedicated to Farel and Viret. He compared their work in Geneva to Paul's
on Crete, and wrote, "I do not think there have ever been such friends who
have ever lived in such close friendship as we have in our ministry." Here
too, though, it should be noted that Calvin immediately and exclusively tied
their bond of friendship to the work they shared in God's Kingdom. The
three of them had recognized their tasks and could get along well even after
they had not seen each other for quite some time. In that, Calvin thought,
they showed that their friendship "was devoted to the name of Christ and
was to this very day useful to his church." In this respect, Calvin's idea of
friendship always remained humanistic in concept, though some Reformed
principles were added. This also surely explains how Calvin could so easily
keep himself at a distance when necessary. This, indeed, proved necessary
when at the age of sixty-nine, Farel decided to marry a seventeen-year-old
girl—something which turned into quite a scandal. The pastors of Neuchâtel wanted to forbid it, but Calvin thought they were going too far. In Calvin's opinion, their poor brother suffered from an incurable disease (malladie
incurable). Why else would he do such a thing? They should not abandon
him, otherwise he might no longer know what to do at all. In spite of Farel's
pleading, however, Calvin refused to attend the wedding. Calvin told him
he was too busy, but even if he were not, he still would not come. After this,
Calvin rarely wrote to Farel again.

Almost exactly the same thing happened with the other friend in that
triumvirate. Viret left for southern France on a doctor's recommendation in
September 1561. What exactly happened between Calvin and him before his

departure is not known. Perhaps Viret was jealous of Theodore Beza, the rising star. Whatever the case may have been, there was a marked decline in letters exchanged between Calvin and Viret. While more than 400 letters passed between them in the period 1537-1563, after September 1561 there were only twelve from Viret to Calvin and three from Calvin to Viret.

STOIC

Though hardly necessary in light of much of the above, it may still be useful to treat the old myth of Calvin the emotionless stoic. If we are permitted to use his own testimony, it is more than clear that he experienced deep emotions. After the death of his colleague Courault, he wrote that he was a wreck and that in his grief he hardly knew the time of day. Throughout the day he would think back to it and could hardly do his work, and these torments during the daylight hours were followed by the horrors of the night. When he heard of the persecutions of the Waldenses, he got cramps in his stomach and could barely keep working. He regularly wrote of his tears and pain. Sometimes he claimed to have no idea what to do, and wanted to die. When he heard that Bucer had passed away, he was overwhelmed by a feeling of loneliness and wished that all his friends would outlive him so that he at any rate could die in joy.

Calvin's own adversities, as well as those of others to whom he spoke and preached, led him to question God. He had no question as to God's existence, nor his election, but rather his ways. God had a plan for each person's life, and the trick was to accommodate oneself to it. That plan, at any rate, was not written in the stars. In 1549 Calvin published a work about astrology in which he characterized it as a "demonic superstition." If astrology occupied itself with the position of stars and planets (what would now be regarded as the field of astronomy), there was no problem, but the discipline should not go beyond those boundaries. People who put stock in horoscopes diminished God's might, behaving as if he could be bound to what was written in the stars. Horoscopes had nothing to do with science at all, and it was not for nothing that the Bible forbade similar practices. Satan tried to turn people from their dependence on God by tempting them to trust horoscopes instead. Here, as in other matters, Calvin tried to free the people from their fears, turning them away from the complicated patterns in the stars to the simple confidence of faith, and turning them also from a dependence on horoscopes to an independence in which everyone could make their own choices before God. Calvin's rejection of horoscopes, however, brings back the question of God's ways with even greater force. He tried to understand God, but it never worked. He was like one who tried to climb a high mountain, threatened by the dangers of falling into a chasm *(abyssus)* or of losing the way *(labyrinth)*. The mountain he climbed was God, and though Calvin made his way higher and higher, he would never reach the summit.

PATIENT

(1551-1554)

GOD'S CHOICE

According to Calvin, God was to blame for sin's entrance into this world. At least, Jerome Bolsec (d. 1584) argued, that was the only conclusion one could reach if Calvin's doctrine of predestination was taken seriously. Jerome Bolsec had an interesting past. He began as a Carmelite friar, then earned his keep as an itinerant doctor. After that, he was employed at the court of Renée de France in Ferrara, first as a doctor and later also as a spy. In the spring of 1551, he settled in Veigy close to Geneva, where he showed himself to be a fervent supporter of Calvin in all things but one. Shortly after his arrival, Bolsec began to attack Calvin's teaching on predestination. He knew well that Calvin had not invented the doctrine himself and that it was one taught by many respected theologians throughout the centuries. One of these was Augustine, who comes up so often in Calvin's works that you would think he read nothing other than the Bible and Augustine. Calvin agreed with this church father that, although part of predestination remains hidden from us so that we cannot understand it, we should not refrain from speaking about what is revealed in the Scriptures.

But as always, Calvin tried to think through and give expression to the doctrine as well as he could. This brought him to the conviction that the Bible teaches double predestination, that is, that God has chosen one group of people to live eternally with him, and that the other group would remain in darkness. The issue was not whether there were two types of people, some who would go to heaven and others who would go to hell. The issue was instead whether anyone could make a saving decision for himself or herself, or whether everything depended on God's choice. For Calvin, there was no question. The Bible showed most clearly in both cases that everything depended on God, and that it was by his decision and choice that the eternal destiny of all people was decided. Calvin had no use for a solution like single predestination, which held that there was only an election to salvation. If God had decided to preserve one group, his decision was automatically a choice not to save the other. There was simply a double predestination. Calvin also had no desire whatsoever to leave even a small part of their salvation to people; that would only lead to uncertainty, and at the time there was already so much uncertainty in the world. This was something that particularly upset Calvin about Rome, where he thought people were only made to fear God. If one had to contribute even only a pebble to one's own salvation, one would live in lifelong fear that one's pebble was just not big enough. A life of Christian fanaticism would displace any joy in faith. The families of the departed would also find no rest, not knowing whether or not their loved ones were in heaven. For the dying, the prospect of death in the face of uncertainty would be all the more difficult. No, Calvin preferred predestination, which brought the certainty and comfort people needed. Even more, predestination was a further testimony to God's glory, and for Calvin this was the most important consideration. If humanity had even a small role to play in these things, it would be to the detriment of God's honor. If I have even only that little pebble to contribute, God can no longer receive all of the honor. He could, perhaps, receive the most honor, maybe even almost all, but not all. For Calvin, this was not good enough; to him, God's glory was everything.

There would also be nothing left of the church without the doctrine of predestination. It was a simple matter: predestination had to be preached, "first of all to bring to God the glory he deserves, and secondly to assure us of our salvation, so that we call out to God as Father with all freedom. Woe to us if we do not hold to these two elements, because then there will no longer be faith or religion. You can still speak of God, but it will only be a lie."

BOLSEC'S ATTACK

Bolsec found Calvin's theology very interesting, and although he was a medical doctor, he had immersed himself deeply in theology. He also regularly attended the meetings of the *Compagnie des Pasteurs*. Calvin's doctrine of predestination just went too far for him, though. From Bolsec's perspective, if everything depended on God in the way Calvin described, one could hardly come to any other conclusion than that God was the author of sin. Calvin's teaching, taken to its logical conclusion, would arrive at a God on whom everything depended, including sin. Bolsec had spoken to Calvin about this issue before, but they had not been able to come to a resolution. On October 16, 1551, Bolsec began to criticize Calvin in the midst of the Friday *Congrégation* after someone had preached on this topic. Bolsec really went at it, suggesting that anyone who held Calvin's position made God the cause of sin and a tyrant. Furthermore, it was nonsense to claim that the church fathers, and particularly Augustine, held to this doctrine. Burning with self-righteousness and indignation, Bolsec did not notice that Calvin had entered the room and was present for this outburst. The unexpectedness of Bolsec's attack, as well as Calvin's own nature, combined to produce a fierce counter-attack from Calvin, which according to witnesses was as fiery as it was learned. Bolsec was therefore arrested by a representative of the magistrate who happened to be present, the charge being that he had broken the law by attacking the received doctrine so fiercely. With that, it became the problem of the council, which was actually not sure what to do, and decided to ask several of the neighboring cities for advice. This did nothing to help. Basel considered Bolsec a dangerous heretic, but Zürich thought they should all relax and settle down a bit in Geneva. Calvin himself was highly irritated by this weakness. The city council also found the whole issue of predestination difficult, but said that they were ready to believe the theologians, and therefore banned Bolsec from the city forever. Back in France, Bolsec was so disturbed that he not only returned to Catholicism, he wrote a malicious book about and against Calvin that has shaped and dominated the image of Calvin in the French-speaking world for centuries.

TROLLIET

Bolsec was banished from the city because he had transgressed the laws of Geneva, but at bottom was of course the matter of Calvin's zeal for predestination. For Calvin this teaching was so essential both to God's glory and to the happiness of humanity, that he would permit no criticism of it. In addition to Bolsec, Jean Trolliet was to discover this as well. This former monk from Burgundy, who had converted to Reformed Christianity and was eager to become a pastor in Geneva, was opposed by Calvin on his road to the ministry. Instead, Trolliet got a job as notary and took his revenge from this position by publishing one of Calvin's letters in which he was rather critical of the magistrate. Later, in June 1552, almost a year after the Bolsec affair, Trolliet registered a complaint against Calvin's sermons. The ensuing discussions revealed that Trolliet also had difficulties with Calvin's doctrine of predestination and that he too thought Calvin turned God into the author of sin. There was much discussion back-and-forth, and the council decided to read the *Institutes* for itself—a most uncommon event among politicians. This turned to Calvin's favor; the *Institutes* appear to have been so clear that the members of the council declared his view to be fully biblical. They further officially ratified his doctrine of predestination, which was another rather uncommon event. Everyone was required to hold to it, and not even one bad word was to be uttered against it. Calvin had succeeded and was rewarded for his persistence. "I could do no other," he said. "I had to be so persistent if I did not want to become a betrayer of the truth." Here God's watchdog, who barked at the slightest danger, had dug in his teeth. Anyone who threatened Calvin's doctrine of predestination was actually threatening God, and anyone who undermined what Calvin taught on the matter actually shortchanged both

God and humanity. Calvin's strong reactions can only be understood in this light.

HUMANKIND

Predestination was also closely tied to Calvin's view of humanity. It is God who has to choose, because humans are unable to do so. Humankind is, without question, "the most beautiful jewel on earth," but sin inflicted great damage. What remained was, in fact, but a ruin of that original, lofty creation. Humanity had become "a ruined being without any worth." "Although humans were equipped with magnificent gifts, they have yet been corrupted by the fall and have become nothing." Humanity has remained special and set apart—people have not been reduced to the level of animals—but they are no more than religious wrecks before God. This had far-reaching consequences, for sin "has claimed the soul and the body." Calvin reproached papist theologians for reducing original sin to an inclination to sin and for locating sin especially in the physical desires. According to Calvin, there was much more wrong with humankind. Everything that constituted a human being, including the soul, was out of kilter because of sin, and every human heart was an abyss of confusion. The truth was painful, but it was still true. Human nature was inclined to idleness and lies. According to Calvin, human hearts were rebellious and full of sinful thoughts, while human nature longed for all that is wrong. People had become so detached from God's justice that all that they willed, longed for and did, was ungodly, impure and blasphemous. The heart was so riddled with sin that even what appeared to be good was really cloaked in hypocrisy and deceit. Free will had no value whatsoever anymore, and as a result, for anything good to come of humankind, it had to be given by God. While this might be seen as a negative view of humanity, one needs only think of the awful things people have done since Calvin's time to see it as a realistic view.

RADICAL

Calvin's relationship with the de Fallais family provides evidence of how deep the Bolsec affair went for him, how tightly he tied his own business to that of the church and theology, and, in fact, how greatly his attitude informed that of Calvinism. The de Fallais couple—named after one of their estates in the Netherlands—was made up of Jacques de Bourgogne and Yolande van Brederode. Calvin had been in contact with them since 1543, and their relationship was quite close from the very beginning. The de Fallais family wanted to leave the Netherlands because they could no longer live in a country where Christ was not worshiped in the right manner. Calvin suggested that they move away, although he knew well what a great sacrifice this would be. For Calvin, obedience to God and a clear conscience was to carry more weight than possessions and family ties. There may have been no divine command to leave one's home country, but if God could no longer be worshiped in body and soul, the words heard by Abraham also applied to the faithful in the present: "Leave your country."

This theme appears frequently in Calvin's writings. "For that reason this is the best, namely to leave before you get bogged down in the mire, are no longer able to free yourself and about to drown. The earlier, the better." Jacques and Yolande first left for Cologne, and then went to Strasbourg where they met Calvin in 1545. By way of Basel they ended up in a little chateau in Veigy, close to Geneva. Here they had even closer contact with Calvin, but after four years it came to an abrupt and permanent end. The de Fallais family had a different doctor than Calvin did, and their doctor happened to be named Bolsec. They befriended him as they had Calvin, but in the controversy between the doctor and the Reformer, they chose for Bolsec, and for Calvin this indicated that the relationship was nearing its end. In a last letter to de Fallais, Calvin made it clear that their friendship was over. Anyone who wanted to be friends with an enemy of the truth could no longer be a friend of Calvin. The matter was as simple as that for Calvin, and displays an attitude that has become typical for many Reformed people. People who cannot sit in the same church cannot sit in the same living room, either. Calvin's pettiness became more evident in 1546 in the second edition of his commentary on First Corinthians, where he took back his dedication to the de Fallais family that had been included in the first. Furthermore, since we have copies of Calvin's letters to de Fallais, but not of those of de Fallais to Calvin, we can only conclude that Calvin himself made sure they disappeared. He no longer wanted even their letters in his house.

DISCIPLINE

Calvin remained radical in his stance on church discipline, and in October 1552 a new conflict broke out when he refused to baptize the child of Balthasar Sept. Calvin could not understand why he should do it. Sept had never recognized Calvin as a legitimate pastor, but now that his child needed to be baptized, he suddenly appeared ready to do so. With Calvin, things did not work that way. This was the beginning of a dispute that would last for months in which the real conflict was between French pastors who expected a Christian lifestyle from their people, and Genevan citizens who refused to be told what to do by these foreign Frenchmen. By the middle of 1553, when the Little Council gave Philibert Berthelier permission to attend the Lord's Supper, the controversy over church discipline became so intense that it seemed Calvin might need to leave Geneva once again. Calvin was not at all willing to accept the council's decision, and in a sermon he preached on September 3 (which he knew might well be his last) he stated that he was ready to accept exile as a consequence. He did not really want to go, and if God were to leave him in Geneva, contrary to his present expectations, he would continue to devote himself wholeheartedly. It was the same God, however, who now would not permit him to administer the holy sacrament to people who were consciously living an unholy life. Once again it was that struggle with God's will. Calvin was more than ready to be finished with all the hustle and bustle and hardships, but every time he tried to pull back, God returned him to the center stage of public life. One can become sick from always having to do what one does not actually want to do, and Calvin indeed became sick, or rather, he became sicker than he already was.

SICK

Just as it would of anyone, it says a lot about Calvin that the things he had once enjoyed became unpleasant for him and that he solicited assistance for things he had formerly preferred to do himself. Early in 1551, Calvin wrote

to Bullinger that he was exhausted from writing, and was in fact so tired
that he regularly just about hated having to write letters. At the end of the
year he gave in to the appointment of secretaries to whom he could dictate
his letters and who were to assist him in any of his other work that involved
writing.

Every chapter in this book could include a paragraph on the maladies
Calvin suffered during the particular times under consideration, but to prevent the reader from falling victim to the monotony of his chronic bad
health, all of his illnesses will be gathered together and treated here. It is
easy to present a wide and detailed medical report on Calvin. He often
wrote about his health, and two other reports exist from shortly after his
death. We should also remark as an aside that it should come as no surprise
that someone who suffered as much illness and pain as Calvin did also had
less resistance and patience in other matters, and had a tendency to
overreact.

Calvin was actually a sickly person throughout his entire life, and his work
ethic only served to pad his file with the doctor. Whether or not he had a
weak constitution as a child is not known, but we do know that the terrible
food and lodgings at the Collège de Montaigu—to which Erasmus had also
fallen victim—left their mark on Calvin's physical well-being. After that,
things only got worse. Stress, way too much work, lack of exercise and sleep-
lessness were only some of the factors that led to the further breaking down
of Calvin's already fragile constitution. The number of pills he had to swal-
low, as well as the frequent bloodlettings he describes, were both intended to
benefit his health but may well have done more harm than good.

The physical pain was also aggravated by mental anguish.

> Courault's death has left me such a wreck that I can no longer put up with
> the pain. By day there is nothing that can occupy me without continually
> thinking about it. Added to this terrible pain by day are the severe agonies
> by night. Not only do the sleepless hours continually torment me, to which
> I am accustomed, but the entire nights in which I do not even close my eyes
> drain all my power, and there is nothing that could be worse for my health
> than that.

Psychological

In a letter he wrote soon after his marriage to Idelette, Calvin made clear the degree to which external pressure and fragile health affected his mood. The fact that a noble lady and her son were still living in their house at this time apparently did not help the situation, either.

On September 3, I had a very bad headache, but I am so accustomed to them that they barely bother me any longer. As I suddenly began to feel hot while preaching on the following Sunday, I noticed that the fluids that had stuffed up my head were suddenly turning liquid. Even before I left the church, I caught a punishing cold that left me with a constantly runny nose until Tuesday. When I preached on that day as usual, I had a very hard time speaking because my nose was so congested from that flow, and I was so hoarse that I almost felt like I was being choked. And then I suddenly felt a shudder go throughout my whole body. The cold stopped, but too early because my head was still congested with those nasty fluids. For on Monday something had happened that seriously galled me. For when the lady who boards with us and speaks more freely than she should, insulted my brother, he could no longer put up with it. He made no commotion, but quietly left the house, swearing that he would never come back as long as that woman was also there in my house. When she saw that my brother's departure was so lamented, she left as well. Her son, however, remained with us for a little while.

Now when I get wound up by some irritating thing or by a great fear, I usually let myself go when eating, and scarf everything down more quickly than I really should. And so, because at dinner I had burdened my stomach too heavily with too much and unsuitable food, the next morning I had incredible pains in my stomach. It would have been best to do what I usually do, namely to fast. But because I did not want the son to think that I was trying to hint to him that he too should leave the house, I decided to ignore my health and simply overlook my illness. But the Tuesday when the cold went away as mentioned, I became very dizzy around nine o'clock after dinner. I let them put me to bed. Then followed a heavy fever attack, great heat and terrible dizzy spells. When I wanted to get up on Wednesday, my limbs were so weak that I had to admit that I was really sick. In the afternoon I ate a little, but after eating I had two more dizzy spells. Then there were again and again fever attacks, but irregular, so that it was impossible to determine what kind of fever it was. I sweat so much that my whole pillow was soaked. This is the state I was in when your letter arrived, but I was in no way able to do what you asked of me since I could hardly take even three steps. Whatever it had been before, my illness finally became the tertian fever, which was first severe but in the third phase subsided a bit. When I began to regain my health, the point in time for which you had invited me had already passed. I did not have the strength to endure a journey.

These are the words of someone who is a case not only for physicians but also for psychologists. This is someone who got so physically worked up over stress, who so tied himself into knots to avoid giving the wrong impression to another, and who so struggled with feelings of guilt as to make himself sick. Then he would feel guilty for being sick. "Because I have been struck down by a migraine, I am forced to be lazy and to do nothing." Others will recognize Calvin's difficulty: when sick, one becomes irritable especially over not being able to work. Then one simply keeps working, trying to recover the lost hours and so following a schedule that only makes things worse.

Now I am suffering from another migraine, although the last hour things are going better. Fortunately I am just able to pull myself through to take care of the necessary things, but things are moving slowly, as they always do with me. In the meantime, more time that I could have devoted to more useful things is being wasted through my illness.

In this respect, Calvin was often torn between two things, as he wrote to Farel in the late hours of the night: "I must actually still prepare for tomorrow's sermon, but if I think of my health I should actually go to bed now."

PAIN

Calvin often complained of headaches. He wrote that even as a student he had suffered from terrible migraines that regularly made it impossible for him to write and at times confined him to bed for several days. The stomach problems mentioned earlier resulted in regular experiences of the two extremes of digestive problems, but thankfully Calvin spared his readers the details of his constipation and diarrhea that Luther never hesitated to give. While Luther often encountered the devil on the toilet, Calvin sat there with his own problems. Sitting also later became difficult for him when he developed hemorrhoids, which also made it very painful to ride a horse and caused him to lose much blood.

A feeling of constriction that was anything but psychological and chest pains that once kept him from his work for six weeks form another category of ailments. In his long letter to the doctors of Montpellier, written several months before his death in 1564, Calvin related that he had been having attacks for some five years already during which he coughed up blood. In a letter to Heinrich Bullinger, Calvin spoke of the pain his kidney stones caused him, which came toward the end of his life. He wrote of acute, indescribable pains that almost caused him to lose all sense of feeling, and after passing a kidney stone he could describe their journey with the detail of a medical expert. After a doctor-prescribed horseback ride, "the stone passed from the bladder to the urinary tract" and became stuck there, causing unbearable pain. "For more than half an hour I tried to rid myself of it by shaking my whole body." Only a day later did he finally pass the hazelnut-sized stone. Calvin claimed to feel reborn—"I feel as if I am only now alive again"—but also reported that the stone had cleared a path for others to follow, so the pains did not cease. Calvin's kidney stones were principally caused by a severe case of gout, and all these maladies were on top of the other pains he already suffered in heavy bouts of fever. In one report about his many health problems, Calvin described the treatment of his gout. Some kind of small tent was placed over his foot since he was unable to bear having even a sheet cover it. His foot was then rubbed with an oil that was so disgusting that Calvin said he almost had to vomit. The gout became so intense that Calvin said he could hardly even move, and was forced to lead a sedentary life. As we noted before, however, sitting was also a problem. The fevers made work difficult and life hard to bear. A fever that he caught in October of 1558 lasted until May of 1559, and came on with acute attacks that made others fear for his life. The fact that Calvin's doctors massaged his lower belly and regularly applied pressure to it makes clear that the fevers also caused his spleen to swell considerably.

IDEAL

Calvin's respect for authority made him an ideal patient who took care "not to depart even a hair's breadth from the doctors' prescriptions," even though he had to admit that his thirst always impelled him to drink more wine than was actually allowed. He also obeyed when they forbade him to preach and teach, but then during the same period dictated letters from his bed and managed to publish the definitive edition of the *Institutes* in both French and Latin. In the time since his death, Calvin's own descriptions of his maladies have been subjected to medical analysis by specialists. Their findings have suggested that he probably suffered from malaria and tuberculosis, and also had a heart problem or two. All in all, it is a wonder that he reached the age of fifty-five with such a frail body, and in light of all of the above it may be surprising that there were health problems he never did experience, or which he at least never reported. Thus he appears never to have had a toothache, even though it was only in his time that Geneva got its first dentist. In spite of his fragile physique Calvin outlived his doctor, Benoit Textor (ca. 1509-1560), although the latter did live to see that Calvin's commentary on Paul's second epistle to the Thessalonians was dedicated to him in 1550. This was in gratitude for the great care Benoit had given to Calvin, and especially his wife Idelette, and as reward for the fact that Benoit had never charged him for his services.

In the course of time, attempts have been made to add a psychological file to Calvin's medical record. It has been suggested that he suffered from terrible panic-attacks, which supposedly provide a partial explanation of aspects of his theology. Even though Calvin certainly experienced anxieties, there are no grounds at all to suggest that such anxieties were felt more acutely by him than by his contemporaries. Calvin and his peers lived in a time when death threatened a person's life at every turn in the form of robbers, war, plague, spoiled food and other enemies, a time when there was more than enough cause for fear. Calvin has also been put on Freud's couch, but the conclusion that he must have suffered from certain obsessive-compulsive disorders can only be maintained by ignoring the vast amount of contradictory evidence from and about him. It is thus prudent to let these speculations be, and to concentrate instead on his physical ailments.

Of course Calvin found a way to connect his own illnesses and those of others to God's providence in such a way as to be left with positive consequences. When Madame de Coligny recovered from yet another illness, Calvin wrote a letter to congratulate her, and therein noted that we can interpret illnesses as discipline from the heavenly Father, and that we can turn such discipline to our advantage.

> Our illnesses are surely not only to humble us by showing us our weakness, but they should also encourage us to examine ourselves so as to acknowledge our weakness and take refuge in God's mercy. They should also serve as remedies that free us from the desires of this world and burn away all that is unnecessary. Further, they are messages from death that ought to teach us to lift one foot, ready to leave when God so decides.

This attitude was to become typical of Reformed pastors, who, acting in faith in God's providence, tried to turn the question "Why?" into the question "What for?" These endeavors, however, met with varying success.

DEFENDER

As a student Calvin had been known as *accusativus,* but throughout his life this accuser was also a defender, especially of what he saw as God's cause, which he closely identified with his own. Calvin's troubles of the 1540s tempted him to abandon his homiletical principles and to defend himself in his sermons. He was unable to resist this temptation, and the man who wanted nothing more than to let God speak now frequently spoke on his own behalf. As a result, the word *I* occurs with unusually high frequency in the sermons from this period, while it all but disappears again as soon as calm was restored in 1556. Despite using the word *I* and defending himself, Calvin nevertheless claimed to want to avoid repaying evil with evil. Although slighted by another's insult, Calvin knew that he himself was not without guilt before God. Should sin committed against him not be for-given while the million other sins he committed against God be overlooked? Calvin was not particularly stoic in the way he suffered injustices but claimed to do his best to turn his strong feelings in upon himself when they did well up. He discovered thereby that God was showing him through these feel-ings that he himself was nothing, and that God calmed them again. Calvin also admitted an awareness that he was by nature no better than the people who were being punished for breaking Geneva's laws.

Calvin's need to defend himself appears to have arisen from the criticism that was brought against his preaching. Seeing himself as an Old Testament prophet, he stood in confidence and pulled no punches. During his ser-mons, Calvin chided the politicians who were present for looking after themselves financially a little too well and for not doing nearly as much as they could to fight immorality and to make the streets safe.

> How are things over here? An honest person hardly dares to go out into the streets when it is dark. You get insulted, harassed, assaulted, and if attacked you can hardly defend yourself. And what are they doing against these evil-doers, this lot worthy of the gallows? Years before they should already have been hanged.

A month later, in October 1554, Calvin merrily continued his criticism. "Just look at the people who are in authority and how they serve themselves. What is the state of the judicial system these days? You see only arrogance. The only thing that counts for them is pomp and circumstance, and they no longer think they are mortals." Calvin called them a bunch of weaklings who exploited the people. These were pointed sermons and did not simply go in one ear and out the other. In 1546, seven people were arrested be-cause they began to shout during a sermon, showing most clearly that they disagreed with Calvin when he called the Genevans wild beasts. Calvin continued on, however, because he believed himself to be a prophet and that he should be as direct and radical as his Old Testament colleagues had been.

Behind the sharply critical sermons of 1554 was the arrest of a prostitute who, as Calvin saw it, was put in prison only for show. Instead of only bread and water, she received all kinds of good foods and was also treated very well. "Now, I ask you, can you call this justice?" The following Sunday Calvin addressed the criticism that had been brought against his earlier sermon. It had apparently come from the authorities, since Calvin noted "that they began to justify themselves, conspired against God, and to hide amongst themselves what everyone could see." No one understood the point of his sermon, which was that they might humble, not harden, themselves. Even more criticism followed. "They do not say, 'I do not want him to preach for me any longer,' but rather, 'Does he really think that God's promise is to be preached like this? Should it not be preached more warmly?' . . . Some say that we are too harsh and that for that reason God's Word is not received." Every pastor is accustomed to these kinds of remarks. One congregant thinks the pastor is too direct, another that he is not straightforward enough. One wants greater comfort, another more admonition. One wants to be entertained, another to be confronted. Upon reading Calvin's sermons, one finds a balanced mix of rhetorical strategies that clearly reveals these supposed shortcomings to be largely a matter of perception. Calvin's own socially critical approach was much more pronounced than that of many of his later followers.

SERVETUS

Questions as to whether or not Calvin was mentally disturbed, and perhaps even a psychological case, are raised most often in connection with the Servetus affair. These questions can be answered negatively very quickly upon consideration of the facts, but this is precisely the problem. Over the years, books have created such a clearly crystallized mental image of Calvin that even the facts can hardly change it. Calvin has been best known for two serious wrongs. The first was leaving Reformed Christianity with the awful heritage that is the doctrine of predestination. The second crime was that he all but single-handedly set fire to the stake to which Servetus had been tied. He is therefore seen as no less than a murderer of both souls and people. Concerning the first, nothing needs to be added to what has already been said. But what about the second accusation?

Servetus was a doctor who came from Spain, but not with any intention to help Calvin with his many health issues in Geneva. So why did he come to Geneva? Servetus was, in fact, already a dead man before he came to Calvin's city; an effigy of him had been burned in Spain following an official order of the Roman Catholic Church. This was often done if the person concerned could not be captured, and was intended to burn into the mind of the perpetrator the message that he was as good as dead even if he had not yet actually been executed. The reason Servetus had for all intents and purposes been burned by Rome was that he thought the doctrine of the Trinity was a bunch of nonsense. He called God a three-headed monster, and also had other names to make his opinion clear. What he did and said was against the law. Emperor Charles V had established a law that everyone in his empire who denied the doctrine of the Trinity was to be punished with death. A denial of the Trinity was a frontal attack on the Christian faith, and thus on the established power of the empire as well. This meant that Servetus could just as well have been burned in Cologne, Strasbourg or Antwerp. Unfortunately for Calvin, and for all Reformed believers in fact, it happened that Servetus was executed in Geneva. One might almost think that Servetus had intentionally chosen Geneva in order to smear Calvin eternally with a bad name in a sort of suicide mission. If this was indeed his intention, it has certainly been a considerable success. If, however, Servetus went to Geneva in the hope that he could get the council on his side, and thereby bring Calvin into problems, his mission was a rather painful failure.

CONTACT

Calvin and Servetus had actually already been in contact before. Calvin had invited him to Paris for the purpose of dialogue. A date was set, but Servetus never showed. Thereafter Calvin never made the least effort to respond to him, and ignored every single one of the thirty letters Servetus wrote. Calvin remarked to Farel that Servetus offered to come to Geneva should Calvin want that. Calvin, however, did not want that, and immediately added that if Servetus decided to come anyway, he would make sure the

Spaniard never left the city alive. In that he clearly succeeded.

There can be no doubt that Servetus was looking for a confrontation. What else would have possessed him to go to Calvin's church on the afternoon of Sunday, August 13, 1553? After the service he was spotted by someone while eating, and this person informed Calvin. Calvin, in turn, fulfilled his civic duty by reporting this man, a known threat to the state, to the authorities. Nothing would ever have been made of this had the event not been interpreted later as evidence that Calvin was a basket-case heretic hunter, who maniacally tried to get rid of anyone who did not agree with him. At the time, in any case, no one thought anything of it. This is clear from the letters of advice Geneva received from neighboring cities upon request. Servetus was arrested and interrogated. At a certain point in the proceedings he was offered the chance to be returned to France, but on his knees he pleaded that he might be tried in Geneva. His request was honored.

The council could come to no other decision but to have Servetus burned at the stake: if this step was not taken Geneva itself ran the risk of being seen as a city that threatened the state. Calvin went to seek out Servetus and convince him to recant his statements, but he did not succeed. He also did not succeed in securing a less painful death sentence for Servetus, asking that he be hanged instead. Once again, it is more than clear that Calvin by no means had the final say in Geneva. Servetus was burned, but the smell of smoke has clung to Calvin's clothes for centuries.

It hardly makes sense either to attack Calvin as an intolerant fanatic or to defend him as a child of his time who simply did what the law required of him. The fact of the matter is that people often know nothing about Calvin except a simplified version of this event, which they consider enough to, as it were, tie him to the stake himself. One author who has greatly contributed to this is Stefan Zweig, whose 1938 novel described Calvin's demeanor in such a way that alleged similarities with Adolf Hitler could not escape even an illiterate person.

The Servetus affair took place at a time when there was great tension in the city. Calvin's colleague Wolfgang Musculus assumed that Servetus had come to the city to take advantage of the council's dissatisfaction with Calvin. It is remarkable that Servetus was condemned by a government that was actually not at all favorably disposed toward Calvin, but they saw no other option but to carry this punishment out. Any city that became known as tolerant of those who would deny the Trinity would be abandoned by friend and foe alike. This also relativizes the whole Servetus affair a little. It may be interesting as fodder for debates on the extent of religious toleration, or a study to find out why Calvin has for so long been implicated in it. At the end of the day, however, the Servetus case was just one among many others.

ENOUGH

By this time, Calvin had had enough of his struggles, but in the 1550s the situation only worsened. "Here in the republic there is such chaos that the church is being tossed back and forth by God as Noah's ark was by the waves of the flood." He claimed that the people of Geneva were so fanatically opposed to him "that by now everything that we say is considered suspect. If, for example, I were to say that it is light in the afternoon, they would immediately begin to doubt it." Calvin also claimed that they played on his weaknesses, for they knew "that I am irritable and thus they try to test my patience by provoking me often and in many ways." To a professor in Leipzig he wrote that if the situation in Geneva was known, he would understand "that you must go far from here to find rest."

In his sermons on 1 Timothy from late 1554 to early 1555, Calvin was very open about the situation. He said that he would most gladly withdraw from Geneva, that he would go as far away from it as possible, that he wanted to ask God to make sure he put at least one hundred cities between him and Geneva. Calvin thought things had turned into a complete disaster there and was ashamed to be the city's pastor. Even a blind man could see that things were wildly chaotic in the city. Calvin's view was that what had taken place here could in no way be called a reformation. All efforts from, and on behalf of, God had come to nothing, and all that could be done was to wait and see how God would react. According to Calvin, "God would burst out in tears over it" *(pleurer)*. Calvin himself wanted nothing more than to leave. "If it were up to me, I would wish that God would take me out of this world, and that I would not have to spend even three more days in this mess."

Much of this had to do with the frustration that not everyone was as Calvin himself was. Calvin seems to have known the full range of human emotion, including the experience of that awful feeling of tiring oneself out only for minimal results. It was the doubt as to whether any of his work had been worth the effort, made especially difficult by being completely on his own. Calvin could well imagine that God also had had enough. Our heavenly Father had invested so much time and effort in us, but in light of what has been done with it, "He has more than enough reason to reject us, and no longer count us among his children." Calvin noticed that people outside of Geneva were fairly impressed with the way things went within the city. They were awed by the order that prevailed and by the fairness of the market. For Calvin, however, this was nothing but a front: Geneva remained a city full of scandals. Calvin could not understand why, when God gave so much grace, the people did so little with it; when he gave so much love, the people still remained unfaithful. No matter how the city may have appeared to those on the outside, Calvin knew that within Geneva "we carry about as traitors."

FAREWELL SERMON

According to the Scriptures, the words of institution for the Lord's Supper were pronounced shortly before Christ's death. It was a sort of farewell sermon accompanied by a sacrament, but that sacrament was intended to promote unity between Christ and believers. It is thus sad that both the schism between Rome and Reformation, as well as the schisms within the Protestant camp, essentially stem from disputes over this sacrament. The Lord's Supper also provided the context for Calvin's farewell sermon on Sunday, September 3, 1553, which he preached on these words of Acts 20:32: "Now I commit you to God and to the word of his grace." Calvin had had enough, but this, of course, was not the motivation behind Christ's farewell sermon. Calvin's situation was informed by nothing other than the old struggle for ecclesiastical power between the church and the state, between the church council and the city council. The consistory had ex-

pelled—or, to use that awful word, excommunicated—Philibert Berthelier. He, however, still considered himself a member of the church and
appealed his case to the Little Council as if he were still in good standing.
He was successful: the Little Council ruled that he had the right to participate. By this decision, the state overruled a decision of the church. Calvin,
however, wanting to obey God rather than man, felt bound to a higher authority and declared that even if Berthelier were to come to church, he
could forget about participating in the Lord's Supper because Calvin would
serve him neither the bread nor the cup. Calvin was fully aware as to how
this would end, because it had ended the same way in 1538. He was certain
it would mean another exile. Calvin's sermon, however, turned out not to
be a farewell message after all, because the following Monday there was a
fierce dispute within the Little Council after which the other pastors decided to stand behind Calvin. The case dragged on for about a year until, on
March 20, 1554, the council declared that they alone ruled the city. This, of
course, brought no manner of resolution to anything, and so the advice of
Basel, Bern and Zürich was once again solicited. The other cities kept themselves out of it. Basel simply stated how things were done there, telling the
Genevans nothing they did not already know. Bern noted that they did not
use excommunication at all. Zürich said that Geneva should return to the
old way, and that each city thus had its own customs.

REBELLION

A meeting of the Council of the Sixty and of the Two Hundred was held on
January 24, 1555, in order to discuss what should be done next. Calvin of
course had a pretty good idea. Speaking on behalf of the consistory, he made
it clear to the politicians that the Scriptures gave the right of excommunication and readmission to the church. To everyone's surprise the council
agreed. It was decided that the church should simply be allowed to do its
work, and thus Calvin wrote to Bullinger that "after a long struggle, we
have finally had the right of excommunication conferred upon us." Calvin's
sermon was thus no farewell at all, but the announcement of a new period
in the history of the city. In February the political tide turned as well when

the four newly elected syndics all turned out to be supporters of Calvin.

Support for Calvin grew within the council, but so did the number of conflicts between the Children of Geneva and the refugees from France. In autumn 1547 the *Chambre ardente* was instituted in France. This was a royal body charged with the adjudication of heretics, which meant anything and anyone that was not Roman Catholic. Hundreds of Protestants were sentenced to death, while thousands fled the land of King Francis. Many sought refuge in the city where another Frenchman appeared to be king, though he was not, and so they came to Geneva. This influx of new refugees brought about a resurgence of that ancient and ineradicable xenophobia, but they were still given the opportunity to buy citizenship, which many did. Ami Perrin, the same man who had brought about Calvin's return in 1541, and his friends did everything in their power to prevent this, and so a rumor was started that the new citizens were forming a fifth column intent on secretly delivering the city into the hands of the French. Tensions escalated, people took to the streets, and when the mayor came out on May 16 to try to calm the crowds and prevent violence, Perrin attempted to grab his staff, which was viewed as an act of treason. Perrin and several of his friends were forced to flee and condemned to death *in absentia*. Four others confessed and were executed. This rebellion that had come about as the result of growing tensions between the Children of Geneva and those who sided with the refugees resulted in so great a defeat for the former group that a large part left the city. Geneva lost a large number of citizens, but also gained many, which was desirable because citizens paid taxes, defended the city and worked to its general welfare, especially if they happened to be promising businessmen. Geneva thus came to owe no small part of its wealth and standing to the Reformed refugees.

New Winds

With the elections of 1555, the political winds shifted. In the preceding period, many refugees from France had already obtained citizenship. Citizenship meant that you became *bourgeois* and that you had all the rights of the natives, the *citoyens* born in Geneva, with the exception of a place in the senate. These new citizens were also greatly needed, because while refugees did not pay taxes, citizens did, and while refugees might just stand around, citizens could be called to arms to defend their city. The refugees, therefore, had been given certain rights and (especially!) duties, but nevertheless were still kept from political power. The supporters of Calvin in the council thought this too was to their gain politically, for citizens were entitled to vote. In full agreement with a policy of *ora et labora,* and propelled by the idea that those who were not strong had to be smart, the Calvin party began to push for more rights for the foreigners, even if not all refugees were Calvinists. This roused angry protests from some people who were quick to see what was going on, but the anti-French party was unable to resist the new citizenship policy. Slowly the Calvinist party gained a small majority, not only through direct supporters but also through the votes of those who saw that the Perrinists' policy had not exactly brought about peace and quiet for the city, and that they were further a rather exclusive and cliquey bunch who only provoked and aroused suspicion. Many votes for Calvin were protest votes from those who had had it with Perrin and were now ready to give another political party a chance. Such a chance need be offered to Calvinists only once, because they are glad to take on a project and to see it through. In this way, the Calvin party aimed at a second, comprehensive reform of the city.

MIRACLE

Those who could not see in these events the miracle from God that Calvin saw will still need an explanation for this dramatic turn of events. An explanation can indeed be given, even if it must be composite. First, there was the influence of the Reformed elders in the consistory, people who were devoted to, and kept in close contact with, the people and the pastors. Over the years, Calvin had managed to populate the consistory with people who were both ecclesiastically and juridically well informed and who were committed to the right theology. Those elders made family visits during which they heard what was going on in the lives of the people, and by means of which they could give instruction as to what a Reformed view of church, politics and society ought to look like. Their close interaction with the pastors ensured that they were well-prepared for these tasks. Even greater was the influence that was exercised simply through preaching and catechetical instruction. If one wonders how Calvin ever managed to turn a chaotic, politically volatile Geneva into a city that experienced rest and prosperity, and that exerted influence throughout Europe as an independent state, one need look no further than the sermon and the catechism. It is difficult to estimate the influence of the daily exposition of the Bible and the years of biblical teaching given to the youth in Calvin's Geneva. Instruction was given by well-trained pastors, strong ministers who knew the languages and the rules of rhetoric, and who could hold their own against church people and politicians. Their instruction formed the people of Geneva from childhood on, corrected them, gave them knowledge in the Scriptures, and instructed them in how the world fits together and how the church ought to fit together. In addition, this education that was given within the triangle of church, school and family was supported by a theology that taught that though humanity might well be completely corrupt, God's grace could completely change people, and God's Spirit could spur them on to great deeds of blessing and renewal. What Calvin did from 1541 on is proof that a society can be changed. It also attests to his conviction that simply leaving things as they are is completely un-Reformed.

DRIVE

There is a question that presents itself, certainly with respect to the years of Calvin's life presently under consideration, but which could also be asked of the whole of his life. What drove Calvin to devote himself to his cause with such conviction, or if you will, fanaticism? The answer has everything to do with his walk with God.

> From my very birth, God has cared for me. I have gone through a million dangers, and he has delivered me. And would I then not repay my Father for his protection? I further have been oppressed on every side, but God always took heed of me. And how often have I not become Satan's prey, and yet God did not a single time will that I should perish?

Once when Calvin drew up an account of his life, he saw that God had brought him from birth through so many illnesses and difficulties that he could not but serve this God. In short, Calvin's motives were thanksgiving and obedience to God the Father.

He was further fully convinced that God had given him his office, and that he had to fulfill the duties of that office faithfully. He thought the same about making good on promises. If Geneva had committed itself to a church order, that church order must be followed. If Calvin was to be hindered in the duties of his office, he would rather be forced to flee than to abandon it.

What does not fit with the present-day image of Calvin is that he could laugh even as he was caught up in his drive. Of course, there was never any such thing as a Calvin who rolled on the floor with laughter—even here there ought to be restraint and moderation. Besides, Calvin's frail body would only have given him shooting pains if he laughed that hard. Calvin's sense of humor was that of a humanist, that of the intellectual elite. Calvin said he laughed heartily when he read in the *Christian Disputations* how Viret had unmasked the "superstitions of this poor world." Even laughter must have a goal. So when Calvin wrote to the de Fallais in 1547 on the occasion of the birth of a child, he said he would be glad to spend an hour with them, to laugh together in order to make their little child laugh as well, "for that is after all the first sound we make in the beginning of our lives; and we can only really laugh once we have left this life." For Calvin, life both began and ended with laughter, but in between there was a vale of tears. In spite of the difficulties of the French Protestants, Calvin allowed himself a joke when he heard that Jean Mercier, in contrast to the earlier reports, appeared not to be dead after all. The rumor had not just frightened but completely crushed him, and Mercier ought to have been impressed by this. In Paris Mercier had been beaten and left for dead in the Seine, but he was later taken out alive. Calvin was overjoyed by "this happy catch," and told Mercier he should now make sure Calvin could continue to be happy.

Laughing, however, was not the same thing as mocking God, and that was something Calvin could not bear. Aside from the deeper theological issues, this was one reason why Calvin could not stand the Lutheran Osiander. Calvin thought he was a bit of a strange fellow. "From the first day that I saw him, I was disgusted by the unholy and terrible conduct of that man. Every time he wanted to praise a sweet, fine wine, he would say: 'I am who I am' (Ex 3:14), or, 'This is the Son of the living God' (Jn 6:69). That is outright mockery of God."

The last laugh is the best laugh, Calvin could well have said. In 1552, full of worry, he wrote: "It is good that we are anchored in heaven, for otherwise we would never be able to sail safely through these storms." In 1555, the weather turned. Calvin became a phenomenon, even a tourist attraction, and before he was to finish his course in heaven, things would settle down for him even on this side of life.

SAILOR

(1555-1559)

In 1555 the political winds were finally at Calvin's back. After the elections the makeup of the city council was such that it consisted of a majority of Calvin supporters. This was a considerable change, but the party that had first effected the revolution, reformation and independence of Geneva fell apart and disappeared from the stage on account of its internal divisions and snobbery.

The number of refugees who obtained the right of citizenship grew by 127 in 1555 and by 144 in 1556. They were almost without exception people who supported Calvin and his policies, and their qualities ensured that they soon took on important functions in the ecclesiastical, political and social spheres. In this way, Geneva became a forerunner of a phenomenon more particularly associated with the nineteenth and twentieth centuries, where cities underwent social and political transformation through the immigrants who began to determine the city's shape and to take control from the locals. In Geneva no French ghetto was created in the process. Instead, the city became a completely international and internationally oriented city. This had everything to do with Calvin's view that the world had taken on a different look. His theology of the experience of being a stranger, of having heaven as one's true home country, reduced the need for strong ties to one's earthly home country, increased mobility and produced a pioneer mentality. Calvin's political outlook also informed this new view of the world: the time of the old world had passed, and Europe was now divided not into east and west, or north and south, but into Catholic and Reformed. For Calvin it was not nation, region or locality that was important, but the overall direction of a people who had come together in one city from many different cultures, united by religion.

According to Farel, it was God who brought people from all over Europe to this "asylum." This statement has a pious ring to it, so it must be added that these people came to Geneva because of Calvin. Also noteworthy is that while Farel focused on Geneva as a praiseworthy earthly city, Calvin made a point of looking beyond it. "Improve the world, begin with Geneva," was Calvin's motto. Others could praise Geneva all they wanted, but Calvin had a different opinion of the state of the city, and he wanted to set out from Geneva as a starting point into the rest of the world. This makes it all the more remarkable that just when the party supporting Calvin gained the upper hand, he made the decision to leave his office and the city. Little is known as to what may have moved him to this, except that Viret reported there were many things that vexed Calvin. Viret convinced Calvin to stay and exhorted him not to let anything and everything bother him. The fact that Calvin did stay probably had more to do with another terrifying visit from Farel, who, when he had heard of Calvin's plans, immediately traveled to Geneva and preached there on March 22, 1556. Soon thereafter, Calvin dropped his plan. His change of mind will surely have resulted more from Farel's assault than from the power of God's Word.

DISCIPLINE

The church had finally gained the right of discipline, and, as the numbers reveal, it readily made use of it. In the first year after the rebellion of 1555 there were 80 cases, in the following year 160, and each of the years from

1557 to 1561 there was an average of 240. In 1559, there were even 300 excommunications. These numbers are impressive for a population of some 20,000.

As early as November 12, 1557, it was decided that those who ignored the discipline administered by the church were to be banned from the city for a year. Three months later it became even more clear that the church had become independent: it was decided that the mayor was no longer allowed to take his staff to the consistory meetings because he was there as church official rather than government representative. In this way, Calvin showed himself much wiser than Ami Perrin in making a grab at the mayor's staff.

All of these discipline cases give a good idea of the kinds of things that were happening in the city and of what Calvin and his colleagues thought could, and could not, be permitted. Before considering these matters, it is wise to remind ourselves that the world at that time was very different from the one we live in today. We should also be mindful of our tendency to think we have come so much farther than our ancestors, not only knowing much more but also doing much better. To keep things in perspective, we would also do well to remember that in Calvin's context, church discipline and civil law all but coincided, and that breaking the law immediately meant the involvement of the church as well.

The notion that Geneva must have been a terrible place to live during Calvin's lifetime does not fit at all with the fact that thousands took refuge there and were more than glad to stay. Many horror stories have circulated for centuries about a supposed reign of terror, but the facts leave us with a different picture. Despite the reports of certain books that claim to be historical, no one was ever put to death for blasphemy or for disobeying one's parents in Calvin's Geneva.

Moreover, the government and consistory not only oversaw the city but also themselves. The consistory first introduced the *censura morum,* a round-table discussion within the consistory where each elder took a turn standing outside while the others discussed whether or not he was doing his work well. The council later decided to do the same, and during the meeting preceding the celebration of the Lord's Supper no less! How could they keep good oversight of the people if they were not putting in their own good efforts? How could they promote harmony in the church and state when there was disharmony within their own ranks? This practice has been maintained in many Reformed churches outside of Geneva, but in politics the *censura morum* has been abandoned even in Geneva itself.

INTERNATIONAL

If Calvin had wanted to turn Geneva into a New Jerusalem, he succeeded at least in the sense that, just as at Pentecost, people spoke, preached and sang in different tongues. There were English, Italian and Spanish communities, each of which had its own congregation and worship services. People came from countries as far away as Crete, Tunisia and Malta in order to settle in Geneva. At Calvin's Academy, there were students from such territories as Catalonia, the Netherlands, Scotland, Calabria and Venice.

Not every foreigner, however, was a benefit, and Calvin ran into problems, particularly with the Italians. There was, for example, Matteo Gribaldi, an expert in law from Padua, who denied the doctrine of the Trinity just as Servetus had. His lot turned out better than that of Servetus, for he was merely banished from the city. His countryman Giovanni Gentile was put into prison for similar opinions, but escaped with his life by the skin of his teeth when he claimed that, on second thought, he had changed his views. His recantation appeared to be either short-lived or not heartfelt when some time later he took up residence in Bern and was subsequently beheaded for heresy. Two other Italians, Giorgio Blandrata and Giovanni Alciati, also left Geneva after they got into trouble with Calvin over the doctrine of the Trinity. Calvin had the same sort of difficulties with certain Poles. Lelio Sozzini, who would later become one of the founders of Unitarianism, paid Calvin a visit, and although they disagreed, Calvin nevertheless gave Sozzini a recommendation to the Polish prince Radziwil. Calvin was not happy with all of the French refugees, either. He thought there were some who took advantage of the situation in France to come and live an easy life in Geneva. Pretending to flee for the sake of the Word, "they come here to corrupt and defile the church with their sinful and licentious life."

WEBER

We turn now to the issue of work. Weber's thesis concerning the Protestant work ethic is well-known in scholarly circles, but this early twentieth-century theory may need some explanation for those outside of academia. It is really not all that difficult. Weber's theory basically comes down to the supposition that good Calvinists are almost by definition capitalists, because Calvinism typically combines piety and fiscal discipline. Calvinist predestination leads to an inner isolation and a pessimistic individualism, and these are useful attributes for a budding entrepreneur. One who truly hopes to be counted among the elect will also anxiously look for proof of his or her election, and will avoid doing anything that is not allowed. What is allowed, moreover, he or she will do only in moderation. Therefore, one might be assured of one's election by certain qualities of lifestyle, thus one makes greater and greater attempts to live a Christian life. This would mean wasting no time, working steadily, not living in luxury and not throwing money around. Following these guidelines, one ends up a capitalist. If one were to decide to do some social work to prevent beggars from doing nothing all day, one might open a business. By taking people in off the street, theft is reduced, work has been provided to others who had none, and a thriving business is created. Again, Calvinist virtues coincide with capitalism. Weber was honest enough to admit that Calvin himself was not a capitalist, but maintained that his theology tended toward it.

Much can and has been said against this thesis, but considered in light of what actually happened in Geneva during those years, it has to be admitted that Weber had a point. Calvin tightened moral laws, and a well-organized ecclesiastical institution kept a close eye on everything and everyone. Marriage was protected, prostitution was forced back. Laws were introduced against fancy clothes and overindulgence in food and drink. Parties were to be held with moderation. A small weaving mill was set up to create jobs. Although usury was prohibited, reasonable interest could be charged because it was seen as good for the economy. The common argument against charging interest—that the practice allowed some to make money without doing any work, which was perceived as unchristian—Calvin dismissed as not only weak but also bad for the economy.

Money

In spite of the above, however, Calvin cannot be made the father of capitalism. This is in part because his doctrine of predestination differs from the version described by Weber but also because he himself reacted fiercely against the capitalism that was already coming up in his time. Calvin was not oblivious to the role money played in society and to the harm it did, but he continued to see it as a useful means and thereby became the first theologian to give a biblical defense for charging interest. Of course, Calvin had nothing against lending money without interest, especially since Jesus had said that Christians should lend without expecting anything back (Lk 6:35). Calvin saw it as an Anabaptist confusion of the two kingdoms if this rule was applied to regular economic activity. Calvin thus had a positive view of bankers, but also of farmers, who were God's coworkers in a very special way, since in their work God's work is more visible than in the work of others. Those too who were employed in intellectual or technical fields received theological support for their career choices from Calvin, whereby they could hold themselves proudly in their work. If God's Spirit is the only source of truth, the truth—wherever we encounter it—may not be rejected or despised, for this would be to hold God himself in contempt. It is impossible to despise the gifts of the Spirit without also despising and scorning the Spirit himself. Calvin saw the work of God's Spirit particularly in the discoveries of science, which teach us more about God. It should then come as no surprise that there are so many scientists among the Reformed as well as bankers. Calvin had nothing against private possession, so long as Christians were ready to share what they owned with others. One who possessed anything "did not receive by simple chance, but by the allotment of the highest Lord of all things." In effect, we are not possessors but "distributors" (*dispensateurs*).

Calvin himself had little use for money. When he was accused of being greedy, it only made him and others laugh, "for everyone knows that just this year I turned down an offer of a raise, and did so with such persistence that I swore under oath that I would not preach a single sermon more if they did not stop offering it." Calvin also discarded as ridiculous the rumor that he had sold a piece of land for good money. In and around Geneva, everyone knew that he did not own even a square inch of property. "For I have not made it this far, and in fact I use the furniture that belongs to someone else. Neither the table from which we eat, nor the bed in which we sleep, belongs to us." Nevertheless, Calvin was very sensitive to these kinds of accusations. When he heard that it was being rumored in Bern that he had embezzled large sums given by the queen of Navarre for the aid of the refugees, he reacted at length and pointed out that even his greatest enemies knew money did not interest him. This accusation was complete nonsense. "Everyone knows how simple things are in my home. They can see that I spend no money on nice clothes, and it is further well known that my brother is not rich, and that what he does have he did not receive from me."

WORK

For all of this, however, Weber's thesis that Calvin's work ethic boosted capitalism is not totally without ground. Calvin worked virtually night and day. On April 20, 1539, he wrote to Farel:

> I cannot think of a day this year in which I was so overwhelmed with all kinds of things to do as today. For because the messenger wanted to take also the first part of my work, I also had to look over the first twenty pages of the manuscript. On top of that I had to lecture, preach, write four letters, settle several disputes and receive more than ten visitors. I thus apologize for being a little brief and less clear than usual in my letter.

Calvin got up at four o'clock every morning, and went to bed late. He worked systematically and as efficiently as possible. When he was busy with the corrections to Olivetan's Bible translation, he wrote that he "cut an hour from each day" to be able to work on it. All of this helps us to understand how he became so highly irritated when he lost the manuscript of a commentary. He got so worked up over it that he could get nothing else done anymore: "Whatever it was that I started on, nothing worked." What bothered him most was not the loss itself, but that he had only his carelessness to blame for it.

Calvin barely took any time for himself. Even when he was sick, he attempted to keep working, claiming that he could be useful when sick in bed by patiently and willingly adapting himself to the situation and resisting the temptation to rebel. What time he did take for himself was devoted to meals with others, where he could drink from the wine the council had apportioned to him in 1542 as reward for his efforts on behalf of the city. Calvin endlessly remarked that he was too busy, that he had no time and that he was not doing enough. Even in his earliest letters he complains of his laziness, and this continues throughout almost every other letter until the reader becomes bored by the assertion. To Hubert he apologized that he was dictating the letter: "I am dictating this letter because I am suffering from a migraine. So that you will not think that I am doing this out of laxness." On August 10, 1548, he apologized to Farel that he had recently allowed two messengers on their way to Neuchâtel to pass on without a letter for Farel, and now "I fear that you may accuse me of laziness." Two weeks later he repeated this, and anticipated what Farel would say: "I think that deep down, you will probably accuse me of laziness."

FRUSTRATION

Calvin could become hopelessly frustrated when his work did not progress as anticipated, as he let Farel know when the latter inquired about two commentaries:

> Why do you even talk about Acts and Genesis, which are hardly even like newly conceived fetuses in the womb? I am ashamed to tell you how slowly I am progressing with Acts. Now that I have finished a third of it, I see that it will become a large volume. Genesis I have had to put aside for some time. The last four months I have been busy with the corrections [of the translation] of the New Testament. Now I am against my will being involved with the Old Testament. I had urged the printers to look in time for people who are qualified for this task, as I am not. Since they did not follow my advice, I now suffer the punishment for their own sluggishness.

Farel could praise Calvin's diligence kindly, but Calvin himself was all too aware of his own slowness and laziness: "May the Lord grant that, in spite of my slow pondering, I may yet get somewhere." Farel apparently persisted in pressuring him at times, but Calvin could not take that. "So you would gladly see a couple of commentaries appear from my hand as if I just produce books like that and then immediately have them published, commentaries for which one actually needs a lifetime of intense work? How much free time do you actually think I have?" More exasperating, but also very recognizable for many readers, was Calvin's opinion that so many other people were at least as lazy. As one who lived to work and still thought he was not doing enough, it can be no surprise that Calvin would surely consider others lazy as well.

Even if Calvin had wanted to take more time, that would simply not have been possible. His correspondence alone took an incredible amount of time, and there were yet all the other daily tasks on top of that. A colleague from Neuchâtel invited Calvin to his wedding, but he had no time. "For a month now I have not even left the city, not even to relax." Nicolas Colladon gave a brief overview of how Calvin might spend a day in 1549:

> In that year he preached on Sunday mornings on the letter to the Hebrews, and when he had finished with it on the Acts of the Apostles. . . . In the Sunday evening services, he preached from the Psalms. . . . The other days of the week, he preached on the prophet Jeremiah. In his lectures, he expounded for students, preachers and other auditors on the prophet Isaiah, with which he had begun a long time ago. Fridays in the *Congrégation* he treated the letter to the Hebrews, and thereafter took up the catholic letters. As to his writings, in that year he published his commentary on the letter to Titus and on the letter to the Hebrews.

Starting in 1549, Calvin preached twice every Sunday, and every other week preached no less than daily, which worked out to some 4,000 sermons. Three times a week he lectured on biblical exegesis. Each Friday he was an active participant in the *Congrégations*. In all of these things he wanted to be as prepared as he could be, but this proved impossible, as he also complained to Farel in a letter from June 1554. The council repeatedly asked for his advice, sometimes even about things that were not really Calvin's specialty. In 1557, for example, he was asked by the council whether or not a new heater should be purchased.

Never Stop Working

In spite of the above, it would be too much to propose a thesis to the effect that "Calvinists never stop working" on the basis of Calvin's own work schedule. After all, who at that time did not work day and night? Everyone did, except, if we are to believe Calvin, the Catholic clergy. Calvin's anti-Rome bias may well have led to some hyperbole, such as in his claim that most clerics followed a work ethic diametrically opposed to his own. Calvin wrote to an unidentified clergyman that he was both overjoyed and amazed that this particular man was different. "I first of all want to congratulate you from the heart that you are not one of those clergymen who throughout their entire lives are so busy eating and drinking, playing and sleeping, and with their vile lusts, that they do not even in their dreams ever think of honest labor." We do not know about Calvin's dreams, but when he was awake he wanted to spend his hours differently from the aforementioned clergymen. He still thought, though, that life could be enjoyed. Neither should one's enjoyment of life be too constricted, because enjoyment was a part of Christian freedom. The conscience should not be needlessly worked up, "for when the conscience has once let itself be entrapped, it enters into a long and convoluted maze." What Calvin says about the trap into which the conscience can fall is best related in his own words:

> When you begin to doubt whether you may use linen for sheets, shirts, handkerchiefs and tablecloths, you will thereafter not be sure whether you can use hemp. And then you will also have doubts about using flax. You will consider whether you could do without a tablecloth at dinner, and whether handkerchiefs are really necessary. If you suppose that you may not permit yourself a nicer meal, in the end you will not eat normal bread or an ordinary dinner with a clear conscience before God when you realize that even more simple nourishment would do for your body. When you doubt whether or not you may drink a fine wine, you will soon no longer be able to drink

even a flat wine with a peaceful conscience, and in the end not dare to touch
any water that is sweeter or better than others. Finally, things will go so far
that you think it sinful to step over a straw that blocks your path.

SUNDAY

Calvin sometimes also escaped from the city for a few days, and he did this
on Sunday of all days. He once suggested to Viret that he should come to
Geneva from Lausanne on Saturday. "On Sunday morning you can preach in
the city, and I will go to Jussy. After eating, you follow me and together we
will go to Sieur de Fallais, so that from his place we can cross over to the
other side and take a vacation of several days with Sieur de Lisle and Sieur
Pommier." This reveals that the rumor that Calvin went sailing every Sunday afternoon is based on a significant misunderstanding—whether one
likes it or not. Nevertheless, that Calvin had no difficulties crossing Lake
Geneva in a sailboat in order to begin a midweek holiday is certainly true—
again, whether one likes it or not.

Traveling on Sundays was not uncommon. A year earlier Calvin had suggested that Viret should depart after the morning service so as to be in
Geneva before lunch on Monday. Calvin also sometimes left the city for
several days to be able to work without interruption, and here it is clear that
he was certainly no Puritan. He wrote that he "had intended last Sunday to
go to the country in order to concentrate fully on my work for three days,
free from all other things." That very Sunday, however, Calvin could not
find his papers, thought they had been stolen, and became so worked up
over it that he—as was typical!—became sick and could not leave until
Monday. One who has even the slightest Puritan tendencies could find in
this irony the opportunity to reproach Calvin's intended use of the sabbath,
pointing out that God immediately punishes such sins.

What is most remarkable is the rumor that was circulating in that time
that Sunday observance had been completely abolished in Geneva. Calvin
was glad to know that Bullinger did not believe it, and added that it had
probably arisen from Geneva's decision to move Christmas to whichever
Sunday immediately followed it. Calvin was not responsible for this be-

cause, as he complained, the council took decisions in these matters without asking the pastors for their advice. "For that matter, already before I came to this city for the first time all the holidays but Sunday had been abolished here." After ensuing protests, four holidays were later reintroduced. Calvin decided to leave things be, but he did protest the fact that Jesus' circumcision was commemorated, but not his death. Similarly he preached every year against the fact that the conception of Christ was celebrated as a Marian feast. In these things, Calvin stood more or less alone between the two sides, especially in order to prevent pandemonium from breaking out between the advocates and enemies of the celebration of these holidays.

In the Reformed tradition, Sunday has become a bit of a problem, and in many circles it is above all a day on which many things are *not* allowed. For Calvin, however, it was to be above all a day on which many things *were* allowed, such as going to church, praising God, prayer and confession of faith. It was for this reason that there was a safeguard for servants, so that they could be free from their work and able instead to assemble on this day. To continue to allow them their rest, others should not call on their services, either. Restaurants were to be closed on Sunday, since everyone had the right to rest, and besides, whoever was in the bar would not be in church.

> For if the stores and businesses are closed on Sundays so that no one has to work as during the week, we have a much greater opportunity to devote our time to things to which God calls us, such as instruction in his Word, coming together to confess our faith, to call on his name and to participate in the celebration of the sacraments.

SOCIAL

On the one hand, enjoyment was to be had in moderation, even of some things which might to some degree be seen as potentially sinful. On the other hand, care must always be taken to look out for one's neighbor in society. This view of life is an aspect of Calvin's thought that has received little attention, but it would certainly be well worth the while to do so. Calvin was convinced that one who was justified was also sanctified. Or, to put it in less theological terms, when things were right between you and God, you would readily do what God asked. Thus the law not only shows that you are a sinner but also shows what, as a Christian, you ought to do. One important aspect of this is that a Christian should defend the poor. Calvin thought that the injustices one suffered ought to be endured as a kind of spiritual exercise, but that injustices suffered by others ought to be resisted and fought. Thus Calvin could become extremely fierce when people were, sometimes actually, stripped of their clothes to pay their debts. What kind of people ensure the repayment of loans they have made by forcing their debtors to sell their furniture and clothes? We have been placed on the earth to help, not to trample, one another. God loves the poor, and so whoever loves God must also love the poor. For Calvin, things were as simple as that, and this social concern also informed his opposition to excessive partying, clothes and other possessions. "Jesus Christ was not a tailor" was the sober reminder Calvin directed to the big wheels in the city who followed the latest French fashions while the city was crawling with poor wrecks and refugees who had lost everything.

Calvin was averse to all individualism and saw humanity as a collective whole where each one was responsible for the others. We are not here for ourselves, and we have nothing of our own. One who has more than another has that only so as to be able to better serve others. Calvin's social vision was based not only on the thought that God had bound people to each other but also on the conviction that, just as God cares for us, so we also ought to care for one another. Here, each person must realize the image of God, which should govern everyone's outlook, so that he or she is heartily ready to care for widows and orphans, beggars and refugees, in short, for anyone who has a hard life. Toward this end no collection was taken in Calvin's church, but rather there was a gathering of gifts. A collection supposes that you need to ask people to give money, but a gathering of gifts supposes that people are ready to give. Calvin believed that everyone who lived from Christ's sacrifice was ready to make sacrifices for others.

LUTHERANS

Calvin could put his own social views into practice with the Lutherans. He corresponded with a number of Lutheran theologians, such as Jacob Andreae, Veit Dietrich, Johann Marbach and Johann Brenz, but what characterized his relations was that he saw himself as being in line with Luther, and accused the Lutherans of departing from him. Calvin did not have a very high opinion of Marbach and called him a beast because he had brought about the closure of the French refugee church in Strasbourg. "So that small congregation that flourished for twenty-five years has been ruined under the raging attacks of this beast."

According to Calvin the Lutherans prevented any chance for Protestant reunification because they continued their disputes over the presence of Christ in the Eucharist, while Calvin claimed that Luther himself had realized this question was of secondary importance. According to Calvin, those who appealed to Luther's name in their battles were fanatics, by which they must have been offended, considering that Luther himself once wrote against the *Schwärmer* ("fanatics"). Calvin did not have an easy time with the Lutherans. In the summer of 1554 he dedicated his commentary on Genesis to the three sons of the Saxon elector Johann Friedrich, who had passed away in March of that year. The dedication was turned down, however, on the grounds that Calvin departed from the Lutheran view of the Lord's Supper and had further repeatedly insulted Luther's interpretation of Genesis. In 1555, Calvin lamented, "O, if only Luther were still alive. He could be fierce, but he never went as far as his followers, who cannot be called his students but rather imitators, or apes." Calvin was of the opinion that Luther, had he still been alive, would not have chosen for the Lutherans.

WESTPHAL

Calvin's most intense disputes were with Joachim Westphal (1510/11-1574), the pastor of Hamburg. When the Swiss abandoned the view that the bread and wine are merely symbols with the *Consensus Tigurinus* of 1549, Calvin hoped in vain that the Lutherans would be open to greater unity. Westphal reacted sharply to the publication of the *Consensus Tigurinus* and was also the

first to introduce the concept of "Calvinism" in order to put Calvin's view of
the Lord's Supper in as negative a light as possible. It was also through Westphal that Calvin came into contact with the Lutherans in Frankfurt am
Main, because in 1555 Westphal incited the Lutheran preachers there against
the Dutch-speaking Reformed refugee church, which had by that time existed for several years and had its own building to use. In the preface to his
commentary on Acts, Calvin praised the council of Frankfurt for helping
the refugees, but he asked the Lutherans why a book from Westphal should
cause so much strife when the Reformed and the Lutherans actually had so
much in common. When the situation further worsened due to the refugee
church's internal disputes, Calvin decided to make the journey to Frankfurt
in September 1556. His visit was a failure: the disputes continued, and the
Lutheran pastors did not want to talk to him. In 1561 the government decided to close the church of the refugee congregation because they were not
willing to give in to the Lutherans on certain points of doctrine and liturgy.
Then the question was whether Reformed believers could bring their children to be baptized by a Lutheran pastor and participate at the Lutheran
Lord's Supper. Calvin answered that the sacrament did not depend on the
one who administered it, and that while the Lutheran ceremonies were not
unimportant, they were not essential either. As long as one was not forced
to confess a Lutheran view of the Lord's Supper, one was free to partake in
it. This was how the pastors from Geneva saw it. Here, Calvin was in essence giving the same advice he had given to the refugee church of Wesel,
which had been forced by the city council to conform to the Lutheran confession in 1553. It was better to adapt and preserve the unity of the church,
in this case with the Lutherans, than to lose a whole Reformed congregation. Yet when the Reformed remnant was forced to subscribe to the Lutheran confession in 1563, Calvin wrote that a number of corrections on
baptism and the Lord's Supper would first need to be made.

It does not give a fair picture of Calvin to suggest that he only disputed
with the Lutherans. His contact with them was, to be sure, dominated with
controversy surrounding the Eucharist, but Calvin also had many friendly
exchanges with the likes of Justus Jonas (1493-1555). Jonas even offered to

translate Calvin's second treatise against Westphal, an offer that Calvin readily accepted.

THE ARK (*INSTITUTES* 1559)

It can be difficult to sail an ark, or a battleship or even a container ship, but Calvin somehow managed it. The final edition of Calvin's *Institutes* could be compared with any of these types of vessels. The *Institutes* had drifted onto the market in 1536 as a sailboat, but by 1559 it had grown into a cargo ship, increasing from six to eighty chapters. It had become fully loaded with containers carrying theological freight, which, in Calvin's opinion, ought to be shipped worldwide. It had, however, also turned into a battleship with which Calvin wanted to defend God's glory and human salvation, beating back every enemy's attack on the gospel, and ready to turn and launch attacks on menacing submarines and old fortresses. Of course, the *Institutes* could also be seen as a sort of Noah's ark, where the great variety of Christian thinkers, pastors and professors found their places together, where church fathers and scholastics, fellow Reformers and mystics, were given an orderly shelter and thus survived the flood of the ages. Only in such an ark could the truth be kept safe from the waves of heresy and unbelief.

There are also other factors that make comparison with the ark apt. In the introduction to the 1559 edition of the *Institutes*, Calvin wrote that a fever had almost finished him and that his condition had driven him to finish the work as a repayment to God for sparing him. As Noah steadily worked on the ark under the threat of the oncoming waters, so Calvin kept working on his magnum opus under the threat of his own death. Or did he simply want to do something in return for God's saving him?

The book became very big. It was heavy, which is something also said at times of its content, even at times by those who have never read it. Calvin is sometimes supposed to have taught everything that could possibly make him unappealing. Some consider his theology a total disaster on account of that horrible and untenable doctrine of predestination, as well as his pessimistic and fatalistic view of the human condition. In contrast, the fact that the longest chapter of the *Institutes* is devoted to prayer is quickly forgotten.

Furthermore, this was the work that particularly brought Calvin worldwide success, and for centuries it has spurred on church planting, edification and theological renewal. These facts, however, can hardly be accounted for by the negative image of Calvin.

At any rate, Calvin himself was satisfied with the *Institutes,* at least as far as the format was concerned. Calvin spoke of an *ordo,* something he sought all his life for all aspects of his life, but also for this book the text of which he never seemed to stop cutting and pasting. By 1559, however, he had found the right order, and nothing more needed to be done to it. The ark was finished. The flood could come. And indeed the *Institutes* survived the flood of theological works that continually swept over theologians as well as regular church members within the Reformed tradition. Calvin had not intended it as an arsenal of weapons for use in theological battles. For him the theologian's task was not to fill the ears but rather to strengthen the conscience.

Calvin claimed to use different writing styles depending on the audience to accomplish this purpose. For example, when it came to the Lord's Supper, he intended his short treatise on the subject particularly for the common people. "The simple, popular writing style, intended for unschooled people, shows my original intention, since for those who know Latin I have the habit of using more careful formulations." He added that he had written the same thing in the *Institutes,* but with greater clarity and more arguments. There was also the catechism, intended for the instruction of believers. For each target audience, Calvin had a different style. For students of theology it was that of the *Institutes.*

BARE BONES (LITURGY)

Sailboats need strong winds and a small cargo. Churches that want to move ahead, stay on course and maintain speed must unload all that might hinder them. The extent of Calvin's unloading can immediately be seen from the inside of the average Reformed church and is also evident in the liturgy during a service.

Images had to be removed. Luther had said that it was better to remove images from the heart before taking them out of the church, but Calvin could not understand why the two could not be done at the same time. Nevertheless, the problem was not with images or statues in themselves but rather with images of God. For Calvin any attempt to portray God did him an injustice. However humanity might represent him, we will always reduce our omnipresent God, and by shortchanging God we actually shortchange ourselves. Some might claim to worship God himself through the image, but in reality such people are only kidding themselves. History teaches that people do after all expect results from such images, and come to place their trust in wood or stone. Calvin also rejected the argument that images were books for the illiterate laity. Instead, efforts should be made to teach them, and one line of the catechism was worth at least as much as 5,000 crucifixes. Furthermore, there were many prostitutes in the whorehouses who were more modestly dressed many images of Mary in the churches. With all of this, however, Calvin did not intend to say he was against all art as such, whether paintings or sculptures. Artists ought to paint all that the eye might see. Calvin knew, of course, that the eye might at times see nudity, and added that what artists saw and depicted ought not to be indecent. After all, if artists are given a chance, they will usually take it.

Nevertheless, Calvin opposed iconoclasm. "God has never given us the command to destroy images unless they be in our own house, and in public the command is only for those whom he has given such authority." Calvin had difficulties with images, but even more with such destructive actions.

Feast Days

Calvin also had difficulties with the celebration of many holidays, which produced superstition rather than edification. Calvin, who was no big partier to begin with, also had little use for Christmas Day, and expressed his opinion clearly in a sermon on Micah 5 from Thursday, December 25, 1551:

> I see that today more people than usual have come to the sermon. How is that? Because it is Christmas! But who says it is? It appears to be that way for

those poor beasts, for is that not what they are, those who came for the preaching today only because it is the holiday? What then? Do you think you are honoring God with this? Shall we consider how obedient you actually are to God? You think to make a feast to him today. That is one thing. Indeed, as has been brought to your attention more often, it is a good thing that there is one day in the year on which we are shown what use it was to us that Jesus Christ was born into this world, and that the story of his birth is related as it will be on Sunday. But if you think that Jesus Christ was born on this day, you are but beasts, even mad beasts. If you think you can honor God by organizing a couple of holidays, you in fact honor the idols. To be honest, you think that you are honoring God, but in fact you are honoring Satan. . . . Specific days are not important when it comes to the birth of the Lord. We can speak of it Wednesday, Thursday, any day. But if you are so wicked as to worship God as is most convenient for you, it is blasphemy.

This was Calvin's problem with holidays. People worshiped God in the way that best suited them, which was blasphemy, because they had conjured up their own images of God and did not worship him as he wanted, but as they wanted. It was as simple as that. "When you realize this, you will also not find it so strange that we have abolished the celebration of Christmas on this particular day, and that we will celebrate the Lord's Supper this coming Sunday and tell of the birth of the Lord."

In spite of the above, when it came to liturgy Calvin allowed for more than many of his later followers did. The English congregation in Frankfurt became divided over liturgical rites because one party was of a more Anglican orientation, the other more Calvinistic. Calvin himself did not understand why they were making such a big deal over it. He even found it "absurd that division arises among brothers who have been banished from their home country and who took flight all together for the sake of the same faith." Were they now quarreling over prayer formulas and other ceremonies? Calvin thought that there were many follies in the Anglican liturgy, but these could not be changed in a day, and furthermore they could easily be tolerated. Something should be done about it, but not at that moment, and not at all in the situation in which the refugees found themselves. As

Calvin saw it, they should have been glad that there was a church in Frankfurt that they could join, and with respect to the rest they should simply accommodate themselves.

Baptism, Lord's Supper, Shut-Ins and Funerals

There were also other things in Calvin's church that were rather barren compared to a Catholic or Lutheran service. Calvin expressed his thoughts on liturgical customs in a letter to the pastors at Monbéliard, who had asked him for advice. He could only wholeheartedly reject emergency baptisms performed by midwives. Baptism ought to be administered by one who held the pastoral office, but more important was that such emergency baptisms were based on the false assumption that baptism was absolutely necessary for a child's salvation. Here too Calvin aimed to provide assurance for the people, and wanted to prevent baptisms performed out of mere panic. A child was taken up into God's covenant, and on the basis of that covenant she received eternal life if she died at a young age. When Rome denied the kingdom of God to unbaptized children, it did a great injustice to God's promises. Baptism is a sign and seal of his promise, and nothing less—but nothing more, either. It was as simple as that.

Calvin had no problems serving communion to shut-ins, even if they were on the point of death and requested to receive the sacrament that one last time. He wrote at length about this to Olevianus at Heidelberg. If a believer saw that the time had come to depart from this world, all kinds of temptations would assail her, and in that period the sacrament could be a help in the spiritual battle. "May one deny her this one help that so strengthens the conscience that she enters the battle with joy and receives the victory?" The Lord's Supper was also a symbol of the unity of the church, and by receiving it, one who had been confined to bed for a long time could yet confess and experience being one with the church. Calvin did have difficulty with the fact that this was not practiced in Geneva, but he did not want to start a quarrel over it. Opponents will point out that the Lord's Supper is a communal event and that providing communion to shut-ins individualizes it, but Calvin found this reasoning unconvincing. Communion for shut-ins was "a part of, or appendix to, the public celebration." Calvin was indeed aware that one had to be careful against the curiosity of those who simply found it exciting, and against the superstitious belief that this outward symbol would effect salvation. "For that reason I would prefer for the Lord's Supper to be administered to the bed-ridden but rarely, with careful consideration and not without good knowledge of the situation."

With respect to funerals, Calvin had little use for the custom of bringing the casket all the way into the church. He thought it best to go directly to the cemetery and deliver the funeral message there, so that people heard the message right by the grave. He also considered the tolling of bells unnecessary, but he did not want to make an issue of it where it was already an established custom.

BERN

In the meantime the problems with Bern appeared to have come to a definitive end with the political agreement that was forged between the two cities early in 1558. There was no real congeniality, but the threats of France as well as the Duke of Savoy made the agreement necessary. This also explains why there was also little in the way of a theological peace. In Bern, Calvin's view of the Lord's Supper had always been seen as too Strasbourgian and therefore too Lutheran, and not Zwinglian enough. Added to this was the dispute on predestination. After his exile from Geneva over this issue, Bolsec sought and found refuge in Bern, and his arrival resulted in disputes between followers and detractors that were not in the least appreciated by the city. The city council therefore decided to forbid discussions on subtle doctrinal distinctions, specifically naming predestination as a prime example of a doctrine that caused nothing but strife. The pastors from Bern who sided with Calvin in this matter were admonished, and the academy of Lausanne was even forbidden to use the *Institutes*. Of course, Calvin could not keep silent over this and wrote a long letter to the senate. He admitted that "we must be sober and humble with respect to this great, incomprehensible mystery," but added that one could not pretend as if the Bible said nothing about it. If this were to be the case, many texts would have to be cut out of the Scriptures. For the same reason, Calvin could not understand why the pastors from Bern took such a neutral position, which remark of course justified his own reaction as well. Calvin wished that the duty of his office and his conscience would let him keep quiet, but they would not. "When I then see how the heavenly teaching of Christ, for which he wants me to be a servant, is everywhere scornfully torn down, how scandalous would it be for me to tie a knot in my tongue and keep silent?" Calvin was also very surprised when Farel suggested that he dedicate his commentary on the Gospels to the council of Bern. Calvin had sweated over this commentary, and was he now to "cast it before the snouts of swine, so that they can tear it apart in shame and scorn"? Calvin worked himself up into a fit over Farel's suggestion. "I would rather let my tongue and hand be cut off than that I would let myself be moved to dictate or write what you propose." In the end, Farel's suggestion was neither dictated nor written down, and so Calvin entered the last phase of his life with his body still fully intact.

SOLDIER

(1559-1564)

SERVICE

Calvin may not have supported celebrating Christmas, but it was on Christmas Day 1559 that he received the gift of Genevan citizenship. He himself was above all glad that he had not needed to ask for it: he would have felt guilty because people might have been given the impression that he had asked out of selfish ambition. Calvin wanted his only ambition to be God's cause, and in the last years of his life, this was the cause with which he continued to be occupied and in which he continued to find success. Calvin's struggle for the church's jurisdiction was crowned by the revision of the *Ordonnances ecclésiastiques* of November 13, 1561, which included new marital laws among other things.

Calvin persisted. Throughout his life he had sought rest, but clearly he served a Master who would not give him any. "I would prefer nothing more than peaceful, scholarly work, if only he under whose command I stand would give me the freedom for it." He did not receive this rest and freedom on earth, and so he sought them in heaven instead. Calvin frequently wrote that he longed for death, or that he at least expected it to come soon. Life had become a struggle for him, and he spoke of it as military duty from which he soon hoped to be released. Calvin wrote this in 1555, but would have to endure another nine years of soldier's service in God's army.

MILITANCY

Calvin often used military terms and metaphors, calling the life of the believer "a continuous active military service." God calls us to arms because there is a war raging with Satan, and it is so fierce that there is little opportunity for down time. Believers, however, scorn the obstacles of this life and are ready to do battle at any and every moment, as well as to suffer injury, "for it is simply so that they are there to do battle on this earth." This was true especially of the pastors, who were also engaged in the internal battle, that is, the one inside the congregation. "The faithful servant knows the war" is a phrase that Calvin repeats time and again in his sermons on Jeremiah. If there is a militant tendency or a willingness to fight among Reformed believers, they did not get it from a stranger. Nevertheless, if they go out looking for a battle, they did not learn this from Calvin.

In any case, it is not clear whether Calvin's militancy came from his view of the Christian life as a battle or from his inherently militant nature, which might have led him to adopt such terminology. Most probably it was a combination of the two. What is clear is that he saw himself as the kind of soldier who, just when the army has been thrown into confusion, "grabs the banner from the commander and returns the people to their ranks." That banner was the cross of Christ, and it meant more suffering than triumph, which was also why "so few are found who are willing to take up this military service." For Calvin the courage needed to go back out into battle time and again was rooted in the fact that the Commander he served could not be beaten. In fact, in the paradoxical nature of this battle, the more Christ was attacked, the more he triumphed. The military service of the Christian life was like a training camp, "which is not only tough but also produces little honor, so that we realize we should not seek human approval and crowns of victory."

It was from this perspective that Calvin defended the right of the church to oversee the Lord's Supper. When he heard that the council was going to decide to keep this right for itself, he said that they would be able to accomplish this only if they killed or banished him. Calvin made his life a life-or-death battle. In such a state of war, neutrality was not possible, and for Calvin there had to be a choice between Rome and Reform. As has been made clear repeatedly, this choice had to be made radically.

Calvin's strongest weapon was his pen, and with it he launched a powerful offensive, in part by way of his commentaries. After careful consideration, he usually dedicated these to princes, in the hopes that the honored rulers would be able to do something for the cause of the gospel—that is, to help the Reformed church. Sometimes Calvin won a victory, sometimes he did not. His academy became another weapon—a sort of boot camp for the army of salvation.

BACK TO SCHOOL

Calvin's time at the Collège de Montaigu had not harmed him so much that he could no longer stomach well-run educational institutions. He did his best to push for a solid education backed by a tight curriculum until the establishment of the beginnings of what eventually became a university in Geneva. The three-year interruption that was his work in Strasbourg had fully convinced him that the training of pastors and others who could lead and serve church and society was of the greatest importance. In Bucer's city there was that beautiful and renowned gymnasium, set up by Jean Sturm, which later became the city's university. Calvin wanted the same for Geneva, and he succeeded. In 1556 he traveled to Strasbourg to ask Jean Sturm for advice. Calvin evidently made use of the tips he received, for on June 5, 1559, festivities—in moderation, of course!—were held for the opening of the Academy of Geneva, modeled after that of Strasbourg. Calvin had needed to do his best to convince the council, and even after receiving its approval, money had to be raised, because the government was not willing to put any funds toward the academy. Calvin's fundraising drive was a success. Both the first five-penny gift from the wife of a baker, as well as the 312 florins donated by the wealthy printer Robert Estienne, ensured the construction of a beautiful new building overlooking the lake.

The Academy consisted of a *schola privata,* a type of primary and secondary school, and a *schola publica,* which was intended more as a university where one could study theology, law and medicine.

In Bern they thought nothing would ever come of this school, but in Geneva Bern was once again ignored. Beza and Viret gave notice at Lausanne and went to work in Geneva, and in the very first year 162 students matriculated. In the year of Calvin's death (1564), the *schola privata* had 1,200 students and the *schola publica* 300. The new building thus soon became too small, and in 1562, Calvin and Beza began to lecture in the old church building of the Notre-Dame-la-Neuve, which became known as the *Auditoire,* close to the St. Pierre cathedral. At first, the school was only a theological university, but after Calvin's death faculties of law and medicine were successfully added. To ensure the Reformed character of the institution, students had to demonstrate their adherence to the Reformed confession. Nevertheless, since even in those days universities needed income, there appear to have been students who did not subscribe to the Reformed confession of faith and thus were not matriculated but could still follow the lectures and also paid school fees.

There were five professors at the Academy. One for the so-called *artes,* which consisted of the general subjects of mathematics, rhetoric and logic. Additionally, there was one professor of Hebrew, one of Greek, and two for Old and New Testament. On Saturday afternoons the students practiced their preaching under the direction of several pastors, who also benefitted from the presence of the professors in the Friday *Congrégations.*

BARRACKS

In keeping with the military terminology and strategy of its founder, the Academy in fact became the barracks where Reformed students from all over Europe were molded into theologians who were taught to preach with enthusiasm, establish congregations, and be faithful and diligent shepherds for the people. The distinctive foundation of this Academy was the combination of two late medieval phenomena: humanism and the *devotio moderna.* As was typical, Calvin once again managed to combine the positive features of different traditions. People were attracted to this institution by the prospects of a thorough knowledge of the languages, solid training in rhetoric and logic, and a form of instruction that was fully permeated with piety. This last was to be the enduring concern of the Academy's graduates in their own lives and in those of others. The heart and armory of the institution was, of course, the library. It was a storage room filled with the tools needed to fight Satan, sin, the world and, naturally, Rome, but above all to reach the hearts of men and women and through them to conquer territory for the kingdom of Christ. Calvin's Academy was both the Pentagon as well as West Point, the goal of which was to make the whole world as Geneva. The school was an immediate success, and for several decades one could hardly be considered a good Reformed pastor unless he had studied for some time in Geneva.

Calvin himself taught Old Testament, which meant very little change from before: he had been professor of the Holy Scriptures since 1536. This was, in fact, the position with which he had started in Geneva. It is said that Calvin took no more than half an hour to prepare for a lecture. The question is, of course, whether that was all the time he needed, or whether that was all the time he had. Whatever the case may have been, he could work as efficiently as many later Calvinists. Since the Academy stood beside the St. Pierre cathedral and because the clock of this church struck every hour, Calvin knew exactly when he was to begin his lecture, and more importantly, exactly when to stop so as to be able to move on to the next task. Thus he ended his 123rd lecture on Jeremiah with the words: "I cannot continue now, for the clock is tolling."

ARMY

Calvin set an entire campaign in motion simply by staying at home and writing. He engaged in literary warfare against Rome and other errors, and above all against everything he saw as unbiblical. As noted before, his pen was his most effective weapon, and it should come as little surprise that a small army of printers gathered around him. Between the years 1551 and 1564, they saw to the printing of some 500 titles, 160 of which were editions from Calvin, most of which went to France. Calvin was able to persuade businessmen to finance the production of these books and to convince merchants to smuggle them into France or transport them to other areas. Like a general he commanded the entire publication process, including the lines of the network along which his words would reach the people. The works produced and distributed included bestsellers such as the *Institutes* and the catechism, but also calendars that noted important biblical and church-historical facts instead of saints' days. The absolute bestseller was the Psalter, which went through nineteen Genevan editions, seven from Paris and three from Lyon. By 1562, some 27,400 copies were printed in Geneva alone. Calvin knew the power of music and made positive use of it. Realizing that a line sung from a psalm would touch the head and heart more deeply than a phrase read from the *Institutes,* he used the Psalter to combine word and music. His letters too were weapons, and he knew that they were largely also public documents that would not be read by the addressee alone.

Then there was also that small army of pastors that went out from Geneva to invade the world, and particularly France. They were educated at the Academy, characterized by Calvin as a training school for people "who will soon be spread all over France." In the period from 1555 to 1562—in addition to one pastor who was sent to London, one to Antwerp, one to Turin and two to Brazil—ten pastors were sent to Piedmont, and fifty-six to France. Calvin was unable to keep up with the high demand for pastors.

> They come from everywhere to seek pastors from us, no less eager than the papists when they go after their prebends. Those who pick them up besiege my very front door, and as if they need to approach me in supplication as is customary at the courts, they piously vie with one another as if they already possess the kingdom of Christ. We would be glad to fulfill their desires, but we have completely run out. A long time ago already we took from the workplaces the last man who had even the least bit of literary and theological training.

Thus Calvin sent warriors out into the world with Christ as their banner and the Word as their coat of arms. They were not clones of Calvin, but they did became the type of pastor for whom the pulpit was a battleship from which the allied Father, Son and Holy Spirit began a process of liberation, and from which shots were also fired on everything that was, or appeared to be, hostile. They would be pastors who were not afraid to hold up the truth to both friend and foe, just as the prophets, and Calvin himself, had done. This was also the way in which Calvin described their function. According to him, they must

> boldly dare to do all for God's Word, and force every power, fame, wisdom and highness to submit to the majesty of the Word and to be obedient to it; supported by the power of the Word, to command all, from the highest to the lowest; to build up the house of Christ, to overturn that of Satan; to pasture the flock, to tear apart the wolves; to educate and spur on the teachable; to punish, rebuke and subdue the rebellious and obstinate; and finally, if necessary, to break out with words of thunder and hurl verbal lightning bolts. But everything through the Word of God.

This was quite a task, and has continued to be felt as such by pastors throughout the centuries.

ACTION

Calvin sent his soldiers out into the world, but he stayed home and hardly ever left his post as a field commander. After 1541, Calvin only left Geneva once in a while. In July 1543 he was back in Strasbourg for some time. In May 1545 he made a tour of Bern, Basel, Konstanz and Strasbourg to drum up support for the persecuted Waldenses. In September 1546 he visited Neuchâtel; in January 1547 and once more in 1548 he was in Zürich for discussions with Bullinger, resulting in the *Consensus Tigurinus*. He also made several shorter visits to Swiss cities and a journey to Frankfurt in 1556, but in general he made no more than one trip per year.

In 1559, military metaphors gave way to actual military duty for Calvin, when he and his colleagues and others assisted in the reinforcement of the ramparts. In that year the peace of Cateau-Cambrésis was put into effect, and this meant that Philip II of Spain and Henry II of France decided to bury the hatchet and join forces against the Reformation. Under the new treaty, Henry received the rights to lost territories, one of which was Geneva. The entire city prepared for war, and even though it never saw battle, Geneva managed to remain free and independent.

In the meantime, Geneva's population grew to around 18,000–20,000 inhabitants, largely due to the influx of French refugees. During these years, Calvin was at the height of his work and influence. It might have seemed only natural to push through an agenda that would make Geneva into a completely Calvinist bulwark that could function at least as a miniature model of the New Jerusalem. The facts of what actually happened point in another direction, however. Between February 1562 and February 1563, 197 criminal cases came before the courts. More than half of them involved theft, extramarital relations and commercial laws. There were only three cases of heresy. These statistics suggest that Geneva did not act any more forcibly than other cities. It is true that a proportionally high number of citizens were arrested, but at least the punishments dealt out were moderate. Calvin did not introduce, much less lead, a theocracy, although it is true that the opponents he labeled as Libertines were not nearly as licentious and liberal as he made them out to be.

Vive la France!

Calvin loved France and was homesick.

> Our common home country, which is so lovely that it attracts many foreigners even from far away, I have by now had to miss for twenty-six years. But it would in no way please or agree with me to live in a country from which God's truth, the pure teaching and the doctrine of eternal salvation have been banished.

At the time, Calvin felt little urge to return to France, but he did feel strongly connected to the French people "because if I were to forget my people to whom I belong and not pay any attention to them, it would be inhuman and sinful." Calvin was sure that in all of his activities he had shown "how serious and sincere his wish was to be useful to our people." He thought that his usefulness had only increased through his absence, because, free from the troubles that he would have had in France, he was better able to give the nation the fruits of his study. This thought comforted him in the pain of his exile and even made his stay abroad enjoyable.

According to some, exile was so enjoyable for him that he had little idea as to how difficult life actually was for Reformed believers in France. Here it cannot be determined whether or not this criticism was justified, but an example of the way Calvin advised his countrymen and fellow believers can be given. Antoine de Crussol was in a moral dilemma. Catherine de Medici, widow of Henry II king of France and thus no friend of the Reformation at all, made a journey through Languedoc where de Crussol, who was Reformed, happened to be governor. His question for Calvin was whether he as Protestant could participate in a procession to be held in honor of Catherine's visit, because his office would hardly allow him to escape from this responsibility. Calvin was glad to see that de Crussol had really wrestled with this question and asked for his advice, which he was glad to give. De Crussol was to remember two things. In the first place, he had to be careful not to grieve the children of God. Second, he was to ensure that God's enemies would have no chance for mockery. Given these two considerations, the answer was clear enough. How many faithful souls would be torn when they saw Antoine participating in such an idolatrous event? And wouldn't the enemy have cause for mockery when they saw how he trimmed his sails to the wind by participating? Antoine had compared himself with the Syrian Naaman (2 Kings 5), but Calvin rejected this argument on the ground that the latter was the only believer in his country, and thus could not offend anyone. Further, Naaman expressly built his own altar to distinguish himself from others. Calvin saw how much Antoine could do for the church from his position, but on this point it came down to a choice between honoring God and honoring people. Calvin also hoped that a refusal to participate would impress Catherine more than a compromise. Antoine was not to feign illness, for that too would be to the shame of the gospel. In short, he was simply to say he would not participate, to pray to God for courage and to place his trust in God's care. According to Calvin, that was the best that could be done.

POLITICS

Calvin cared dearly for the French people and identified with them, though of course particularly with the Reform-minded. The Protestants in France had a hard time but managed to keep their heads above the water, and did so in such a way that they had an organized church life. When they held their first synod in 1559 and established a church order and confession of faith, Calvin was their most important advisor. Calvin also gave unsolicited advice, however, which was fully in line with his conviction that pastors were not to spare the elite. One such example is the letter of admonition he sent to Antoine de Bourbon, king of Navarre. Antoine had apparently fallen in love with "Mademoiselle du Rouet." This would have been fine had the "mademoiselle" not been a lady in waiting to Catherine de Medici and had Antoine's infatuation with her not led him to become somewhat less active in his initially Reform-oriented politics. Calvin apologized for having to say these things but did so in keeping with the apostle Paul who had said that sometimes people first had to hurt in order to make them happy (2 Cor 7:8-9). It would, after all, have been a grave fault for Calvin to keep silent about the things that he had heard, and so he admitted that he had been deeply shocked at the news that Antoine was so deeply in love that he gave in to many things where he should have remained firm. He should consider the sins of his youth and remind himself how gracious God had been to him, so that he might do his best not to fall back into them. Antoine would do well to remember that he would have to account for his sins before God and that he was not just a political leader but that God had appointed him to be a father to the believers in France. Should he desire to take this task seriously and to receive the crown of glory at the end of his life, he ought immediately to "fight against your inclinations, distance yourself from the worldly amusements and to keep in check the desires that tempt you to dishonor God." In another context, the same message was given to Louis de Bourbon, prince of Condé. It was high time for him to show that he had understood something of the teaching of salvation, and he should hasten to put an end to all his love affairs and instead devote himself to his task. This was the kind of clarity and directness that we have come to expect from Calvin.

With regard to kings and princes as such, we remark that Calvin had difficulties with monarchy as a political system. Monarchy was at bottom problematic because it was not ability, but birth, that determined who would rule a country, and Calvin was well aware that some strange and unsuitable people were born even into royal families. The greatest risk of this system of governance, however, was that all governing power was put into the hands of one person. This could only exacerbate the human tendency to exploit power and to view oneself as a demigod, free to pillage and murder. Moreover, countries with monarchies were also often more heavily taxed. Calvin warned the king of France against such temptations because he tried by legal avenues to gain possession of surrounding lands, while in fact he "was after their riches." In view of his own life, the example he gave to kings as to how they should conduct themselves is not surprising: "If kings want to be considered legitimate and as servants of God, they need to show that they are real fathers to their nation."

RESISTANCE

People listened to Calvin in political matters less than they did in ecclesiastical ones. Here we come to the theoretical question as to whether Calvin advocated that absolute obedience be given to the authorities. This question must be answered in the negative. The practical issue at hand was the Amboise Conspiracy of 1560, in which a number of Reformed fanatics broke out in violence against the power of the Guise family and against other anti-Reformed figures. Calvin thought it a foolish plan and considered the plot to have been "organized in a childishly mischievous manner." It ended in a bloody failure.

This also raises the issue of the degree to which Calvin recognized the right of rebellion, an issue that has received considerable attention. Calvin promoted passive resistance, adding the right to active resistance only at the end of his life, and this he accorded only to the so-called lower magistrates. His insistence on passive resistance had to do with his conviction that Christians were called to bear their sufferings patiently, and that in his own time God would ensure that wrongs were avenged. It also related to his political insight that active resistance produced much bloodshed but little result, as well to his aversions to chaos and war. When he referred to endless rivalries between France and Germany, it was as if Calvin was able to look ahead across the centuries. This also led him to make his own small addition to the biblical text: where Paul says that in Christ there is neither male nor female, neither Jew nor Greek (Gal 3:28), Calvin added, "and there will be neither Frenchman nor German."

We return, however, to the question of when passive resistance may become active. For Calvin this was not difficult to answer: if an assault was made against God, one simply had to jump into action. The imposition of idolatry—which could take the forms of compulsory attendance at, or the reintroduction of, the Mass or processions—was the point at which Christians may, or rather must, resist. "If princes demand that we turn from honor of God, if they force us into idolatry or superstition, then they have no more authority over us than frogs and lice do." False religion was first to be resisted passively, but if such efforts proved unsuccessful, active resistance was to follow. It would be better to die a hundred deaths than to abandon the true worship of God. Bucer was of the same opinion and said—while the emperor's cannons were turned on Strasbourg—that it was better to let cannon fire rain down on the city than to reintroduce the Mass.

All the same, Calvin did not approve of rebellions rising up from the people. To Edward Seymour, duke of Somerset, he wrote that those who had been renewed after the image of Christ would not rise up in rebellion but would show by their conduct that Christianity did not cause chaos. If Christians lived quietly and moderately, showing themselves not to be abominable and uninhibited people, they could close the mouths of the mockers and receive God's reward for obedience. Calvin warned Antoine de Corfy, prince of St. Porcie, that he should maintain a balance in these things, "since Christianity reveals itself not only in that we arm ourselves and risk life and possessions in the battle for the sake of the gospel but also in that we obediently submit ourselves to him who has bought us at a high price, so that he might be praised by us in life and death." The real battle was not the one fought against other people with the sword, but the one fought against the sin in our hearts and against Satan who tries to keep us from God's way.

Right of Rebellion

Only in the most extreme cases do the magistrates, in this case the highest-ranking nobles of France, have the right of rebellion. Thus when the de Bourbons, Louis de Condé and Gaspar de Coligny, defended the Reformation cause with weapons, Calvin could admire their deeds as the fruit of God-given courage that sought the advancement of God's kingdom. When the Huguenot war broke out, Calvin supported it fully and even actively engaged in the collection of funds for the Huguenot armies.

Church leaders, however, were not to involve themselves in battles with weapons. The pastors of Lyon who did do this in 1562 received a forceful letter from Calvin. Calvin was saddened by what they had done, because it was not fitting for a pastor to leave the pulpit and take up arms. Calvin had heard how violently these pastors had acted and was horrified by what they had done. "These were the words reported to us, and from dependable witnesses we heard that you said: 'Sir, you are to do what we say, for the power is in our hands!' Such words, we tell you straightforwardly, are downright horrible." The iconoclasm that occurred there came, in Calvin's opinion, from thoughtless zeal, even though it may have originated in piety. "But what are we to say of this thieving? What right do you have that allows you to pillage what does not belong to any individual, but is public property?" Calvin was thus also of the opinion that this offense must be undone.

Calvin had a completely different message for the persecuted church, because he knew just how difficult things were for believers. Work and endurance, zealous devotion and patient suffering, were the two pillars of Calvin's strategy to provide comfort. This, of course, amounted to perseverance. "Rather die a hundred deaths than give in." In all of this, Calvin's conviction was that a gentle demeanor would more readily break through the defenses of the enemy than would active resistance. Violence would resolve nothing, and according to Calvin, there was hope only when the monarchs kept their hands from the women, and the theologians embraced one another. Ecclesiastical unity, theologians who loved one another and politicians who did not render themselves impotent with their love affairs could make the Reformed cause into a worldwide success.

STRATEGY

It used to be that no war was waged without preliminary meetings to work out a plan of attack. Calvin knew that. He was one who thought things through, who was cognitively oriented and approached many things rather rationally. Calvin's plan for church building was thus also thought through strategically, and conceived of in terms of building up faith. When Olevianus asked Calvin how this was done in Geneva, Calvin pointed him to the specifically Reformed phenomenon of the home visit. Every year, said Calvin, a sort of checkup was made of every family, and for that to be done well, the city was divided into wards. The pastor would then take an elder to pay a visit to each home. Those who had recently joined the congregation were examined. This was not done for those who had already been members for some time, but an effort was made to check "whether things are done in an orderly and peaceful manner in the home, whether there are conflicts with neighbors, or drunkenness, and whether they are lazy and lax in church attendance." For Calvin this flowed over into church discipline, which was not meant as a military drill but as a means to help keep the people close to God and to each other.

It is not difficult to see how a Reformed lifestyle developed from these policies that were put into effect in Geneva. That lifestyle was promoted in the preaching, catechetical instruction, schooling and home visitation, and it was further spurred on by church discipline. Calvin noted that those who disregarded personal admonition, or gave a bad example to the congregation with their offensive behavior, had to appear before the consistory. Calvin gave a list of the type of people concerned: "blasphemers, drunkards, adulterers, thieves, brawlers, dancers and such people." Those who had committed lesser sins were admonished "with some kind words," but those who had committed graver sins could be kept from the table, but only for a short time. "With that they are excluded from the Lord's Supper until they ask for forgiveness and under the same pastor are once again reconciled with the congregation." The one who hardened himself or herself in sin and showed no sign of repentance could be banished from the city for a year. This possibility was not available to most Reformed consistories and so later turned into expulsion from the congregation. Calvin wanted to prevent the people from complaining that their pastors were too strict and therefore insisted that the pastors were also subject to these rules. Sins that would exclude a lay person from the table would, if committed by a pastor, automatically lead to his deposition.

Of the home visit, it could be said that Calvin's strategy was like house to house combat, moving from one street to the next. Home visits were a type of peace mission in the form of guerilla warfare. It was a lot of trouble but was necessary because of the strength of the enemy. The cause, after all, was well worth the effort.

LOOKING BACK

Calvin became older, and he thought that was what life came down to: getting older. He could write of it rather darkly:

> If you look carefully you will see that things are such that someone who gets up in the morning cannot take a step, cannot eat a meal and cannot move a hand without continually becoming older. Life becomes shorter. For that reason we must simply acknowledge that our life disappears in the blink of an eye and flows away. . . . We are always heading toward death, it comes near to us, and we must in the end go to it.

On July 23, 1563, Calvin wrote a long letter of thanks to Frederic III, elector of Pfalz in Heidelberg, who had taken in refugees from Flanders and France. The letter was like a backward glance, a look back taken by someone who knows his days on earth are numbered. Calvin spoke of his labors and noted that there were people who claimed to have benefited greatly from his exegetical work. That appears to have pleased him, as when people thought it worthwhile to publish his lectures, "for their simplicity could help other authors all too intent on making an impression be healed of this illness." He also knew there were others who thought his work was not academic enough, but he claimed he had always done his best to write nothing other than what would be of use to the church. This should not be taken as an attempt at self-justification but as an effort at most to make clear one more time that he was concerned for the well-being of the church, and that there were apparently people who had much use for his work.

Now Calvin ended in Geneva:

> Thirty years have passed since I voluntarily banished myself from France because the truth of the Gospel, the pure faith and the right way of worship were banished from it. I have become so used to life abroad that I no longer suffer from homesickness. Here [in Geneva] (for I do not have to be ashamed of the banishment from way back when, since they called me back) I am indeed a foreigner, but the citizens look at me as if my ancestors already were citizens of this city.

Calvin remained a stranger, and though he said he was not homesick, his homesickness jumps out at the reader from the words of this letter. Calvin was a stranger who felt at home only where the gospel could make its home. Calvin was the forerunner, or rather the father, of those Reformed Christians who went out into the world, taking the gospel with them and claiming not to be homesick. Nevertheless, wherever they ended up in the world, they turned some of their home country's distinguishing features into part and parcel of what it means to be Reformed.

DEATH

Calvin of all people cannot be behind the image of Calvinists as people who show no emotion at death, who bury their loved ones without shedding even a tear and who thereby show that they are ready to receive whatever comes from God's fatherly hand. It is true that his only comfort was "that even death could not be an unhappy circumstance for a Christian," but Calvin's letters are at the same time full of tears over loved ones who had died. He thought that his grief did not conflict with his belief that God was in control over all things. When he heard of the persecutions suffered by the

Waldenses, he wrote to Farel: "I am writing in tears, and worn out with grief I sometimes burst out in tears so that I have to stop writing." And when his friend Guillaume de Trie, lord of Varennes, passed away, Calvin became sick with grief. "I have to dictate this letter from my bed in great grief, for my dear Varennes has been taken away from me."

Calvin tied into a well-known medieval song when he wrote that we are surrounded by death in the middle of this life, but that we can be sure we will be surrounded by life in death. In such situations, Calvin always explained God's direction of life in such a way as to make it constantly clear that God intended these things for some good. When Claude Féray, a deacon to whom Calvin had become very close, died from the plague, Calvin wrote that he was a complete wreck. When he realized, however, how much this man had meant to him, and how he had been his support and refuge in all kinds of circumstances, Calvin could only conclude that God was gravely pointing out his sins by taking this friend away. Calvin said the same when his own child was taken. He thanked Farel for the letter of comfort he had written to Idelette. She herself was unable to respond because of her grief, so Calvin wrote: "The LORD has dealt us a heavy stroke in the death of our little son. But he is our Father. He knows what is good for his children."

These are beautiful words, and yet we find other things in Calvin's writings as well. He expresses his fear of death, his fear of having to appear before God as a sinful person, a fear that according to Calvin only increased the better one came to know God and desire more and more to live for him. It was the realization that "a sinner is confronted here with a judge whose wrath and severity count many deaths besides the eternal death." What dominated, however, was the conviction that believers ought to have no fear of death.

GLAD

Amidst all the sadness, Calvin could still also rejoice over the death of some. When the sister of de Fallais passed away, whose husband had become lukewarm to the Reformed cause while she remained an ardent supporter, Calvin remarked that she could be glad to have been freed from this life, that is, from this man. "The woman would have had to live in an unhappy captivity had she been forced to continue to live on this world." Now she was free of it, and her brother could think of her without continually worrying.

Well known and typical is the letter Calvin wrote to the lord of Richebourg to comfort him when his son Louis died from the plague. It reveals everything about how Calvin viewed life and how he saw God's guidance. Anyone who wants to know what Lord's Day 10 of the Heidelberg Catechism (both greatly despised and much loved) looks like in practice needs only to read this letter.

Calvin began by telling of his own sorrow over the death of his friend Claude Féray, who had been Louis's teacher, and about the worries he experienced for his own family when the plague raged in Strasbourg.

> When I received the message about the death of master Claude and of your son Louis, I was so shocked and so despondent that for several days I could only cry. And although I tried to find strength in the presence of God and wanted to comfort myself with the refuge he grants us in time of need, I still felt as if I was not at all myself. Really, I was no longer able to do the normal things, as if I myself were half dead.

There is no hardened Calvin here, who, rooted in God's almighty power, undauntedly and emotionlessly lets things pass over him. Rather, we see Calvin at his wit's end, overwhelmed by grief. He spoke of these things so as not to give the impression that it was easy for him to talk when offering comfort to de Richebourg and exhorting him to stand firm. Calvin knew the pain of losing a child, he knew the pain of that hole, and he knew the burden of the question "Why?" Nevertheless, this was exactly why he pointed de Richebourg to God's providence.

> There is nothing that robs us more of our power, nothing that dejects us more than when we let ourselves fall into such complaints and questions as: Why did things go like this? Why not another way? Why like that just here? There would be reason to utter such words if we on our part had made a mistake and if we had neglected our duty, but if we have done nothing wrong in this matter, there is also no place for these types of complaints.

In this way Calvin tried to set this father free from such endless questioning as well as from self-reproach and to guide him to the only conclusion that Calvin thought could offer comfort: "And so it is God who has reclaimed your son, that son whom he entrusted to us to care for under the condition that he ever remain his possession."

For this reason, Calvin contrasted the present life with the life to come: "If in your pondering over your son you were to consider how difficult it is in these dark times to bring our life in a pure manner to a good end, you would surely consider happy one who has been delivered from this at an early age." In this context, Calvin used the image of our life as a journey through stormy seas, and spoke of what a blessing it was to arrive at a safe haven earlier than expected. Calvin also praised the boy for his conduct and faith, and spoke of the good things that were expected of him. He also immediately anticipated the objection he thought de Richebourg would raise, namely that though the father knew his son was now in heaven, the reality remained that he had lost a child. It is clear that Calvin himself knew the questions and the difficulties that could take the wind out of the sails of any form of comfort. The fact that this is God's way does not mean we may not grieve over it.

> You will say that all of this is too heavy to drive away or suppress the grief of a father so as to suffer no more pain at the death of your son. But I am not asking you to suffer no more pain. For this is not the view of life that we are taught in the school of Christ, that we lay aside the God-given human emotions and that we turn from people into stones.

Calvin was not made of stone, and if there are Reformed Christians who are, they are not Calvinists.

DYING

In order to understand Calvin, one should actually begin with the end, when he died still dressed in full armor. On Wednesday, February 2, 1564, he gave his last lecture on a passage from Ezekiel, and he preached his last sermon the following Sunday, when he was carried to the pulpit on a bed.

On Easter Sunday, April 2, he was once again carried to church, this time to participate in the Lord's Supper. Calvin then turned his deathbed into a pulpit when he invited first the Little Council (April 27) and then the consistory (April 28) for one final discussion with each. Even when facing death, he wanted to see the politicians and church officers one last time, and above all to speak with them. He did this as a patriarch, but without making a scripted scene of it. Calvin was a lawyer, not an actor, and did not speak dramatically, but in a businesslike and pastoral manner. He made use of the fact that he did not die suddenly, and remained—by his own account— clear in spirit until his dying day, so as to give a clear testimony. In this way, he continued to work until the very end.

In both of his final meetings, Calvin asked for forgiveness for his conduct and his weaknesses. The people were willing to forgive. Beza related that Calvin's illness left him in low spirits toward the end of Calvin's life, and at times made him a difficult person, but that God used even that to the good. Colladon also referred Calvin's quick temper to God's providence, for God was able to make good use of this weakness. Calvin spoke openly of the things he had done wrong, claiming there was little use in hiding them since God and the angels already knew of them. During his time in Geneva, numerous disputes had arisen and many quarrels were fought that were not the fault of the council, but his own. Nevertheless, it would be hypocritical to say that God had not wanted to use him in his service. That Calvin claimed he wanted to remain in line with the Scriptures and to do everything to the glory of God is not surprising. What is surprising is that he did not remark once but twice that he had not acted out of selfish ambition. This would thus appear not only to have been an impression that others tended to get from him but also one that had not entirely escaped his own notice either. All the same, this part of Calvin's address is dominated by self-awareness and admission of errors. "I have always been but a poor, timid student. I am a miserable creature. What I have done is in fact worth nothing, and I beg you to forgive me all that I have done wrong but to hold on to anything there might have been that was yet good." That he claimed his work was worth nothing could be readily used by his opponents, but what should be remembered is that he always had good intentions. To the council, he declared that he had never sought anything but the best for the city and immediately added that his work was not always appreciated. "I have lived through many battles here. In the evening I was mockingly saluted with some fifty to sixty carbine shots. How afraid do you think that made me? Me, a poor, timid scholar as I am and always have been, as I readily admit?" Such was his first visit, but his second was no better. He related that when he walked the streets to go to work, people sent their dogs after him and shouted, "Sic 'em! Sic 'em!" *(criant Here, Here.)*

Both speeches are in the style of Moses' last words—Moses, who had to pass on his leadership and was not permitted to enter the Promised Land, but of whom the Scriptures still tell that he was taken up into God's glory. What remains remarkable, however, are the things Calvin did not say. He gave no resumé of the high points of his career, made no reference to his contact with kings, politicians and other renowned theologians. The whole was limited to his service in and for Geneva. What is left is the report of someone who had envisioned his whole life differently, who had at decisive moments been unable to do what he wanted to do, but under the threat of God's judgment let himself be directed to another way to which he adjusted—not stoically, not unwillingly, but still against his will. That is the way things sometimes go in life. You can always get someone to do something, if only you know how to get him or her that far. If you wanted something from Calvin, you could simply threaten him with God's judgment. This has resulted in the fact that, after the deaths of Luther and Bucer, Calvin became the leading Reformer in Europe, and one, in fact, who was more effective in the expression and dissemination of his thoughts than the majority of his colleagues.

CHANGE

Both of Calvin's final speeches began with pleas for forgiveness. Calvin also went on to give comfort to those present, but especially stiff exhortations to stay on the right path. He told the pastors to leave all things as they were and to change nothing because change brought little good. Such words sound rather strange, coming from one who had almost single-handedly changed an entire city, developed a new theology, and in fact helped bring about a complete transformation of the Western world. What is more, in 1543 he had explicitly told a pastor that change was always necessary because traditions could so easily obstruct God's glory. After he had given an exhaustive list of things that ought to be changed in the church, he dealt with the argument of those who wanted to leave things as they were and who claimed that the old ways were good in their experience. At that time, Calvin admitted that he could not handle such reasoning. Sorcerers and fortune tellers also appealed to their experiences, proving that this was no valid argument at all. It was better to live by the rule that reflection should come first, and could only then be followed by experience.

Then again, that was Calvin in 1543, when he was thirty-four years old. In 1564, at the age of fifty-five, he said all things should remain as they were. In Reformed circles, Calvin's last words have stuck more than his warning from 1543.

On April 25, Calvin dictated his will to the notary Pierre Chenelat. Calvin's armor was not the pulpit, or the lectern, or a horse or his bed, but rather the position in which he stood before God. After enumerating and confessing his sins, he came to his apology, which was at the same time his confession: he had done everything out of his fear of God *(que la racine de la crainte de Dieu a esté en mon coeur)*. This Old Testament term can hardly be translated without turning fear into an *Angst*-filled faith, or else losing the element of fear altogether. This fear was the armor in which he deflected criticism and attacked his enemies, and with which he was ready to serve in God's army. In his last words he also continued to show himself reliant on God, remaining the type of soldier who blindly follows his commander even without understanding his strategy. Calvin spoke of his desire to communicate with others before God brought his life to an end, but he added that things could well go very differently. He knew it would be arrogant on his part to encroach upon the decisions of God's council.

To use Calvin's own words, it was the decision of God's council that he should permanently withdraw. Beza wrote a rather detailed account of Calvin's death, depicting it as the death of a hero of faith. The Carthusian monk Laurentius Surius, born three years after Calvin's death, described in his chronicles Calvin's death as that of a worthless bloke. According to Surius's account, Calvin cursed and ranted and raged on his deathbed from the pain his venereal disease was causing him, which was also reported to be the cause of death. Even those who know only a little about Calvin would know that venereal disease was about the only illness Calvin did not contract throughout the course of his life.

On Friday, May 19, 1564, the pastors held their regular meeting, and in view of Calvin's situation they decided to meet in his house in a room next to the one in which he lay. They even carried him in for a short time, but that was his last official action. On the evening of Saturday, May 27, 1564, Calvin died. He was buried the next day, and so made also his last journey on a Sunday.

FEAST

Unlike the Tomb of the Unknown Soldier, Calvin was a well-known soldier who wanted an unknown grave. He wanted his end to be like that of Moses, without a grave, for fear of posthumous hero worship. He appears to have overlooked the fact that his grave might just as well have been liable to desecration. At any rate, Calvin did not even want a gravestone, just in case. At two o'clock in the afternoon of Sunday, May 28, 1564, he was buried in a common wooden casket in the cemetery of Plein Palais, in conformity with his request. The well-attended funeral was as sober as the casket. The principle of "everything in moderation" held even for funerals.

It was, however, a busy afternoon that Sunday, and no wonder. The man who had continually submitted to father figures throughout his life had himself become a father figure. In their first assembly after Calvin's death, the Venerable Company of Pastors noted that he was "as a father to everyone in this *Compagnie*." It is also remarkable that every year until that one they had been able to choose no one other than Calvin as their president. They maintained he had received so much grace and authority from God, and had always helped his colleagues with such good advice, that it would have been an insult to God's gifts to have chosen someone else. Who would now take over in Calvin's absence? He had been a father figure, but also someone against whom a lot of criticism was directed, and who had not been above admitting his own errors and failures. It is thus somewhat strange how many Calvin scholars have defended him so fiercely. Why should anyone want to do this if his friends and contemporaries openly and honestly expressed their difficulties with aspects of his personality—especially when Calvin himself was fully aware of his shortcomings?

CONVERSATION

This, however, is not the end of the story yet. Calvin assumed that people would recognize each other in heaven, and went rather far in his descriptions thereof. Richard Vauvill, pastor to the refugee church in Frankfurt, received a letter from Calvin on the occasion of the death of his wife with the comfort "that you were able to live with a woman to whom you would gladly return in order to reunite with her when you depart from this world." If Calvin's plans have indeed become reality, he will already have had many discussions and conversations in heaven. In his letter to Luther, which was never received, Calvin wrote that they would soon be together in heaven, where they could continue their discussion in quiet. He wrote the same to Melanchthon, with whom he also wanted to feast in heaven, even though neither was much of a partyer.

In contrast to many later Calvinists, at any rate, Calvin himself had no doubt as to whether or not we would recognize one another in heaven. This would indeed be nice. If I am to end up there myself, there are some things that I would really like to talk to him about.

NOTES

Much more happened in Calvin's life than could ever be described in this book. And his own letters, sermons and books contain more information about him as a person than can be managed. I hope that the pages of this book present enough of that information to give an image of Calvin's life, and of Calvin as a person. It is also hoped that an image might be provided of that unique group of people who should actually be called "Reformed," but, not surprisingly, are often known as "Calvinists" instead.

Calvin's letters form the most important source for this book, but his sermons and others writings have also been used. References to the sources are given in short form, and the translations are my own.

The abbreviations used are as follows:

CO = *Ioannis Calvini Opera Quae Supersunt Omnia*. Edited by Guilielmus Baum, Eduardus Cunitz and Eduardus Reuss. 59 vols. Brunswick: Schwetschke, 1863-1900. (Calvin's collected works)

COR = *Joannis Calvini Opera omnia denuo recognita et adnotatione critica instructa notisque illustrata*. Geneva: Droz, 1992-. (new edition of Calvin's collected works)

Herminjard = *Correspondance des Réformateurs dans les pays de langue française*
. . . Geneva: H. Georg, 1866-1897.

Inst. =   *Institutes*, 1559 edition.

SC =   *Supplementa Calviniana, Sermons inédits.* Edited by Erwin Mül-
haupt. Neukirchen: Neukirchener Verlag der Buchhandlung
des Erziehungsvereins, 1961. (sermons not found in the CO)

Citations and references to the original sources have also been gleaned
from the multitude of books on Calvin. Whoever wants to learn more can
begin with the following:

W. de Greef. *The Writings of John Calvin: An Introductory Guide.* Translated by
Lyle D. Bierma. Grand Rapids: Baker, 1993.

Willam G. Naphy, *Calvin and the Consolidation of the Reformation.* Manchester:
Manchester University Press, 1994.

Herman J. Selderhuis, ed. *Calvin Handbook.* Grand Rapids: Eerdmans, 2009.

Herman J. Selderhuis. *Calvin's Theology of the Psalms.* Grand Rapids: Baker
Academic, 2007.

I would like to express my thanks to Karla Apperloo-Boersma, William
den Boer, Maarten Stolk and Mirjam van Veen for proofreading this work.
A special thanks to Albert Gootjes for his wonderful translation.

CHAPTER 1

p. 9   Regarding Calvin's hometown of Noyon, see *CO* 14.423, 14.412,
14.476.

pp. 10-11 Regarding Calvin's mother as an example of piety, see *CO* 6.442.

p. 12   Regarding Calvin's awareness of class differences, see *CO* 5.5.

p. 12   Regarding Calvin's self-representation, see *CO* 3.21.

p. 12   "dumb man": *CO* 13.526.

p. 13   Regarding the dedication of Calvin's commentary on 1 Thessalonians
to Cordier, see *CO* 13.525.

p. 14   Regarding Calvin's nickname, *"accusativus,"* see *CO* 21.121.

p. 15   Regarding Calvin's greater chances of financial success in law, see *CO*
31.22.

p. 15   "my father sent me to study law": *CO* 13.525.

pp. 15-16   Regarding Calvin's study habits, see *CO* 21.122.

p. 18   "Although I did everything to do the will of my father": *CO* 31.22.

p. 18   Regarding Calvin's conversion to a "purer doctrine," see *CO* 31.21.

pp. 18-19   Regarding Calvin's preconversion obedience to the Catholic Church,
               see *CO* 5.412.

p. 19   Regarding Calvin's initial lack of appreciation for Reformed theology,
               see *CO* 9.51.

p. 19   Regarding Calvin's conversation with François Daniel's sister, see *CO*
               10/2.9.

p. 19   Regarding Calvin's view that God in his mercy had called him when he
               was lost, see *CO* 26.656.

p. 20   "I was his archenemy": *CO* 54.212-13

p. 20   "There were always those torments of conscience": *SC* 6.77.

p. 21   "there is no greater good one can inherit on this earth": *CO* 31.64.

p. 21   Regarding Calvin's view of the transitory nature of life, see *SC*
               5.122.9.

p. 21   "but that the Spirit of God reigns in us" *SC* 5.55.25-30.

p. 23   Regarding Calvin's self-presentation in the preface of his *De clementia*,
               see *CO* 5.6.

p. 24   "The dice have been cast": *CO* 10.19.

p. 26   Regarding Calvin's view of a position as an ecclesiastical jurist as an
               occupation with useless things, see *CO* 10/2.37-38.

p. 27   Regarding the intersection of the political and the theological in con-
               troversy with the Anabaptists, see Herminjard, 3.249-54.

p. 28   Regarding prevailing images of Calvin as one who emphasized law at
               the expense of grace, see Will Durant, *The Reformation* (New York:
               Simon and Schuster, 1957), 6.490.

pp. 28-29   Regarding Calvin's desire for independence and freedom from debt,
               see *CO* 10.17, 10.20.

p. 30   "Who I am, you know": *CO* 12.338.

p. 30   Regarding Calvin's claim that he did not like to speak about himself,
               see *CO* 5.389.

p. 30   "against his nature": *CO* 11.365.

p. 30   Regarding Calvin's unintentionally fiery tone in writing, see *CO* 9.250.

p. 30	"it is not my nature to fight it out with such coarse rudeness": *CO* 12.15.
p. 30	Regarding Camerarius's struggle to understand the combination of Calvin's harsh writing style and friendly personal manner, see Friedrich Lauchert, *Die italienischen literarischen Gegner Luthers* (1912; reprint, Nieuwkoop: De Graaf, 1972), p. 620.
p. 30	Regarding Calvin's preference for living in isolation, see *CO* 15.812.
p. 31	Regarding Calvin's view that God had given him his role to play, see *CO* 14.415.
p. 31	Regarding Calvin's admission to Bullinger that he tried to write in such a way that others would not become angry, see *CO* 15.834.
p. 31	Regarding Simon Grynaeus's admonition of Calvin, see *CO* 10/2.158-61.
p. 31	Regarding Calvin's harshness with Joachim Westphal, see *CO* 15.358-59, 16.11, 16.552.
p. 31	"I have to admit that by nature I am timid, soft and of little courage": *CO* 31.26.
p. 31	"timid as I am and have always been, as I confess": *CO* 9.892.
p. 31	Regarding Calvin's view that he lived as he had taught others to live, see *CO* 9.620.
p. 31	Regarding Calvin's inability not to speak the truth, see *CO* 20.8.
p. 31	Regarding Calvin's love of being straightforward, see *CO* 9.249.
p. 32	"I prefer to make my complaint against you openly": *CO* 14.252.
p. 32	"to give offense in my boorish simplicity": *CO* 13.594.
p. 32	Regarding Calvin's view of anyone who thought he was sycophantic, see *CO* 19.42.
p. 32	Regarding Calvin's view that others should speak as openly with him as he did with them, see *CO* 15.304.
p. 32	"I have always loved simplicity": *CO* 12.666.
p. 32	"My way of teaching is too simple to be considered suspect": *CO* 12.666.
p. 32	"I have so little self-confidence": *CO* 13.374.
p. 32	Regarding Calvin's feelings of shame, see *CO* 6.470, 12.320.
p. 32	"A dog barks": *CO* 12.67.
p. 32	"You will probably say": *CO* 10.141.
pp. 32-33	Regarding Calvin's claim that his openness was a strategy, see *CO* 17.235.
p. 33	Regarding Calvin's debate with Albert Pighius, see *CO* 7.258.

p. 33	Regarding Calvin's vehement reaction against Sadoleto, see *CO* 5.386.
p. 33	Regarding Calvin's view of Servetus' defamations, see *CO* 7.637.
p. 33	"I do not hate you": *CO* 8.495.
p. 33	"If we are not appeased": *CO* 10/2.432.
p. 33	"I was so afraid that I wanted to die": *SC,* 2 Sam, 122.

CHAPTER 2

p. 34	"We are always on the road": *CO* 26.291.
p. 34	"just sojourners on this earth": *CO* 31.63.
p. 35	Regarding Calvin's view of the world as a place of upheaval and instability, see *CO* 32.13.
p. 35	Regarding Calvin's view that the whole world has been turned on its head, see *CO* 31.461.
p. 35	Regarding Calvin's view that an abhorrent disorder overshadows the order of God's providence, see *CO* 32.11.
p. 35	"since God everywhere lays traps for us": *CO* 32.234.
p. 35	Regarding Calvin's view that it is as if God is toying with us, see *CO* 32.66.
p. 35	Regarding Calvin's view that God soon takes humanity back to himself after the short course of life, see *CO* 31.834.
p. 36	Regarding Calvin's view of the events of life as a prelude to the final destruction, see *CO* 32.73.
p. 36	"As humans we are like dry grass": *CO* 32.66.
p. 36	"hangs as if from a silk thread": *CO* 31.302.
p. 36	"surrounded by a thousand deaths": *CO* 31.302.
p. 36	"leaving the womb is the entrance to a thousand deaths": *CO* 31.656.
p. 36	Regarding Calvin's view that life simply flies by, see CO 32.73.
p. 36	"If only you look up": *CO* 40.135-36.
p. 36	Regarding Calvin's view of the risks to human life in the city and the countryside, see *CO* 32.136.
p. 36	"If you step onto a ship": *Inst.* 1.17.10.
p. 36	"it appears as if the heavens are crashing down": *CO* 31.460-61.
p. 36	"a churning river": *CO* 31.834.
p. 36	"as desperate as that of someone in the grave": *CO* 32.308.
p. 37	"in an ominous labyrinth": *CO* 31.368.

p. 37	"since there is no more terrifying agony": *CO* 32.144.
p. 38	"When I thought things would settle down": *CO* 10/2.37-38.
p. 39	Regarding Calvin's "campaigning" for "God for president," see *CO* 12.317.
p. 39	"I would most like to withdraw": *CO* 52.315.
p. 40	"I am advancing very well in my studies": *CO* 10/2.37.
p. 41	Regarding Calvin's six sermons written to promote the hearing of Reformed doctrine, see Wilhelm H. Neuser, *Johannes Calvin: Leben und Werk in seiner Frühzeit 1509-1541* (Göttingen: Vandenhoeck and Ruprecht, 2008).
p. 41	Regarding Calvin's *Psychopannychia*, see *CO* 5.165-232.
p. 42	Regarding Calvin's view of those who felt compelled by conscience to act upon the words, "Leave your country," see *CO* 11.629-30.
p. 42	Regarding Calvin's view of the ways in which Reformed believers should be exemplary Christians, see *CO* 6.561.
p. 42	"that you can only be a Christian if you have first been in Geneva": *CO* 8.412.
p. 43	Regarding Calvin's view of the king of France as Pharaoh, see *CO* 20.393-95.
p. 43	Regarding Calvin's view that he could not live in a country from which God's truth, true religion and eternal salvation had departed, see *CO* 18.615.
p. 43	Regarding Calvin's view that his departure was necessary, see *CO* 20.78.
pp. 44-45	Regarding Calvin's criticism of Olivetan's translation in the foreword to the Geneva Bible, see *CO* 9.827-28.
p. 45	Regarding Calvin's view that keeping silent and not assisting persecuted Reformed Christians in France would be an unjustifiable betrayal, see *CO* 31.21.
p. 46	"contain more than I would be allowed to say without being immodest": *CO* 12.659.
p. 46	Regarding Calvin's view of the *Institutes* as his most important work, see *CO* 17.578.
p. 48	Regarding Calvin's view that the term "Nicodemite" dealt an injustice to Nicodemus, see *CO* 6.609.

CHAPTER 3

p. 67	"watchmen . . . who always have to be on guard": *SC* 5.216.8-15.
p. 68	Regarding Calvin's view of his calling revealed in a letter to Renée de Ferrara, see *CO* 11.324.
p. 68	Regarding Calvin's view of the reasons why the divine teaching simply had to be recorded, see *Inst.* 1.6.3.
pp. 68-69	"If someone were to ask what the essence of our faith really is": *CO* 6.459.
p. 69	"Just as one who cleans toilets": *CO* 6.595.
p. 69	"extraordinary writings": *Inst.* 3.19.13.
p. 70	Regarding Calvin's view of idolatry as the real problem faced by Reformed Christians in France, see *CO* 13.99-100.
p. 70	Regarding Calvin's view of the distortions of the Roman mass, see *CO* 12.715-16.
p. 70	"a crime that is incompatible with the Christian faith": *CO* 17.135.
p. 71	"And then I am not saying much when I call you a murderer and traitor": *CO* 5.292.
pp. 71-72	"For as long as you suck the blood from the poor": *CO* 5.312.
p. 72	Regarding Calvin's views on Geneva as like and unlike the Promised Land, see *CO* 41.490, 14.363.
p. 72	Regarding Calvin's view that Geneva ran the risk of underestimating the degree to which they had benefited from God's mercy, see *CO* 26.214.
pp. 72-73	"Was the city not headed for ruin and destruction": *CO* 27.88-89.
p. 73	"an eternal rule for a pious and holy life": *CO* 45.171.
p. 74	"They are right to take offense": *CO* 1.546.
p. 75	"They in their turn sin in that they go too far": *CO* 1.546.
p. 79	Regarding Calvin's polemics against Caroli under des Gallars's name, see *CO* 7.293, 12.107-8.
p. 82	Regarding Calvin's statement from his deathbed that he had been chased away from Geneva, see *CO* 9.892.
p. 82	"There is no one at all who can lay even a little guilt on us": *CO* 10.247.
p. 83	"Sir, the admonishments and reproaches contained in your letter": *CO* 10.269.
p. 83	"Yet for the children of God": *CO* 15.162.

CHAPTER 4

tive lack of wealth, see *CO* 31.32.

p. 104   Regarding Calvin's dispute with Melanchthon on free will and predestination, see *CO* 11.595.

p. 104   Regarding Calvin's view that there was room for public disagreement with Melanchthon on the basis of their mutual esteem, see *CO* 14.381.

p. 104   "in a three-hour conversation": *CO* 15.321.

p. 104   Regarding Calvin's high esteem of Melanchthon as commentator, theologian, and friend, see *CO* 10/2.403-4, 10/2.432, 11.147, 11.515.

p. 105   Regarding Calvin's uneasiness with respect to Luther, see *CO* 10/2.139.

p. 105   Regarding Luther's praise for Calvin's Eucharistic theology, see *CO* 10/2.432.

p. 105   "liberate himself from the darkness of the papacy": *CO* 9.51.

p. 105   "the Gospel went out from Wittenberg": *CO* 11.705.

p. 105   Regarding Calvin's view of Luther as the one who first made the papacy waver, see *CO* 14.31.

p. 106   Regarding Calvin's desire to consult with Luther, see *CO* 12.7ff.

p. 106   Regarding Calvin's pleasure upon receiving Luther's greetings and approval, see *CO* 10/2.402.

p. 106   Regarding Calvin's inclusion of Luther's approval in the preface of his commentary on Romans, see *CO* 10/2.432.

p. 106   "immoderately ardent and violent in character": *CO* 11.774.

p. 106   Regarding Calvin's view of Luther as a danger to the church, see *CO* 12.99.

p. 106   Regarding Calvin's defense of Luther, see *CO* 15.305.

p. 106   Regarding Calvin's view that Luther's shortcomings should not overshadow his achievements, see *CO* 11.775.

p. 107   "The articles were delivered to me very late at night": *CO* 10/2.398.

p. 107   "I ended with the words": *CO* 10/2.398-99.

p. 108   Regarding Calvin's exhortation to Caroli, see *CO* 11.72-75.

p. 108   "I could not help but laugh": *CO* 11.36.

p. 109   Regarding Calvin's experience of doubts and trials, see *CO* 10/2.272.

CHAPTER 5

p. 110   Regarding Calvin's view of the preacher as God's ambassador to the church, see *SC* 6.181.

p. 110	Regarding Calvin's view of God speaking through him as a preacher, see *CO* 26.394-95.
p. 110	Regarding Calvin's view of his accountability before God for his words, see *CO* 42.142.
p. 110	"the throne of God": *CO* 53.520.
p. 111	Regarding Calvin's view that the preacher should speak only after first listening respectfully to his Taskmaster, see *CO* 35.424.
p. 111	"it would be better if were to break his neck": *CO* 26.304.
p. 111	"For God there is nothing higher than the preaching of the Gospel": *SC* 8.21.
p. 111	"When I climb into the pulpit": *CO* 34.424.
p. 111	"For of myself I have nothing to say": *CO* 6.602.
p. 111	"It ought to be a hard and fast rule": *CO* 10/2.352.
p. 112	"conceited prig": *CO* 26.474.
p. 113	"when we administer baptism": *SC* 6.131.
p. 113	"swine who peek their heads around the corner": *SC* 8.146.
p. 113	"Let everyone thus be on guard": *CO* 6.452.
p. 114	"so as not to bruise the souls with immoderate harshness": *CO* 49.371-72.
p. 114	Regarding Calvin's view of the pastor as intermediary between God and the people, see *SC* 6.174.
p. 114	"So get rid of all coldness and indifference in it": *CO* 49.123.
p. 114	Regarding Calvin's view that sermons that were more like lectures were "dead," see *CO* 13.71.
p. 115	"Let those who want to do well": *COR* 2.16.60-61.
p. 115	Regarding Calvin's view of God as pedagogue or teacher, see *CO* 26.420.
p. 115	"the school of the Holy Spirit" *Inst.* 3.21.3.
p. 115	"student in God's church": *SC* 7.60.
p. 115	Regarding Calvin's view of the church as a nurturing mother, see *Inst.* 4.1.4.
p. 115	"God calls us to his school": *CO* 54.501.
p. 115	Regarding Calvin's view of the shortness of human memory, see *CO* 28.267.
p. 115	Regarding Calvin's view that sin would constantly lead men and women from the right path, see *CO* 26.241.

p. 115   "for we do not come to the preaching": *SC* 6.138.

p. 116   "The more I balked at returning": *CO* 11.92.

p. 116   "Should I be looking for a way": *CO* 10.271.

p. 116   Regarding Calvin's stated preference to die a hundred other deaths rather than return to Geneva, see *CO* 11.30.

p. 117   "the way the people are there": *CO* 11.91.

p. 117   "If I were able to choose": *CO* 11.100.

p. 117   "Two times a flow of tears interrupted me": *CO* 11.114.

p. 117   "But since I know that I am not my own master": *CO* 11.100.

p. 117   "I could have laid into that entire pack": *CO* 11.389.

p. 118   "When I went to preach again for the first time": *CO* 11.365-66.

p. 118   Regarding Calvin's authorship of *Ordonnances ecclésiastiques,* see *CO* 10.15-30.

p. 123   "The strictness must not be such": *CO* 10/1.30.

p. 125   "Our colleagues are more an obstacle than a help": *CO* 11.377.

pp. 126-27 Regarding Calvin's view that church reform had to take the shape of a complete overhaul, see *CO* 11.485-86.

p. 129   "As long as you live in Geneva": *CO* 12.334-35.

p. 129   Regarding Calvin's view that while perfection remained elusive, efforts should be made to make the church as good as it could be, see *CO* 11.763.

p. 130   Regarding Calvin's happiness with introduction of the consistory and church discipline, see *CO* 11.379.

p. 132   "but of what use is that": *CO* 53.312.

p. 132   "they leave just as they came in": *CO* 34.581.

p. 132   Regarding Calvin's impression that his congregation treated sermons like fairytales, see *CO* 35.324.

p. 132   "whether they know what it means that God appeared in the flesh": *CO* 53.320.

p. 132   "for as soon as they come to church": *CO* 49.736.

p. 132   "In short, by far the majority live according to the old saying": *CO* 8.420-21.

p. 132   "and then they want to know why": *CO* 28.545.

p. 132   "they are eager to explore the rooms in Paradise": *CO* 46.800.

p. 132   Regarding Calvin's displeasure that Muslims, Jews, heathens and papists were more diligent in their superstitions than Christians were in service to the gospel, see *CO* 50.462.

p. 134   Regarding Calvin's comment that teaching was more readily communicated in song, see *CO* 36.102.

p. 134   Regarding Calvin's view of the potential liabilities of music as a distribution method for false teaching, see *CO* 40.625.

p. 134   Regarding Calvin's view of the Psalms as the music of choice for the cultivation of Christian understanding, see *CO* 6.171.

p. 134   Regarding Calvin's view that rays of God's grace could be found even among unbelievers, see *CO* 23.99.

p. 134   Regarding Calvin's view of music's liability to abuse by humanity, see *CO* 23.100.

pp. 134-35   Regarding Calvin's view of tambourines, see *CO* 34.226.

p. 135   Regarding Calvin's view that it was God's will, not David's music in itself, that soothed Saul, see *CO* 30.181.

p. 135   "but also at home and in the fields": *CO* 6.170.

p. 136   "One needs to be very careful": *Inst.* 3.20.32.

p. 136   "What suffices are the simple and pure songs": *CO* 30.259.

p. 136   Regarding Calvin's view that singing for pleasure would neither befit the majesty of the church nor please God, see *Inst.* 3.20.32.

p. 137   "There is thus a big difference": *CO* 6.170.

p. 138   Regarding Calvin's view of the pastor's duties despite the risk of infection with the plague, see *CO* 11.458.

p. 138   Regarding the reproach Calvin suffered for admitting his fear of the plague, see *CO* 11.457.

p. 139   "Recently a conspiracy of men and women was discovered": *CO* 12.55.

p. 141   "As I said, I wish we would find a way to care for Sebastian": *CO* 11.691.

p. 141   Regarding Calvin's high appraisal of Castellio's scholarship, see *CO* 11.691.

p. 143   Regarding Calvin's "Response to a Certain Dutchman," see *COR* 4.1.199-273.

p. 143   "its removal, destruction and abolition": *CO* 5, 256.

p. 143   Regarding Calvin's view of the hypocrisy of participating in the Mass, see *CO* 11.9-10.

p. 143   "Most people find your message extremely depressing": *CO* 11.646.

CHAPTER 6

p. 145   "They appeal to Christ but want to govern without him": CO 12.32.

pp. 145-56 "We brought you a message from God": *SC* 6.26.

p. 146   "and behold, they are doing the same thing today": *SC* 6.124.

p. 146   Regarding Calvin's view of himself as a sojourner, see *CO* 12.251.

p. 146   Regarding the persistence of Calvin's view of himself as a sojourner in Geneva, see *CO* 16.43.

p. 146   "Today I urgently prayed and begged God": *CO* 12.415.

p. 147   Regarding the distance Calvin kept from Genevan politics, see *CO* 16.43.

p. 149   Regarding Calvin's response to the controversy with Ameaux, see *CO* 12.283-84.

p. 150   "As I said before": *CO* 11.378.

p. 151   "an invitation to Satan": *CO* 26.340.

pp. 151-52 "For I did not come back to Geneva": *CO* 12.338.

p. 152   Regarding the controversy over Reformed pastors naming children at baptism against the wishes of their parents, see Willam G. Naphy, *Calvin and the Consolidation of the Reformation* (Manchester: Manchester University Press, 1994), p. 148.

p. 155   "we have the same Christ": *CO* 12.666.

p. 157   Regarding Calvin's exhaustion in the face of controversy within Geneva and readiness to depart for Neuchâtel, see *CO* 12.378.

p. 158   "They talk about it as if we all are lost": *CO* 12.552.

p. 158   Regarding Calvin's prevention of violence between rival factions within Geneva, see *CO* 12.632.

p. 159   Regarding Calvin's view of stubbornness as the source of rivalries between Swiss cities, see *CO* 12.656.

p. 159   "I really do not understand": *CO* 12.729.

p. 159   "How can they reproach me": *CO* 12.729.

p. 159   Regarding Calvin's discussion with Bullinger of a French covenant, see *CO* 13.266.

p. 160   Regarding Viret's attendance of a controversial play and his report to Calvin about it, see *CO* 12.356.

p. 161	"we pray when we get up in the morning": *Inst.* 3.20.50.
p. 161	"The prayers that belong to it I wrote myself": *CO* 11.364.
p. 162	Regarding Calvin's view that God had created the world with no other goal than the happiness of humanity, see *CO* 31.94B.
p. 162	Regarding Calvin's views of the pleasures of food and wine, see *CO* 23.54B, 32.91.
p. 162	"but if wine is a poison to the drunkard": *SC* 6.39.
p. 163	"Through a sort of natural instruction": *SC* 6.194.
p. 163	"The earth demands vengeance when it is polluted": *SC* 6.84.
p. 163	"There was a man who, during the Sunday sermon": *CO* 12.415.
p. 164	"The people want to make a little pact with God": *SC* 6.68.
p. 164	Regarding Calvin's view of satire and mockery in theological discourse, see *CO* 9.863-66.
pp. 164-65	"Although you must know that I am passing through Zürich on the way to Trent": *CO* 14.101.
p. 165	"Those papists do that": *Inst.* 4.19.32.
p. 165	"Do you know why they fight so fanatically": *CO* 1.14.
p. 165	"the living image of my soul": *CO* 17.191.
p. 165	"I get so tired from that endless writing": *CO* 14.51.
p. 166	"while I, swamped with all kinds of work": *CO* 20.393.

CHAPTER 7

p. 167	Regarding Calvin's view of marriage as a means of freeing himself from domestic duties, see *CO* 10/1.228.
p. 167	"those mad lovers": *CO* 10/2.348.
p. 168	"I was presented with a girl of noble origins": *CO* 11.12.
p. 168	Regarding the pressure Calvin felt to marry, see *CO* 11.12.
p. 168	"unless the Lord takes away all of my reason": *CO* 11.30.
p. 168	"I immediately sent my brother and another trusted man": *CO* 11.12.
p. 168	Regarding Calvin's rejection of another possible marriage partner, see *CO* 11.52.
p. 169	Regarding Calvin's view of Idelette as a woman of special qualities, see *CO* 13.230-31.
p. 169	Regarding Calvin's theological interpretation of his postnuptial illness, see *CO* 11.83.

p. 169   "My wife is in my thoughts day and night": *CO* 11.175.

p. 169   Regarding the dangers associated with the birth of Calvin's son, Jacques, see *CO* 12.420.

p. 169   "The LORD has given me a son": *CO* 9.576.

p. 170   Regarding the comfort Calvin took in his spiritual children, see *CO* 9.576.

p. 170   "I would be glad to have her as my own wife": *CO* 12.420.

p. 170   "My wife is recovering slowly": *CO* 12.241.

p. 170   "I am very sorry that my wife was such a burden on you": *CO* 12.732.

p. 170   Regarding Idelette's health problems, see *CO* 12.202.

pp. 170-71 "She was no longer able to speak": *CO* 12.202.

p. 171   "Because she never spoke of her children": *CO* 13.228-29.

p. 171   "Shortly before eight she quietly breathed her last": *CO* 13.229.

p. 171   Regarding Calvin's view of Idelette as his best friend and partner in ministry, see *CO* 13.230, 228-29.

p. 171   "that I continue my ministry without a break": *CO* 13.229.

p. 172   "I am no more than half a man": *CO* 20.394.

p. 172   "What a terrible injury": *CO* 15.867.

p. 172   Regarding Calvin's defense of his decision to live as a widower, see *CO* 11.206.

p. 172   Regarding Calvin's view that he would not make a wife happy, see *CO* 53.254.

p. 172   Regarding Calvin's efforts to bring his stepson to Geneva, see *CO* 12.153.

pp. 172-73 Regarding Calvin's withdrawal to solitude as a result of the shame his stepdaughter brought to the family, see *CO* 19.327.

p. 173   Regarding Calvin's view that, without a woman, a man was only half of what he was meant to be, see *CO* 23.28.

p. 173   Regarding Calvin's criticism of what he thought were typical womanly faults, see *CO* 54.509.

p. 173   "they sometimes leave dinner standing": *CO* 36.92.

p. 173   Regarding Calvin's respect for women demonstrated in his protection of the niece of de Fallais from marriage to a nobleman with venereal disease, see *CO* 12.491.

p. 173   Regarding Calvin's respect for and continuing relationship with Renée de France, see *CO* 18.147-48, 20.244-49.

p. 174   Regarding Calvin's view of women's leadership as contrary to natural order and expressions of both divine judgment and divine grace, see *CO* 15.125.

p. 174   Regarding Calvin's displeasure with John Knox's "The First Blast of the Trumpet Against the Monstrous Regiment of Women," see *CO* 18.490.

p. 174   Regarding Calvin's view of the inappropriateness of women's leadership in the church, see *CO* 20.230-33.

p. 175   "conducted themselves forcefully and with determination": *CO* 16.632-34.

p. 175   Regarding the close relationship between Calvin and his brother Antoine, see *CO* 11.189.

p. 177   "If a frail old man falls in love with a young woman": *CO* 24.455.

p. 177   "It already seemed like a fable": *CO* 11.131.

p. 177   Regarding Calvin's rejection of the idea that men and women were stained with sin by sexual intercourse, see *CO* 26.339-42.

p. 177   Regarding Calvin's claim that those who campaigned against sex and promoted celibacy were clearly going against God's will, see *CO* 23.49.

p. 178   "For that reason a marriage": *CO* 13.307.

p. 178   Regarding Calvin's views of the inappropriateness and validity of mixed marriages, see *CO* 13.485.

p. 178   "If you see one in Strasbourg who would be suitable for Viret": *CO* 12.355.

p. 178   "I think it best if you permit me to ask for her hand": *CO* 12.359.

p. 179   Regarding Calvin's view of the potential for sin in extravagant celebrations of weddings, see *CO* 45.432.

p. 180   Regarding Calvin's view God's punishment of a known adulterer, see *CO* 12.413-16.

p. 181   "that men in the choice of a wife take into account their beauty": *CO* 2.112.

p. 181   Regarding Calvin's view that it was not inherently sinful to choose a marriage partner on the basis of beauty, see *CO* 23.402.

p. 181   Regarding Calvin's admonition of caution and avoidance of sinful thoughts in considering another's beauty, see *CO* 23.185.

p. 182   "If the man and the woman do not agree and do not love each other":
             CO 23.306.

p. 182   Regarding Calvin's view that marriages between Reformed Christians
             and Catholics, Jews, or Muslims were sinful but not prohibited, see *CO*
             13.307-8.

p. 183   Regarding Calvin's view that he had tens of thousands of children
             throughout the Christian church, see *CO* 7.576.

p. 183   Regarding Calvin's reproof of parents who cared more about the secu-
             lar education of their children than the spiritual, see *CO* 54.429.

p. 183   Regarding Calvin's view that parents should invest in their children,
             see *CO* 27.678.

p. 183   Regarding Calvin's encouragement of parental forbearance and pa-
             tience, see *CO* 27.680.

p. 183   Regarding Calvin's view of a middle way for parents between coddling
             and sternness, see *CO* 51.783.

pp. 183-84 "without a catechism the church will never remain": *CO* 13.71-72.

p. 185   "There are different kinds of internal bonds that tie people together":
             CO 13.601.

p. 186   Regarding the friendship shared by Calvin, Farel and Viret, see *CO*
             14.132.

p. 186   "I do not think there have ever been such friends": *CO* 13.477.

p. 187   Regarding Calvin's grief upon the death of his colleague Courault, see
             CO 10/2.273.

p. 187   Regarding Calvin's sadness upon hearing of the persecutions suffered
             by the Waldenses, see *CO* 12.76.

p. 187   Regarding Calvin's tears and pains, see *CO* 10/2.398.

p. 187   Regarding Calvin's claims of having no idea what to do and wanting to
             die, see *CO* 12.642.

p. 187   Regarding Calvin's loneliness upon the death of Bucer, see *CO* 14.121.

CHAPTER 8

p. 190   Regarding Calvin's reliance on Augustine of Hippo on matters per-
             taining to the doctrine of predestination, see *Inst.* 3.23.13.

p. 191   "first of all to bring to God the glory he deserves": *CO* 51.262.

pp. 191-92 Regarding the controversy between Calvin and Bolsec over predestination, see *CO* 8.145-248.

p. 192	"I could do no other": *CO* 14.382.
p. 193	"the most beautiful jewel on earth": *CO* 31.244.
p. 193	"a ruined being without any worth": *CO* 31.91.
p. 193	"Although humans were equipped with magnificent gifts": *CO* 31.91.
p. 193	"has claimed the soul and the body": *CO* 32.320.
p. 193	Regarding Calvin's view that human nature was inclined to idleness and lies, see *CO* 32.226.
p. 193	Regarding Calvin's view of human rebelliousness, sinfulness, and longing for all that is wrong, see *CO* 32.230.
p. 193	Regarding Calvin's view of the heart as so riddled with sin that even what appeared to be good was really cloaked in hypocrisy and deceit, see *Inst.* 2.5.19.
p. 194	Regarding the frequent appearance of the theme of leaving one's homeland to be faithful to God in Calvin's writing, see *CO* 13.63.
p. 194	"For that reason this is the best": *CO* 11.629.
p. 195	Regarding Calvin's view of God's intention for him to play a role at the center of public life, see *CO* 31.22.
p. 196	Regarding Calvin's exhaustion from and professed hatred of writing, see *CO* 12.51.
p. 196	"Courault's death has left me such a wreck": *CO* 10.273.
pp. 197-98	"On September 3, I had a very bad headache": *CO* 11.84.
p. 198	"Because I have been struck down by a migraine": *CO* 14.474.
p. 198	"Now I am suffering from another migraine": *CO* 13.519.
p. 198	"I must actually still prepare for tomorrow's sermon": *CO* 15.686.
p. 199	Regarding Calvin's suffering with kidney stones, see *CO* 19.53-54.
p. 199	Regarding Calvin's suffering with and the treatment of his gout, see *CO* 19.30.
p. 200	Regarding Calvin's dedication of his commentary on 2 Thessalonians to his physician, Benoit Textor, see *CO* 13.598.
p. 201	"Our illnesses are surely not only to humble us": *CO* 20.129.
pp. 201-2	Regarding Calvin's view of his guilt before God, see *CO* 51.663-64; *SC* 1.369; *CO* 54.212.
p. 202	"How are things over here": *CO* 34.377.
p. 202	"Just look at the people who are in authority": *CO* 34.569.

p. 203   "Now, I ask you, can you call this justice": *CO* 34.143.

p. 203   "that they began to justify themselves": *CO* 34.202.

p. 203   "They do not say": *CO* 34.202.

pp. 204-5 Regarding Calvin's rejection of Servetus's offer to come to Geneva, see *CO* 12.767.

pp. 205-6 Regarding the allegation that Servetus had come to the city to take advantage of the council's dissatisfaction with Calvin, see *CO* 14.628.

p. 206   "Here in the republic there is such chaos": *CO* 14.474.

p. 206   "that by now everything that we say is considered suspect": *CO* 14.611.

p. 206   "that I am irritable and thus they try to test my patience": *CO* 14.654.

p. 206   "that you must go far from here to find rest": *CO* 15.478.

p. 206   Regarding Calvin's desire to withdraw from Geneva, see *CO* 52.438.

p. 206   "God would burst out in tears over it": *CO* 53.405.

pp. 206-7 "If it were up to me": *CO* 53.316.

p. 207   "He has more than enough reason to reject us": *SC* 5.62.

p. 207   Regarding Calvin's view of Geneva as a city full of scandals, see *SC* 5.63-64.

p. 207   "we carry about as traitors": *SC* 5.63.

p. 208   "after a long struggle": *CO* 15.449.

p. 211   "From my very birth, God has cared for me": *CO* 26.589.

p. 212   Regarding thanksgiving and obedience to God as Calvin's motives, see *CO* 46.142.

p. 212   Regarding Calvin's dedication to his office, see *CO* 14.655.

p. 212   "for that is after all the first sound we make": *CO* 12.578.

p. 212   "this happy catch": *CO* 20.4.

p. 213   "From the first day that I saw him": *CO* 14.416-17.

p. 213   "It is good that we are anchored in heaven": *CO* 14.412.

CHAPTER 9

p. 215   "asylum": *CO* 15.153.

p. 216   Regarding statistics on excommunications in Geneva, see Willam G. Naphy, *Calvin and the Consolidation of the Reformation* (Manchester: Manchester University Press, 1994), p. 178.

p. 217   "they come here to corrupt and defile the church": *CO* 53.270.

p. 219	Regarding Calvin's view that it is impossible to despise the gifts of the Spirit without also despising and scorning the Spirit himself, see *Inst.* 2.2.15.
p. 219	"did not receive by simple chance": *Inst.* 2.8.45.
p. 219	"distributors": *CO* 34.663.
pp. 219-20	"for everyone knows that just this year I turned down an offer of a raise": *CO* 12.257.
p. 220	"For I have not made it this far": *CO* 12.504.
p. 220	"Everyone knows how simple things are in my home": *CO* 15.825-26.
p. 220	"I cannot think of a day this year in which I was so overwhelmed": *CO* 10.337.
pp. 220-21	"Whatever it was that I started on": *CO* 12.380.
p. 221	Regarding Calvin's rationale for attempting to continue working while sick, see *CO* 12.421.
p. 221	"I am dictating this letter because I am suffering from a migraine": *CO* 12.154.
p. 221	"I fear that you may accuse me of laziness": *CO* 13.26.
p. 221	"I think that deep down, you will probably accuse me of laziness": *CO* 13.35.
p. 221	"Why do you even talk about Acts and Genesis": *CO* 13.655.
p. 222	"May the Lord grant that, in spite of my slow pondering": *CO* 13.656.
p. 222	"So you would gladly see a couple of commentaries": *CO* 15.812.
p. 222	"For a month now I have not even left the city": *CO* 14.456.
p. 222	"In that year he preached on Sunday mornings": *CO* 21.71-72.
p. 223	"I first of all want to congratulate you from the heart": *CO* 11.56.
p. 223	"for when the conscience has once let itself be entrapped": *Inst.* 3.19.7.
pp. 223-24	"When you begin to doubt whether you may use linen for sheets": *Inst.* 3.19.7.
p. 224	"On Sunday morning you can preach in the city": *CO* 13.603.
p. 224	Regarding the custom of traveling on Sundays, see *CO* 12.323.
p. 224	"had intended last Sunday to go to the country": *CO* 12.100.
p. 225	"For that matter, already before I came to this city": *CO* 14.105.
p. 225	Regarding Calvin's preaching against the custom of celebrating the conception of Christ as a Marian feast, see *CO* 14.105.
p. 225	"For if the stores and businesses are closed on Sundays": *CO* 26.292.

p. 226   "Jesus Christ was not a tailor": *CO* 49.681.

p. 227   "So that small congregation that flourished for twenty-five years": *CO* 20.151.

p. 227   Regarding Calvin's view of those Lutherans who prolonged Eucharistic controversy in Luther's name, see *CO* 15.141.

p. 227   Regarding the rejection of Calvin's dedication of his commentary on Genesis to the three sons of the Saxon elector Johann Friedrich, see *CO* 15.260.

p. 227   "O, if only Luther were still alive": *CO* 15.501-2.

p. 228   Regarding Calvin's praise of the hospitality of the council of Frankfurt, see *CO* 15.710ff.

p. 228   Regarding Calvin's view of the needlessness of controversy between the Reformed and the Lutherans, see *CO* 16.53.

p. 228   Regarding Calvin's advice on adaptation in matters of conscience in Eucharistic debates within the refugee churches, see *CO* 15.78ff.

p. 228   Regarding Calvin's view of needed corrections in Lutheran perspectives on baptism and the Lord's Supper, see *CO* 19.619ff.

pp. 228-29 Regarding Justus Jonas's offer to translate Calvin's second treatise against Westphal—and Calvin's acceptance, see *CO* 16.137, 283.

p. 229   Regarding Calvin's view of the *Institutes* as repayment to God for sparing his life, see *CO* 2.1-2.

p. 230   "The simple, popular writing style, intended for unschooled people": *CO* 12.316.

p. 231   Regarding Calvin's disapproval of the depiction of Mary in images used in churches, see *CO* 1.34.

p. 231   "God has never given us the command to destroy images": *CO* 18.581.

p. 231   Regarding Calvin's view of holidays as breeding grounds for superstition, see *CO* 11.625.

pp. 231-32 "I see that today more people than usual have come to the sermon": *SC* 5.172.20-40.

p. 232   "When you realize this": *SC* 5.173.1-3.

p. 232   "absurd that division arises among brothers": *CO* 15.393.

p. 233   Regarding Calvin's view of problems with the Roman Catholic doctrine of infant baptism, see *CO* 11.706.

p. 233   Regarding Calvin's view of providing the Lord's Supper to shut-ins, see *CO* 20.200.

p. 234	"For that reason I would prefer": *CO* 20.201.
p. 234	Regarding the backlash against Calvin at Bern, see *CO* 15.600-604.
p. 234	"we must be sober and humble": *CO* 15.602.
p. 235	"When I then see how the heavenly teaching of Christ": *CO* 15.606.
p. 235	"cast it before the snouts of swine": *CO* 15.726.
p. 235	"I would rather let my tongue and hand be cut off": *CO* 15.726.

CHAPTER 10

p. 236	"I would prefer nothing more": *CO* 14.434.
p. 237	Regarding Calvin's view of life as military duty from which he soon hoped to be released, see *CO* 15.357.
p. 237	"a continuous active military service": *CO* 32.23.
p. 237	Regarding Calvin's view of the Christian life as service in a war with little down time, see *CO* 31.427.
p. 237	Regarding Calvin's view that believers were ready to fight and suffer injury in the spiritual battle of the Christian life, see *CO* 31.296.
p. 237	"for it is simply so": *CO* 32.283.
p. 237	"The faithful servant knows the war": *SC* 6.28ff.
p. 237	"grabs the banner from the commander": *CO* 5.409.
p. 237	"so few are found who are willing": *CO* 12.659.
p. 237	"which is not only tough": *CO* 15.18.
pp. 236-37	Regarding Calvin's struggle with the city council over the rights of the church in the observance of the Lord's Supper, see *CO* 11.521.
p. 241	"who will soon be spread all over France": *CO* 19.170.
p. 241	"They come from everywhere to seek pastors from us": *CO* 18.467.
p. 242	"boldly dare to do all for God's Word": *Inst.* 4.8.9.
p. 243	"Our common home country": *CO* 18.615.
p. 243	"because if I were to forget my people": *CO* 18.615.
p. 244	Regarding Calvin's advice to Antoine de Crussol, see *CO* 20.112-13.
p. 245	"fight against your inclinations": *CO* 18.458.
p. 245	Regarding Calvin's advice to Louis de Bourbon, see *CO* 19.159.
p. 246	Regarding Calvin's view of some of the problems associated with monarchies, see *CO* 36.217B, 36.168C.
p. 246	"was after their riches": *CO* 36.221A.

p. 246   "If kings want to be considered legitimate and as servants of God": *CO* 36.382B.

p. 247   "and there will be neither Frenchman nor German": *CO* 36.226C.

p. 247   "If princes demand that we turn from honor of God": *SC* 8.376.

p. 247   Regarding Calvin's correspondence with Edward Seymour on the merits of Christian obedience and the eschewal of rebellion, see *CO* 13.65-77.

p. 247   "since Christianity reveals itself": *CO* 20.11.

p. 248   "These were the words reported to us": *CO* 19.410.

p. 248   "But what are we to say of this thieving": *CO* 19.411.

p. 248   "Rather die a hundred deaths": *CO* 18.437.

p. 249   "whether things are done in an orderly and peaceful manner": *CO* 18.236.

p. 249   "blasphemers, drunkards, adulterers": *CO* 18.236.

p. 250   "If you look carefully": *CO* 33.212.

p. 251   "Thirty years have passed": *CO* 20.78.

p. 251   "that even death could not be an unhappy circumstance for a Christian": *CO* 6.631.

p. 252   "I am writing in tears": *CO* 12.76.

p. 252   "I have to dictate this letter": *CO* 18.649.

p. 252   Regarding Calvin's view of death in the midst of life and the assurance of life in death, see *CO* 14.561-62.

p. 252   Regarding Calvin's view of the death of Claude Féray as a divine rebuke for Calvin's own sins, see *CO* 11.213.

p. 252   "The LORD has dealt us a heavy stroke": *CO* 11.430.

p. 252   Regarding Calvin's view of the increasing fear of death and the judgment for those desired to please God, see *CO* 31.77.

p. 252   "a sinner is confronted here with a judge": *CO* 31.318.

p. 252   Regarding Calvin's view that believers ought to have no fear of death, see *CO* 31.303.

p. 253   "The woman would have had to live in an unhappy captivity": *CO* 12.423.

pp. 253-54 Regarding Calvin's view of death, grief and hope in his letter to the lord of Richebourg, see *CO* 11.188-94.

p. 255   Regarding Calvin's confession of his faults near the end of his life, see *CO* 9.890.

p. 255   Regarding Calvin's statement to the council of Geneva that he had never sought anything but the best for the city, see *CO* 9.887-88.

p. 256   "I have lived through many battles here": *CO* 9.892.

p. 256   Regarding Calvin's instructions to the pastors of Geneva near the end of his life, see *CO* 9.894.

p. 257   Regarding Calvin's view that reflection should precede experience, see *CO* 11.489.

p. 257   Regarding Calvin's dictation of his will to Pierre Chenelat, see *CO* 20.298-302.

p. 257   Regarding Calvin's confession that he had done everything out of his fear of God, see *CO* 9.893.

p. 257   Regarding Calvin's view of submission to God in death, see *CO* 9.891.

p. 258   Regarding Calvin's burial according to his wishes, see *CO* 21.105-6.

p. 259   "that you were able to live with a woman": *CO* 15.867.

Names Index